BARRY LAZAR

TASTE of MONTREAL

TRACKING DOWN THE FOODS OF THE WORLD

Véhicule Press

Véhicule Press acknowledges the support of the Government
of Canada's Book Industry Development Program

Cover art direction and design: JW Stewart
Back cover author photograph: Thomas Leon Königsthal, Jr.
Special thanks to Vicki Marcok, Bruce Henry, Scott McRae
Inside imaging: Simon Garamond
Printing: AGMV-Marquis Inc.

CATALOGUING IN PUBLICATION DATA

Lazar, Barry
Barry Lazar's taste of Montreal : tracking down
the foods of the world

ISBN 1-55065-175-7

1. Restaurants–Quebec (Province)–Montréal.
2. Ethnic markets–Quebec (Province)–Montréal.
I. Title

TX910.C2L38 2003   647.95714'28   C2003-903242-6

Published by Véhicule Press
P.O.B. 125, Place du Parc Station
Montréal, Québec H2X 4A3

514.844.6073   FAX 514.844.7543

www.vehiculepress.com
vp@vehiculepress.com

CANADIAN DISTRIBUTION
LitDistco Distribution c/o Fraser Direct
800-591-6250

U.S. DISTRIBUTION
Independent Publishers Group, Chicago, Illinois
800-888-4741

PRINTED IN CANADA

For Celina and Sarah, as always

Contents

Acknowledgements

First things first. Long ago I concluded that, when it comes to the kitchen, women make food but men perform. Each week Celina goes shopping and I fulfil the ritual of the hunter and gatherer. She provides sustenance, the flour and eggs, the milk and coffee. I come back with a "look what I have" grin and proudly hold up a half dozen Salvadorian tamales or a bucket of fresh sauerkraut. However, without a family to bring stuff back to, there would be no performance and life would not be nearly as much fun. Celina and Sarah indulge my indulgences. They encourage me on my quests, and, most importantly, they keep me grounded. Our downstairs compatriots Rita, Norman and Sam, who is nine, regularly sit in on family tastings. Panayiota Liakopoulis keeps my notes in order; and Marjorie Dewitz makes sure her son's copy stays honest.

Thanks also to Geoff Stern, who keeps me posted on food trends and has challenged me à la table for more than thirty years; and to Chuck Kaplan with whom I have driven on early morning jaunts for years looking for the next great taste treat. I owe a great debt to Nicholas Robinson, Montreal's least appreciated food critic and the vision behind montrealfood. com. I continue to learn from Nick's knowledge of Japanese cuisine in particular and Asian food in general.

Friend and former publisher Michael Goldbloom was the first to suggest I write regularly for the *Montreal Gazette*. Ashok Chandwani, in his long tenure at the paper, was responsible, with Lucinda Chodan, for hiring me. Ashok was also an astute chef and gourmet who generously offered advice. He died recently and is missed.

David Walker oversaw my copy, winced at my misspellings, and encouraged my à la carte adventuring.

Simon Dardick, co-publisher of Véhicule, gave me the opportunity to write *Taste of Montreal*. He, Bruce Henry, and the Véhicule in-house team bring coherence to my ramblings. Simon and his wife Nancy Marrelli are optimists in a game that has caused many to give up their dreams. Montreal would be poorer without them.

Introduction

This book began as a digression, a series of short articles about herbs and spices for the *Montreal Gazette*. The original idea was to do a few pieces but each time I dropped into a store to do some research I ended up with something else that I just had to try. The columns kept coming over several years, first as "Taste of the World" and then as "Flavour of the Week."

The shelves grew heavy at home as I returned with exotica for my family to try: pierogies, churros, satay, tourtière, bành mí, empanadas, sushi, tamales, gefilte fish, falafel, jerk, carnitas, halvah, verjus, rotis, smoked meat hot dogs, dolmas and on and on. They cried "enough!" when I asked them to test ten kinds of soy sauce.

People ask me why I write about food. While I do love tasting different foods, I like people more. Asking someone about their food—even better, sharing it with them—is the best way to get to know them. Every culture has a doorway to the dining room. Although I have been a working journalist for over thirty years, I'm a lousy reporter. I never developed a good nose for news. I was too involved in people's stories; the smaller voices call out to me. The bigger dramas of the day, the politicians and press releases, always seem less important in comparison.

What I did have, and continue to cultivate, is a nose for what's new—and this sense is sharpest when it detects a subtle flavour from the kitchen. So I became The Flavourguy in my columns, and food continues to be the path that leads me to new friends and old cultures.

Montreal is one of the world's food capitals—fascinating and diverse. And I consider myself lucky to live where I do. The quest for something tasty is the best way to explore our town; all it requires is curiosity and an appetite.

If you have any comments, write to me at Véhicule Press: **vp@vehiculepress.com**
I'll get back to you as soon I've finished eating!

How to Use this Book

Taste of Montreal is an eclectic offering and I've done it alphabetically, with some digressions, from Anchovies to Zershk.

Many of the entries have recipes and suggestions about where to buy ingredients. There is a guide and three indexes at the back of the book. The *Guide to Shops and Restaurants* provides detailed descriptions of over one hundred stores and restaurants. These appear in **bold** type in the text. *The Shops and Restaurants Index, The Tastes of Montreal Index,* and the *Recipes Index* make for quick referencing.

As a *lagniappe* (a wonderful Cajun word meaning a little something extra) there are notes about Montreal's major farmers' markets and our SAQs—liquor outlets.

Happy wandering and bon appétit.

Ten of the Best

To start with, here is a highly personal list of ten great "tastes of Montreal" which make eating in this town an on-going feast.

Beans at La Binerie
This snack bar hasn't changed in decades. Traditional Québecois staples such as tourtière, gras-de-rotis (jellied pork roast drippings...mmm) and fèves au lard fill the menu. The beans are baked for a long time, and sold by the pint or quart to take home. The breakfasts are hearty, cheap and filling. Great before a wintry walk down rue Saint-Denis.

Espresso
Coffee (as in Tim Horton's) is what you use when you need something to wash down a doughnut. But for purists there is only Italian espresso—rich and delectable, with a layer of foam called crema. Bets are off for the best in the city but here are three standouts, all with their own discerning clientele: Olympico (aka Open da Night) in Mile End, **Café Italia** in the heart of Little Italy, and in the north end of town, **Café Guildone**, which is more popularly known as the **Restaurant Without a Name** or Restaurant Sans Nom.

Papas rellenas at La Peregrina
This Latino grocery store has a lunch counter wedged into the back and cooks a variety of South American goodies every day. Papas rellenas is one of their best: cook a potato, mash it and then form it into a ball. Stuff this with hard-boiled egg and ground meat and then deep fry it. This is a common snack in Cuba and the Dominican Republic, where it may be stuffed with cheese. Reheats well in the microwave or toaster oven.

Smoked-meat hotdogs
Take great smoked meat and stuff it into casings. Knocks an ordinary hotdog out of the ball park. Get these locally made beauties at **Quebec Smoked Meat** in Pointe St-Charles.

Licorice at Euro-Plus
This small, bustling West Island café has a superb selection of imported Dutch products. Licorice is a favourite treat in the Netherlands and the selection here is stunning.

Pizza at Roma in Little Italy
Buy it by the slab and take it home. A large variety of vegetarian toppings such as eggplant and zucchini make **Boulangerie Roma** a Little Italy favourite. Also great home-made gelati for dessert.

Sausage subs at Momesso
Fresh Italian sausage seared on the griddle, stuffed into a sub roll with lettuce and tomato. Add a drizzle of hot sauce. Heaven on a bun.

Chinese barbecue at Sun Sing Lung, in Chinatown
This is a small shop with a friendly, knowledgeable staff. There is usually a whole hog roasting in the back and another being carved in the front window.

Barry Fleischer's home-made spruce beer
This was once a common drink in corner stores. Now there is only one place that makes spruce beer and serves it fresh—**Restaurant Émilie Bertrand** on Notre-Dame Street. The recipe is secret. The taste is piney but much more subtle than the commercial bottled varieties. Goes great with an all-dressed steamie.

Quebec "ice wine"
It is similar to ice wine, but this is a vinophile's apple cider with a wonderful syrupy kick. Serve very chilled as an apéritif. Here is a world-class drink that is only just getting the attention it deserves. Similarly, Michel Jodoin's 82 proof Granny Smith-based "Pom de vie" is as worthy an end-of-the-meal digestif as a fine Italian grappa. The SAQ outlet in the **Atwater Market** has a large selection. Ice ciders are also sold in speciality shops such as **Le Marché des saveurs du Québec** at the **Jean-Talon Market**.

The Tastes of Montreal

Anchovies

It's amazing what you can learn about your mate even after a dozen years of marriage. "What is that smell?" she said the other day. "Anchovies," I cheerfully replied, holding an opened tin of Spanish Bertozzi. I was admiring the luscious filets packed in olive oil. "Try this," I added, spearing a marinated 'fresh' anchovy imported from Italy, but by then she had left the kitchen.

For such a small fish—only a half-dozen or so inches (10-20 cm) long—anchovies have a remarkable effect on people. You either love their strong flavour or you can't stand 'em. I am with the group that relishes their thickly-salted, meaty taste. Only an anchovy—or better yet two—can make a salad worthy of Caesar or give an edge to an all-dressed pizza.

Fresh anchovies are a rarity in Montreal. Most of what we see on our shelves is packaged in Spain, Morocco and Italy, even if the fish are caught off Peru. Italians pack anchovies in jars. The other countries use tins and the tinned ones can be foul tasting, particularly if they are not packed in olive oil. Anchovy paste is sold in tubes.

Marinated anchovies may taste closest to fresh ones. Look for the Il Veliero brand. These have a vinegary herring taste, which is not surprising since anchovies are from the same fish family.

The tastiest anchovies are packed salted in large containers and kept on ice or in refrigerators in fish stores and Italian and Portuguese markets. These fish are larger than those in tins or jars. They still have some skin and may have bones as well. They need to be rinsed gently in several changes of fresh water. They can then be sliced and the bones pulled away from the filets. The rinsed filets have a less salty taste than other varieties, with a fresh flavour similar to sardines. Marinate the filets in olive oil with a squeeze of fresh lemon juice before serving.

Anchovy filets are often served as part of an hors d'oeuvre platter. They can be mashed with butter or with garlic oil and lemon and served grilled on toast.

Caesar Salad

Here is how we incorporate them into a Caesar salad.

Tear several leaves of romaine lettuce into bite-sized pieces. Trim the crusts from a couple of slices of bread, toast them lightly and cut these into small croutons. For the dressing, chop two cloves of garlic in a blender. Mix the juice of half a lemon with twice that amount of olive oil, a teaspoon (5 ml) of Dijon mustard, six drops of Tabasco sauce, and one anchovy filet or an inch of anchovy paste squeezed from a tube. Blend everything well at high speed. Put the lettuce in a bowl. Add the salad dressing, a tablespoon of capers, the croutons, and two tablespoons of freshly grated Romano or Parmesan cheese. Toss well. Grate a little black pepper over each plate; add extra anchovies as desired.

Angostura Bitters

This is heady stuff, 44% alcohol. A whiff opens the mind like smelling salts. It is made from oranges and cinnamon bark, carob, cloves, cardamom and perhaps another dozen flavourings. Once it contained Angostura bark, but apparently that was too similar to the lethal poison strychnine and is now left out!

The name originates in Angostura, Venezuela, where, 175 years ago, the elixir was concocted by Dr. J. Siegert. He mixed up this herbal distillation as a remedy for stomach problems, fatigue, lumbago and whatever other ills 19th-century Europeans were succumbing to in the new world. In fact, his wasn't much different than other patent medicines of his time. These all-purpose tonics were potent and popular. They were particularly attractive to women, who were not supposed to drink in bars. A bottle of bitters might indeed be good for what ailed you and could be taken liberally in respectable company.

Today's formula is secret, but Angostura's flavour is as subtle as walking into a barn door. First there is the strong orange zest, not much different from Seville oranges. Then the tongue goes numb from the alcohol. After that, as Hemingway is reputed to have noted, it tastes like varnish.

Fernet-Branca, Peychaud and other brands of bitters are similar but Angostura remains the best known. Its medicinal edge cuts cloying cocktails like Manhattans, Rob Roys and juleps. A few drops added to any sugary cake or custard lends a little of the brass knuckles needed to bring a too-sweet dessert down to earth.

Robin Harding is one Montrealer who has a regular use for Angostura and shares his family's formula for a Christmas highball. For each glass: lace 1 cube of sugar with 2 drops of Angostura Bitters, then add a pudding spoon (½ tablespoon (10 ml) of brandy and fill the glass with a very cold but not expensive champagne such as Cordoniu.

Bacon Bits

Bacon bits (the packaged fake kind) are the ultimate sinless treat. Hurrah for textured vegetable protein (soy flour, caramel colour, red #3, yellow #6). Huzzah for wheat-gluten protein. Yippee for autolyzed yeast, whatever that is.

Welcome to the world of analog foods. Bacon bits are derived from vegetables and grains and made to resemble something else, in this case crispy bits of bacon. They have almost no fat (polyunsaturated or otherwise) and no cholesterol and they aren't a significant source of fibre, calcium or vitamins. It's like eating Styrofoam chips made with a dash of salt and hickory smoke.

Whatever bacon bits are called (chez nous we've nicknamed them "fako bacos"), they are not bacon. Most brands are certified as a kosher food product. We live dangerously. We defy the almighty (doctor, deity, etc.). We eat bacon bits.

A handful (one brand suggests 13 of the little nuggets to the serving) has about 30 calories. But who eats them by the handful? This isn't real food. It's a condiment. We sprinkle them in salad dressings and on salads, baked potatoes, scrambled eggs, vegetable dips and soups.

Here is a bacon bit recipe that takes this treat to another dimension. It is based on the famous Elvis Presley sandwich which combined white bread, mayonnaise, peanut butter, bacon and ketchup (oh be still, my heart!). Here's an updated Montreal version.

Split one warm sesame seed bagel. Lightly butter both halves. Slather one side with peanut butter. Cover this with a thick layer of bacon bits and a dash of ketchup. Close up the sandwich and squeeze it just a bit so that the ingredients meld. The ketchup is the big surprise. The sweetness compliments the smoke. The tomato marries well with the taste of bacon. The flavours meld wonderfully not unlike some Thai dishes that combine sweet with sour. The crispy bacon bits offset the unctuous. The King would have loved it.

Bagels

To my surprise, the bagel has become the essence of la grande bouffe that is Montreal.

More than the faddish crêpe, the guilt-ridden smoked meat or the eccentric poutine, it is the bagel that best defines the city's culinary character. It is a little crusty but quickly yields under pressure. It exists in endless variations although it was founded on two distinct varieties—poppy seed and sesame. It is available everywhere.

The Montreal bagel differs from the New York or Toronto version. The New York bagel is called a water bagel. It is chewier, bigger and not as crisp. Unlike the Montreal bagel, the dough is made without eggs. The New York bagel tastes best with robustly-flavoured cream cheeses.

The Toronto version is usually baked in a gas oven. It is not burnished by the scorching wood-fired heat from which a true Montreal bagel emerges. The Montreal bagel is great by itself. The Toronto one is excellent for dunking in coffee.

"Bagel" comes from the Yiddish "beygel" via the German words "beugel," meaning a round loaf of bread, and "bügel," a ring. Until the 1970s, it was an exotic Jewish bread. You had to drive to St-Viateur Street to get the authentic version. Now, they're as common as croissants.

There are bagel cafés serving espresso and wood-fired bagels in the trendy areas of Monkland Village and Plateau Mont-Royal. There are wood-fired bagel bakeries in Le Faubourg Ste-Catherine and Plaza Côte-des-Neiges. At one supermarket in St-Laurent borough, the bagel bakers speak Spanish. At **D.A.D.'s Bagels**, the common language is Punjabi.

The city's oldest ovens are at the **Fairmount Bagel** bakery and the **St-Viateur Bagel Shop**. Once, the original owners were partners. They were Jews from eastern European families and they sold bagels from a pushcart near **Schwartz's** on The Main. If we had our priorities right, there would be a bronze plaque on the wall.

The key to a Montreal bagel is temperament. It must be coddled in sweet, hot water and tempered in fire. It retains a crunch at the first bite and a malty flavour within. It freezes well and reheats beautifully in a toaster oven.

For an authentic Montreal bagel recipe, it's helpful to know a master baker. Marcy Goldman is one of the best. She shares her knowledge, humour and perceptions with thousands of enthusiasts on her website: www. betterbaking.com. Her latest cookbook, written with web-site guru Yvan Huneault, is called *The Best of Betterbaking.com* (Ten Speed and Random House Canada, 2002) and it has a version of this recipe. It's also in her book *A Treasury of Jewish Holiday Baking* (Doubleday, 1998).

1¾ cups (400 ml) water
½ ounce (15 ml) fresh yeast or 2½ (12 ml) teaspoons dry
    yeast
a pinch of sugar
3 tablespoons (45 ml) oil
2 tablespoons (30 ml) beaten egg
1½ teaspoons (7 ml) salt, optional
5 tablespoons (75 ml) sugar
4½ to 5 cups (1.25 l) bread flour
1 tablespoon (15 ml) malt powder

Marcy likes Fermipan dry yeast for bagels. Malt powder is usually available at health food stores.

Kettle Water
6 quarts (7.25 litres) water
5 tablespoons (75 ml) honey

Garnish
1 cup (250 ml) sesame seeds or poppy seeds (or half and half)

Stir the water, yeast and pinch of sugar together. Let this stand a couple of minutes, allowing the yeast to swell and dissolve. Whisk in the sugar, beaten egg, vegetable oil and malt. Fold in most of the flour. (If using fresh yeast, crumble it into warm water along with a pinch of sugar. Let it stand a couple of minutes and then continue, adding the other ingredients as you would for the dry yeast method.)

Knead this for 10-12 minutes to form a stiff, smooth dough, adding additional flour as required.

Cover the dough with a tea towel or inverted bowl and let it rest 10 minutes. Take out three large cookie or baking sheets. Line one with a kitchen towel and another with baking parchment.

Fill a large stock pot or Dutch oven three-quarters full with water. Add honey and salt. Bring the water to a boil. Meanwhile, divide the dough into 12 sections and form these into 10-inch strips. Form each strip into a bagel ring. Place them on a cookie sheet. Let the dough rise 12-16 minutes until bagels are slightly puffed up.

Preheat the oven to 450° F.

Boil the bagels 1½ minutes each, turning them over once in the process. Place them on the towel lined sheet to drain them. Then sprinkle each generously with sesame or poppy seeds. (Montreal bagels are more seeded than bagels made elsewhere.) Place them on the parchment-lined sheet.

Put the baking sheet in the oven, reduce the heat to 425° F. Bake the bagels 15-22 minutes, or until they are a dark golden brown. Turn them over once when they are just about done.

Baklava

"Fill (the filo dough) with walnuts or pine nuts or custard, and drench it luxuriously with streams of Hymettos honey and cinnamon in abundance."

–Greek Cooking for the Gods

There you have it, this is why baklava is so sinfully divine. Other pastries have their place, I suppose, but for sheer sensuousness, nothing beats a freshly-made baklava. Don't ask me—check with a Turkish sultan. At one time baklava was a pastry for the rich. It was reputed to be a favourite in harems —both walnuts and honey were considered aphrodisiacs.

I'm a texture man myself. That, and the flavour, keep me coming back nibble after nibble. First are innumerable thin layers of pastry that yield after an initial bite. Then the crunch and liquid sweetness fills the mouth. There always seems to be just a little more than you can really eat. Finally there is the surprise within: crushed almonds, walnuts or pistachios with spices that reflect the baker's genes. Arab countries tend to add rose water to the flavourings. Armenians put in more cinnamon and cloves.

While the word "baklava" is Turkish, many in Montreal associate this pastry with Greek cooking. This is because Greeks were among the first immigrants to this city who were not from western Europe. Greek sailors first settled here in the late 19th century and their families joined them. Many were adept at making pastries and set up small bakeries and ice cream parlors. Their skills were appreciated by our fabled Quebec sweet tooth and there have been Greek bakers in Montreal since then. By the way, the Greek word for "leaf" is "phyllo" and from this we get the phyllo or filo dough used for all kinds of cooking and available, usually frozen, in Greek food stores and most supermarkets.

While baklava is the most common dessert using phyllo dough, similar ones include kadayif, which has shredded dough on top, and galaktobouriko with a filling of custard rather than nuts.

Look for them in Greek pastry stores and Middle Eastern supermarkets and bakeries including **Mourelatos** and **Serano**.

Bánh Mì

The signs outside Vietnamese coffee shops and grocery stores say all I need to know: bánh mì. That means, for about a twoonie, I can get a great lunch. It comes in the form of a 10-inch sub sandwich made to order with a thin layer of paté, a layer or two of barbecued pork or chicken, a hit of cilantro, a hint of chili, and a whole mouthful of flavour.

"Bánh mì" means "French sandwich." The baguette and paté are part of Vietnam's history of French occupation that lasted on and off for almost a hundred years and ended in the 1950s. It is one reason many Vietnamese chose to live here.

And it's a good thing they did since, wherever there is a substantial Vietnamese community, there is bánh mì.

The classic bánh mì resembles an American-style sub only in concept. There is the bread and the fillings, but it is not stacked and stuffed. There is an inherent subtlety that would be out of place in any fast food joint where "super-sized" is on the menu. Why not super-flavour?

A bánh mì's ingredients are simple but each is important. The bread must taste fresh—chewy but not doughy with a honey-coloured crisp crust. The fillings are minimal and applied judiciously. There is the heat of the chili, the sweet and sour taste of pickled radish, a snap of fresh herbs and maybe thin strips of sweet pepper. Mayonnaise is spread on the bread in a very thin layer and brings the flavours together. The sliver of pork paté adds richness, but this is not a greasy sandwich. There is no need for the squirt of dressing that seems to be required at franchise sub shops.

Bánh mì is popular in Vietnamese stores and super-markets at lunch time. In the evening, look for them in Vietnamese pastry shops. Several areas of Montreal have Vietnamese stores. You'll find them in Chinatown around the corner of St-Laurent Boulevard and De la Gauchetière; in **Hoàng Oanh** near the intersection of Jean-Talon East and St-Denis; and in some of the south Asian groceries on Côte-des-Neiges, as well as near the corner of Victoria and Van Horne.

Bao-ji

Steamed, baked or fried dough and its endless variety of fillings predominate in the world of street food. Almost always there is a surprise element of something tasty hidden inside. The dough gives the snack body and makes a simple food more filling. The treat within gives it flavour and makes the food fun. Jelly doughnuts do this for many of us. In Chinese street food, it is bao-ji, steamed buns.

Bao-ji are round and usually big enough to comfortably fit in your hand. The ball rests on a small piece of paper that is used to keep this treat from sticking to the pan when it is steamed. The dough covering is thick. It is made from flour, milk , water, yeast, sugar and shortening. The dough itself is bland and light, with just enough sweetness to balance the pungent mix of flavours inside. Classic fillings are chicken, Chinese sausage, barbecued pork, or sweet red bean paste. This is serious eating—several levels beyond the world of jelly doughnuts.

These steamed buns can be bought frozen in many Asian food stores. Ideally they should be brought to room temperature and reheated for about 15 minutes in a steamer. They are equally tasty taken directly from the freezer, covered with wax or parchment paper, and microwaved on high for 2 or 3 minutes. However this method of reheating can make the dough denser and rubbery which doesn't happen when they are steamed.

Bao-ji are more than just a snack. At their best, they are hot and filling and a marvelous comfort food on a cold day. Look for bao-ji in stores and restaurants that have them for take-out. Many dim sum restaurants will sell a couple to eat out on the street or take home. Vietnamese supermarkets like **Kim Phat** often sell bao-ji and other appetizers in their frozen food sections. **Jardin de Jade Poon Kai** sells quarter-kilo wonders (about half a pound) for 95 cents at their take-out counter. One of these is almost a meal in itself.

Barbecue Rub

For many of us, the flavour of summer is the taste of barbecue. It is there but hard to identify. Wood smoke? Mesquite? What is that elusive tang hidden deep in the meat? Serious barbecue chefs know what it is. The flavour of the grub is in the rub.

When it comes to grilling or barbecue, meat can often be given an extra taste-notch with a judicious marinade or rub. Marinades are wet and usually have an acid such as wine, lemon or lime juice, or vinegar. The idea is to tenderize tougher cuts of meat as well as give them more flavour. Marinades are great for chicken thighs, beef brisket and pork roast.

On other cuts, however, opt for a rub.These are spice and herb mixtures that you rub into the meat before cooking. Many commercial styles are available. They range from Jamaican-style jerks loaded with hot peppers to fairly mild blends such as a series of rubs put out by New Orleans chef supremo Paul Prudhomme. Prudhomme gets great publicity, as he should; after all he pushed Cajun-style cooking onto the world stage. However, his style of rub is fairly generic. He gives some recipes in his cookbooks. They are not difficult to make at home. They contain herbs, spices and salt, with his hotter blends having more pepper and cayenne.

The problem with commercial rubs is that by the time they are blended, sent to the wholesaler, distributed to the stores and end up on our tables, they can be stale. It is cheaper and tastier to make your own rub and give it that signature taste of "la maison de la casa house" (or whatever you choose to call it).

Here is a way to start. Think of it as less of a recipe than an approach to give your food the taste you are looking for. First, make a dry rub along these lines (but adjust to your taste): ½ cup (125 ml) of salt , ¼ cup (50ml) of mild paprika, 3 tablespoons (50 ml) of freshly ground black pepper and a teaspoon (5 ml) each of any of the herbs and flavours you like such as cayenne, chili powder, garlic and onion power, sage, or thyme. This will give you enough for several barbecues. Add a tablespoon or two (15-25 ml) of brown sugar if you are cooking at low temperatures. However, don't use sugar in any rub that will be used for grilling meats (which is usually done over very hot coals or high heat) as the sugar will burn long before the food is ready.

This is a standard dry rub for meat or poultry. It keeps well in a covered jar. It is even good sprinkled on a steak just before taking it from the fire.

Better yet is a slightly moist rub. Take a half dozen cloves of garlic and pound them into a mash with a teaspoon (5 ml) of salt. A blender works well but an old fashioned mortar and pestle is best. Add the flavours you want. I usually put in a little olive oil, maybe a teaspoon (5 ml) of Dijon mustard and enough thyme or marjoram to thicken it up.

Whether you use this moist garlicky rub or a handful of the dried mixture, massage it over a larger cut of meat such as a whole chicken, turkey breast, a rack of ribs, or a 3- to 4-pound (1.5-2 kg) roast. Let the meat sit covered in the refrigerator for several hours or, better yet, overnight before cooking.

Then barbecue it in the way you usually would. This also works great in winter. Just cook the meat under the broiler or in a hot oven instead of on the grill. Once the skin has browned and become crisp, set the heat to about 325° F and continue cooking until the meat is done. Baste it occasionally with a simple oil and vinegar salad dressing (a non-sugary Italian bottled dressing is fine and a homemade one with apple cider vinegar is sensational).

Let the meat sit for about 15 minutes on a warm platter before serving. It will be easier to carve. Good bread is a must, to sop up the meat 'juice.'

Ahh, there's the rub! The taste of summer is back.

Bourekas

The singular is bourekas, but these bite-sized flaky pastries are so tasty that it is almost impossible to eat just one. The correct plural is bourekasim, but for most of us, it's one bourekas, two bourekas and so on. It's a good thing that they are cheaper by the dozen.

Bourekas are the twinkling stars of snackdom, easy to miss on an overloaded table of appetizers. When properly made, they are small and flaky, almost dainty. They might be thought of as an aristocratic turnover. They are stuffed and often baked covered with sesame seeds. The pastry should be as crunchy and rich as a mille-feuille, but savoury rather than sweet. While the fillings can include almost anything, the most common are cheese, tuna, mushroom, spinach or potatoes.

Bourekas are Middle Eastern fare and particularly common to Sephardic cooking. Sephardim are Jews who hail from the Mediterranean basin. Many in Montreal's Sephardic community came here from Israel, Morocco, and Egypt.

Pastries similar to bourekas are common to many countries in the same part of the world. In Armenian cooking, they are called beoregs and the fillings can be savoury or sweet. In Turkey, according to Claudia Roden who has written standard reference works on both Jewish and Middle Eastern cooking, boerek means pie, while börek means a cigar. They are often sold as pies or rolled from thin sheets of pastry to resemble cigars and filled with minced meat or grated cheese.

The bourekas sold in Jewish grocery stores and bakeries, however, often look like small empanadas. Traditionally they are shaped into half moons, but they may also be made in other shapes to make it easier for a sales clerk to know what is inside.

Many stores and Jewish restaurants sell bourekas but it is worthwhile to go to a Jewish bakery, such as **Adar** or **Kosher Quality**, that makes them fresh. Note that no store or restaurant which is certified Kosher will be open on Jewish holidays, Friday evenings or Saturday before sundown.

Calzone

The hottest trend in take-out food may be calzone. (It rhymes with "maison, eh?") Pizza Hut sells it as the P'Zone. McCain has had its version—the Pizza Pocket, for a few years. But Italian bakers have known about it for more than a century.

Calzone is pizza that doesn't get messy. The filling stays inside. A classic calzone looks like a turnover and is large enough to be a meal on its own. It can be fried, but it is usually brushed with olive oil and baked. The dough encloses the filling which stays moist and savoury as it cooks. This is a great dish to know about if you make pizza at home and go overboard on the toppings before it's baked. ("I'll have mine with extra, extra, extra cheese? Oh, it's a little sloppy. That's OK, we'll just fold it in half, tuck the edges in and ... hey gang, we aren't having pizza tonight, instead it's ... calzone!")

Calzone proves the cook's maxim: anyone can follow a recipe, but only a cook knows how to deal with mistakes. Calzone, however, is not a mistake; it's a dish with an etymology. "Calzone" is an old Italian word for trousers, or even socks, which seems to fit the concept better. Apparently in 19th-century Naples, men's trousers were cut a little full. Somehow, a folded-over piece of pizza filled with sausage or cheese or peppers looked like a man's pants. However this dish may have an even older etymology. *The Oxford Companion to Food* cites "calsones" as a sort of Sephardic cheese-filled ravioli that was made in the Middle Ages.

Whatever the origin, calzones taste great. If you find the commercial varieties, especially the ready-to-heat frozen ones at the supermarket too greasy and not very satisfying, try them freshly made. Montreal has many Italian bakeries and food stores which bake them daily. This is still an artisanal creation and few of these shops make calzones the same way.

Popular fillings can include a mix of mozzarella, chopped meats and olives. (While it tastes great, I wonder if this is just the easiest way to use the end bits from yesterday's cold cuts.) Other ingredients can include ricotta cheese and chopped spinach, freshly-cooked spinach layered with mozzarella, or slices of pancetta (luscious Italian-style bacon cured with salt and spices but not smoked), or chunks of fresh Italian sausage. The crusts can be as light and flaky as a brioche or as chewy and crusty as a roll. The shapes also vary. Some places make calzones that look like plump half-moons, beautifully fluted around the edges. Others serve them like wedges of pizza with the filling between two layers of dough.

Many bakeries and food stores in Italian neighborhoods make calzones fresh each day. **Salerno**, a 24-hour bakery in the north end of the city, has both a modest version with a few spices and chopped salami baked inside a roll, as well as a wonderful large calzone with chopped olives and meat inside and mozzarella and tomato sauce on the top. This is a calzone for those of us who like everything on top of everything. Near the Jean-Talon Market is **Jos and Basile**. Their specialty is a flaky half-moon calzone filled with either ricotta and spinach or sausage meat and olives. Also in the area is **Motta Boulangerie**. The calzone of choice at Motta looks like a pizza but it has several kinds of meat and cheese layered between two crusts. The spinach and mozzarella calzone is also good here.

Cattails

Euell Gibbons, the ultimate forager, would have liked Bernard Tremblay's pickled cattails. Gibbons devotes a half-dozen pages to cattails in his book, *Stalking the Wild Asparagus*. He calls this plant the "Supermarket of the Swamps" and describes how to make cattail flour from the pollen, how to use the roots for starch, and how to pick the spikes and eat them boiled and buttered like corn, but he doesn't mention pickling them when they are young.

Cattails, or bullrushes, grow in wetlands and are easily identifiable by their tall brown velvet stalks. When they mature in late summer or early fall, they are picked and dried and made into splendid ornamental decorations. Picked young, however, they are short, tender and edible with a taste halfway between asparagus and artichoke.

Bernard Tremblay leads the quest for Quebec cattail cuisine. He is outstanding in his field. His company in Rawdon is called L'Arôme des Bois. It produces mustards, sauces and preserves from wild Quebec plants. In early summer Tremblay looks for cattails. Once they appear, he says that he has just 48 hours to harvest and prepare them while their flavor is at their peak.

Pickled cattails are small, only about 6 inches (14 cm) tall and barely the width of a pinkie. Tremblay cooks them in vinegar with salt and a little lemon. The cattails are packaged in tall narrow jars that hold about two dozen of the young plants. They look delicate. Each has a small stem just long enough to hold while you nibble the thick fuzz. Most people like the taste but some find it hard to get used to the velvety texture. The stalks can be sliced into salads or served on their own as an intriguing part of a selection of vegetable appetizers.

Look for cattails and other unusual Quebec products in specialty food stores such as **Gourmet Laurier** and **La Marché des Saveurs** at Jean-Talon Market.

Cèpes (Dried)

There are people, according to some newspaper articles, who are almost prepared to die for mushrooms. They are harvesters of matsutake mushrooms, the latest gourmet fad. Matsutake grow in the woods of British Columbia and are prized in Japan where a perfect specimen recently sold for $100. With prices at that level, it is not surprising that many pickers pack pistols for protection.

Unfortunately, at least to the untrained eye, matsutake look like amanita mushrooms, many of which have vivid names such as The Destroying Angel. They are—and there is no other way to put this—deadly.

Either way, for mushroom hunters, there is new meaning to the old song "If you go out in the woods today, prepare for a big surprise..." For most of us, it is far better to go out to a good Italian supermarket and pick a pack of dried wild mushrooms.

These mushrooms are not in any way similar to common table mushrooms which are grown in sanitized silage in temperature- and humidity-controlled barns. The dried mushrooms I like have a strong musky taste. They are boletes, known in France as cèpes and in Italy as porcini. A small packet costs a few dollars but a little goes a long way and is wonderful in pasta or rice dishes. Most specialty stores and Italian food stores such as **Fruiterie Milano** carry them.

Dried cèpes are also popular in Eastern European cooking, and you can find them at **Chopin** and **Bucharest Delicatessen.**

Cèpes capture that last moment of autumn just before the ground hardens and the smells of the earth disappear for another season.

There are three ways to savour them. Sold in packages, porcini are dried and sliced thinly. If you buy them this way, wash the pieces to remove any residual sand or earth and then let them rehydrate in water. They can then be chopped and added to sauces, soups or even omelettes. They can also be ground finely and used as you would any flavouring, but you may find that a bit of their grit remains in the powder.

There is a commercial porcini powder but this is rarely found in stores. Restaurants buy it in bulk, however, since it is cheaper and easier to use than grinding dried mushrooms. Try asking for a small amount at your favourite Italian restaurant. Finally, there is now a commercial mushroom boullion cube on the market, made by Aurora. The ingredients include salt and MSG but the mushroom flavour is quite pronounced. A packet of six cubes, which is enough for 12 cups of broth, sells for about $1.50.

Polish-Style Mushroom Sauce
This goes great with meatloaf, hamburger, or on broad egg noodes.

Soak one ounce (35 g) of dried, sliced mushrooms in one cup (250 ml) water for one hour. Then simmer in a covered saucepan for an additional hour. Drain the mushrooms but reserve the liquid. Mix ¼ cup (50 ml) of flour with a little cold water to make a slurry. Add to the mushroom liquid and stir well to eliminate lumps. Add the mushrooms. Bring to a slow boil until the sauce thickens. Remove from heat and let it cool for a few minutes. Add ½ cup (125 ml) sour cream, salt and pepper to taste, and a pinch of marjoram.

Chai

The new hot flavour in summer is chai. It rhymes with "why". There are chai shakes, chocolate chai, non-fat chai, and chai hot drinks. Ben & Jerry's has had a chai-flavoured kind of ice cream it calls a smoothie. What is this thing called chai? It's tea, laddies, just tea.

Well, not *just*, of course. That wouldn't justify the extra couple of dollars charged per.

The chai fad began on the U.S.A.'s northwest coast, the land of lattes and over-priced espressos. Like its limpid liquid cousins, it has now moved east, bubbling over with hype. Chai is lauded as healthful and invigorating. Internet purveyors cite enough anecdotes to make this drink seem like the caffeinated equivalent of the fountain of youth. Tea sellers claim that their chai blends are more aromatic, more authentic than their competitors'. Sites vie for colourful descriptions of how the first cuppa was produced. My favourite starts with a horrific tale of how tea leaves were originally created from the eyelids of a Zen master who slit them trying to stay awake ...this is supposed to make me want to click on and buy the stuff?

Despite its exotic robes, chai is nothing more than what most of us get when we order a cup of "Indian tea" in an Indian restaurant. It's made from an aromatic mixture of spices, tea leaves and milk. Chai, in fact, is a common word in several languages for tea. Where it is commonly drunk—South Asia, China and Russia—it is as exotic as hot water.

So here we are, gullible North Americans, seeking a sip of the "richly flavourful, good-for-your-health" beverage that only the Masala Chai master can bring.

There is no mystery to chai and there are an infinite number of recipes. Rather than look for a secret blend, consider the components and match the flavours you like best. Start with a good black tea (although Kashmiris use green tea for a similar drink called kahva), and brew it as you normally would, with the addition of your own spice blend. Use whole spices, not powders.

A flavourful mixture might consist of a few of the following: a couple of cardamom seeds, an inch or so of cinnamon bark, a clove, a little freshly-grated ginger, maybe a crushed almond or a pinch of saffron, and even whole black pepper. Put the tea in a pot and add boiling water. Stir everything once or twice and then let it sit, off the heat but covered, until the tea is the strength you prefer. Strain it, then add milk and a sweetener to taste.

Charcoal

No one eats charcoal on purpose, at least not unless your stomach is edgy and you remember some elderly aunt saying that's what she chewed when she felt dyspeptic. But there is always a taste of charcoal with grilled food and we look forward to it. It is part of summer outdoor eating. It's what we expect on grilled vegetables or a nicely seared hamburger or a fish—or else why not order it fried or poached? That distinct seared taste doesn't require actual coals as we can see from the cross-hatched grill marks evenly etched on restaurant steaks. But making it black doesn't mean making it good. So here are a few comments in favour of the real thing.

Real charcoal has its own flavour. Its mild tang mixes with food much better than hickory or mesquite or other popular wood chips. These backyard taste enhancers often blur the flavour of barbecued food with too much smoke. There is nothing wrong with burning mesquite or grapevine cuttings or an old hickory log, if that is the flavour you are looking for but, if you want to taste the bird or beef that's on the grill, try using le vrai-de-vrai, just once.

Real charcoal is made from hardwood and it is not briquettes. Briquettes may be easier to find, but hardwood charcoal is common in Quebec and worth looking for.

Briquettes come in different qualities. Cheaper brands are soft and powdery. They leave a huge deposit of ash. Better quality brands are harder and burn a little longer. However, all briquettes are made from compressed charcoal and petrochemicals. They are inherently noxious. Don't give one of these to your Aunt Ida when she feels a little queasy. And don't throw the leftover ash on the compost heap.

Briquettes can give food an oily taste, particularly if it is put on the grill while the briquettes still have some black to them. They should never be used for smoking or covered cooking.

Charcoal, however, burns hotter and longer and leaves little ash. What there is, is easily composted. Real charcoal comes in uneven chunks. It may be a little harder to get started than briquettes but it gives a strong, persistent heat. It is great for grilling, slow cooking, and covered smoking. Many steak houses insist on using hardwood charcoal as do Lebanese and Iranian restaurants and shops that make shish taouk and other grilled meat specialties. If it is good enough for them, I'll continue to use it at home.

When using charcoal, light a small amount first and, once this is burning well, add a layer or two of coals to a half foot below your grill. Put the food on when the coals are no longer red and barely covered with ash. This will reduce flaring and let the charcoal smoke yield its subtle flavour to whatever you are cooking.

Look for hardwood charcoal in hardware stores and Middle Eastern and Portuguese grocery stores.

If you are looking for a portable BBQ grill, consider the Iranian manjal. This is a galavanized rectangular box with short legs that sits on the ground. It's easy to carry and simple to set up. Great for picnics. **Marché Akhavan** sells several models in the $30-$60 price range and offers advice on their uses.

From BBQ grills to olives, Marché Akhavan
has it all.

Chinese Cooking Wine

I did something illegal the other day. I bought a $3 bottle of Chinese cooking wine. I know it was illegal because it was handed to me in a brown paper wrapper. The store owner told me: "If anyone asks where you got it, say it fell off a truck."

This is ridiculous. Chinese cooking wine is a basic ingredient for sauces and marinades. It is common to Chinese cooking but it is also excellent for other cuisines.

Chinese cooking wine is made from alcohol, water and salt. The alcohol burns off in the cooking. Except for the salt, it has almost no flavour on its own. This makes it a perfect mediator. It enhances other flavours. Try mixing it with soy sauce and sugar for a braised Chinese beef as in the recipe below, or blend it into a paste of crushed dried herbs, salt, pepper and fresh garlic to marinate a leg of lamb.

There are several brands—Pearl River, Pagoda, Double Happiness, Golden Star—and what they all have in common is that you are not supposed to be able to buy them in Quebec.

Our food stores can get permits to sell wine and beer, but Chinese cooking wines have at least 17 percent alcohol, which is well above that limit. Go into any gourmet food store and look at the alcohol-based flavourings or fruits macerated in brandy. These bottles have plenty of booze, but ask for Chinese cooking wine? You won't find a drop. And, since it is not a drinking beverage, it's not sold at the SAQ either.

Many recipes suggest using sherry instead of Chinese cooking wine. Aside from being much more expensive, sherry has its own wonderful flavour, a delicious nuttiness that is too strong for many dishes. There is also Japanese cooking sake—Mitsukan is a good brand—on the shelves of Korean grocery stores. It is expensive and has a high alcohol content, 14 percent, but it also contains wheat extracts and corn syrup. It tastes like a sweet cheap sake.

I find that the best replacement is a simple dry white wine with an extra pinch of salt.

However, while not advertised, Chinese cooking wine is available. You might see it on the shelf or you might have to make friends with a Chinese grocer and ask if there is some Pearl River or Pagoda under the counter. Otherwise, next time you are in Ottawa, drop by one of the stores in our capital's Chinatown, such as **Asia Market** or **Kowloon Market.** One clerk said: "Everyone sells it here."

Chinese Braised Beef
Here is a simple braised beef recipe that lets the rice wine (or sherry flavour) seep through.

Cut 2 pounds (1 kg) stewing beef into thumb-sized cubes. Heat a medium-sized wok or frying pan. Add a little oil. When very hot, brown the beef a few cubes at a time, removing them as they are done. Keep the heat on high and when all the meat is nicely browned (really brown, not insipidly grey) put the meat back in the pan. Add one cup (250 ml) of water, a ¼ cup (50 ml) each of soy sauce and Chinese cooking wine (or sherry or some dry white wine with a pinch of salt). Mix in one tablespoon (15 ml) of sugar. Bring this to a boil and stir to dissolve the sugar completely. Reduce the heat to simmer and cover the pan. Let this cook for 1- 2 hours. Stir a few times to keep the meat from sticking to the pan. The liquid should slowly reduce to about ½ cup (125 ml); if it boils off quickly, the heat is too high. Add more water if necessary. Sprinkle finely chopped scallions (green onions) on top and serve rice on the side.

Chocolate

Have some *Theobroma cacao*. It's particularly popular around Valentine's Day. *Theobroma* is Greek for "food of the gods." We call it chocolate. It starts with seeds from the cacao tree which is an evergreen. Originating in Mexico and Central America, it's now cultivated in Asia, Africa and the Caribbean.

The seeds are partially fermented, dried, roasted and ground. In countries where cacao grows easily, people often take the fresh pods and eat around the seeds. Chocolate has protein, minerals and a lot of cocoa butter, which is the natural oil extracted from the seeds or beans as the chocolate is processed.

Chocolate is a great energy booster for cross-country skiers and hikers. Bittersweet chocolate has no cholesterol. Milk chocolate is made with milk and dried milk powder. White chocolate is made from cocoa butter, flavourings, sugar and milk.

Good chocolate keeps well at room temperature. If kept in a refrigerator and taken out and then put back, the natural fat leaks to the surface as a whitish glaze. This doesn't affect the flavour but it isn't as smooth or appetizing.

The chocolate we buy as a sweet likely starts as blocks from a chocolate manufacturer in the U.S.A. or Europe. The chocolatier carefully melts it for hand-dipped candies or pours it into molds such as Easter eggs. Some shops create their own blends of chocolate by using commercial blends from several importers.

Most chocolate used in good candy-making is imported from Europe and manufactured to different tastes. Callebaut chocolate, which is imported from Belgium, has a deep smooth taste. Many of Montreal's best chocolatiers, such as **Un, Deux, Trois Chocolat, Maison Cakao**, and **Cacao Royale** use it. Compare it with Bryan and Tina Stutman's house brand at **Finesse**. They blend chocolate from several suppliers and the result is a slightly spicier and fruitier taste.

Chocolate is usually enjoyed here as a drink or dessert. However, some Spanish and Italian non-dessert dishes incorporate unsweetened chocolate. In Mexico it's essential to many main-course mole sauces. For an unusual Montreal treat, try the chocolate-covered matzohs made at **Finesse** during Passover. During the summer, at **Cacao Royal**, ask for a dollop of their exquisite melted Belgian chocolate over a scoop of ice cream.

Chocolate is not just another flavour of the week. *Theobroma* is forever.

Coconut

In a city where almost every kind of food is available at any time of year, coconuts remain exotic. I don't mean shredded coconut which has a wonderful crunch and gives great texture to pies, cakes and cookies. Nor am I referring to coconut cream—as insanely rich as good butter—sold by the can in Asian food stores and an essential ingredient in South Asian cooking. I mean real coconut with a hard shell and a half-cup (125 ml) or so of cool coconut juice deep within.

A fist-sized chunk of coconut (about 30 g) has a fair amount of fiber, a little iron, and no cholesterol. But it is very high in saturated fat. If you eat coconut occasionally, this probably doesn't matter, but if you use a lot for snacking or in your cooking, you might want to consider substituting coconut cream or milk in a recipe with a blend of one part coconut powder and four parts hot milk or water.

Fresh coconut has a rich, and slightly nutty taste and the juice is slightly sweet. For the freshest taste, both the juice and meat should be consumed within a few hours of opening the coconut. If kept too long both can develop a soapy taste or a moldy smell.

The best way to choose a good coconut is to shake it to hear the liquid slosh around. Try a few and pick the one that feels the heaviest with the most juice. The eyes, or three dark spots at one end, should be firm and almost shiny. Don't buy the nut if any are soft.

Almost as much as the enjoyment of the taste of the white flesh within, is the work necessary to get at it. This is not a simple food that cracks easily like most nuts, or strips cleanly like a banana. This is good, honest work. Cracking the coconut is a time for showmanship. When else can an adult be called upon to demonstrate that real cooking demands brute force? Go ahead. Impress the kids. Get out the hammer and chisel, the awl and mallet, the vise grips, electric drill or whatever tools you need. I know, real men just use a machete. I've seen it done but I'm not there yet.

Whatever way you crack it open, remember to drain the

juice first. This is easily done by poking holes (with an awl or nail) through the softer eyes. Then crack the shell with a few deft blows from a hammer so that the coconut falls apart into five or six pieces. Rest the nut on a brick or cement block when you hit it. A wooden counter is too soft. Slip a knife with a thin blade between the flesh and the shell. The meat should pop out easily.

If you need coconut milk and can't get a coconut (or the recipe calls for coconut cream), buy a can labeled coconut cream or milk. Don't buy coconut water. This is a beverage with a lot of sugar in it. It's not bad as a drink but you don't want to cook with it.

The can of coconut milk will have different layers of cream or milk in it. There is a natural separation with the densest liquid on top. Most cans advise shaking before opening so that the "cream" and "milk" are somewhat homogenized. However, for recipes calling for thick cream, spoon off the thickest stuff from the top. Otherwise, consider stirring it up or adding water or broth to dilute it. Rice puddings and Thai soups made with coconut milk are luscious.

An easy recipe for a Thai-style chicken soup starts with a can of coconut milk with an equal amount of chicken stock (so that the "milk" is the consistency of a broth. Make about a quart (1 litre) of liquid in all. Add to this a dozen or so bite-sized pieces from fresh chicken meat (breast or thigh) with a crushed stalk of lemon grass. Simmer this over very low heat until the chicken is cooked. Add some chopped green onions and a tablespoon (15 ml) each of fresh lime juice and of nam pla or nuoc nam (Thai or Vietnamese fish sauce respectively) and a little freshly chopped chili pepper for heat just before serving. (This is really the minimum amount; you should taste the soup to see how much lime juice and nam pla you want. The nam pla has plenty of salt, so don't add extra salt to this!). Remove the lemon grass before serving.

Dandelions

What do they know that I don't? That is what I ask myself each spring. There they are—dozens of families harvesting greens near the railroad tracks along de Maisonneuve Boulevard or in fields along the Trans-Canada. Why am I not there too?

I know what they're doing—harvesting dandelions. I just keep forgetting how wonderful a plant this is until it is too late in the season. Instead, my first bunch is usually culled from the supermarket.

Dandelions are a green rich in Vitamin A and C. They also have iron, fiber, protein and a little carbohydrate. And, as my family reminds me, they are there for the picking.

If I knew how to use dandelions to their fullest, I would make dandelion wine and jelly from the flowers and a chicory-like coffee substitute from the roots, and use the stems and leaves in salads. Once dandelions were grown indoors, in dark cellars. The white root and stem of these plants were as prized as white asparagus is today. But now dandelions are considered a nuisance and a weed. That's too bad since they are an exceptional wild harvest for those who like greens with more oomph than lettuce.

The trick is to get them young, before the flowers have budded. The younger they are harvested, the less bitter the leaf, and they can be used like any other salad green. Those sold in market tend to be long in the tooth and less tender than homegrown. For these, chop off the roots, wash the leaves and stems and cook them like spinach. Some recipes recommend blanching but even a robust five-minute boil doesn't get rid of much of the bitterness. The stems are not as bitter as the leaves. Chopped into the size of green beans, they are a nice addition to a green salad.

Serve the young leaves simply, either added to a salad or dressed with a fragrant hot olive oil dressing in which minced garlic and crushed hot peppers have mascerated for a few minutes.

Another way of serving dandelion greens is to steam

them, and then sauté with a little finely chopped bacon. Try Italian pancetta for this.

If they are very tender try a traditional pissenlits salad (they are called pissenlits because of the plant's purported diuretic qualities). Slice two hard-boiled eggs. Wash and dry a ½ pound (250 g) of dandelion greens. Cook a clove of chopped garlic with a ¼ pound (125 g) of bacon that has been cut into small pieces, and 6 small cubes of stale bread. When the bacon is browned, toss everything, including the fat, over the dandelion leaves. Deglaze the pan with a few tablespoons of flavoured vinegar (fruit, wine or cider vinegar works well). Pour the hot vinegar onto the salad and toss the greens well. Add the egg slices and serve.

Dolmas

Sink your teeth into a dolma. These are small savoury treats that can be served warm or at room temperature. In Greece they are called dolmadakia and that's how many Montrealers know them. But the root of this word comes from the Arabic and translates loosely as "something stuffed". Dolmas are common to many countries. It is not so much a food as it is an approach to cooking. Think of it as the school of stuffing. Russians enjoy cabbage dolmas while Turkish cooking features tavuk dolma, which is a stuffed chicken breast

Grape-leaf wrapped dolmas is the version we know best. The filling is based around rice and can include meat, tomatoes, scallions, onions, raisins and seasonings as different as dill and saffron.

The most common way to buy dolmas is at a market—almost every supermarket has them—where they are usually sold in cans. The Zenith brand, for example, has vine leaves stuffed with rice and onions, salt, pepper and spices. These and many similar varieties are fairly bland and the leaves can be tough. They are okay if you simply want something a little different for an appetizer but people may taste the canned dolmas and start looking around to see what else the host has put out to munch on.

Far different are dolmas that are freshly made in restaurants and, increasingly, in small stores specializing in Middle Eastern foods. The wrappings are more supple. They are usually from jars of brined leaves, although as we get into spring they can be made from locally-grown fresh vine leaves as well. Stroll through Montreal alleys and you'll see a lot of people growing grape vines in their backyards. The ingredients are apt to be varied and delicious, reflecting cultural traditions and local products. Rice remains the base but there is room for pine nuts in Greek recipes or tomato and split peas in Iranian dolmas.

"Home-made" dolmas are usually thumb-sized and sell for about 25 to 50 cents apiece. Some stores, such as **Marché Norouz** and **Adonis**, will let you sample one to make sure you like them before you buy. If there is a Middle Eastern or Greek grocery store in your neighbourhood you might ask whether they will make dolmas to match specific dietary requirements, such as without nuts or meat.

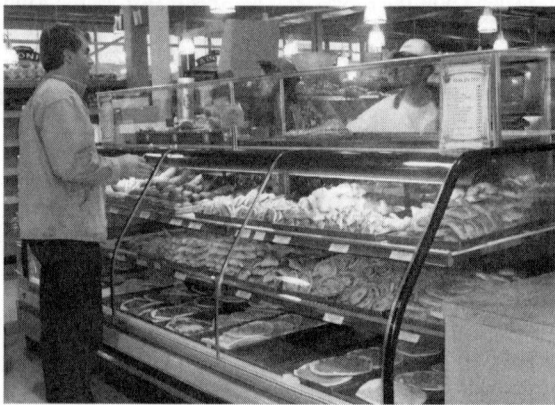

Adonis, on Sauvé (near L'Acadie).

Dulse

Hey man, want some weed? Seaweed, that is.

"Oh, yuck," said my daughter and wife when I brought home a large bag of dried dulse from our nearby fish market. It was thick-lobed, purple and crunchy with that faint perfume of "eau de sea". The fishmonger had it in bags under the counter.

"What should I do with this?" I asked. Everyone in the store had a good suggestion. "Crumble it up and put it on a salad." "Add it to a fish stew." "Munch it straight from the bag." My daughter suggested a recipe similar to the one that Samuel Johnson is said to have recommended for cucumber: slice it thin, salt it well, throw it out.

Without knowing it, most of us eat a fair amount of seaweed every day. Extracts from dulse, kelp and Irish moss are common thickeners in ice cream, salad dressings and instant desserts. They are the suspension agents used in those new gooey soft drinks. And of course sushi lovers are familiar with nori—the thin, toasted, greenish black strip of seaweed folded around thick fingers of rice and raw fish or vegetables.

There are many kinds of seaweed used in food processing but dulse is the most versatile. As a powder, it can be used to thicken sauces and processed foods. As flakes, it can be added to salads and soups.

Think of dulse as nature's original, barely processed, high-fiber, sun-dried vegetable jerky. It's packed with minerals, vitamins, fiber and protein. It can be fried or boiled. It has no cholesterol or fat and doesn't need added salt. Maritimers eat it like popcorn, in dried chunks, straight from the bag. If only it didn't taste like, well, seaweed, it would probably be the perfect snack.

So there I was. One large bag of dulse and no takers. There is so much healthy eating in even a small strand that it seemed a shame to let it go to waste. Fortunately there are some excellent recipes that should work for even confirmed dulse haters. Chopped up dulse can be added to a mayonnaise or a cream cheese dip. Toasted dulse has a lovely smoky flavour that almost, but not quite, covers the flavour of the shore. It's tasty if you get it to the right golden brown state of crispness, but be warned: left a fraction too long in the pan and the house soon smells of burnt vegetation. This is a strong stench and makes even a lousy cigar smell good.

A great way to add dulse to a favourite recipe is to substitute a couple of ounces of dried dulse—soaked in water for about 10 minutes, then drained and finely chopped—for some of the ingredients in a baked dish such as a vegetable quiche, zucchini bread or carrot cake.

"What is this?" said my mate upon returning home from work one evening. "Carrot cake, looks good ... mmm... What are these green things in it? Did you throw in some string beans? Could it be spinach? ... Wait a minute. You didn't!"

Easter Eggs

There are few holiday foods more luscious than Easter eggs. We look forward to seeing the ornately-decorated fragile shells or making homemade hard-boiled hand-dyed eggs or buying them painted red and baked into festive breads as is common in the Greek community. And of course, for many, Easter Sunday morning would be incomplete without children hunting for small chocolate eggs throughout the house.

Eggs symbolize this holiday and predate it. Long before the Easter that we know today, this was a festival welcoming the end of winter and the beginning of spring. Eggs were a universal symbol of this rebirth and at Easter they were often exchanged to bring good luck.

Another common symbol for fertility, by the way, was the rabbit. Supposedly, it is the rabbit that hides the eggs which, if we are lucky, are made of chocolate. Let's face it, there are only so many hard-boiled eggs we are willing to eat on a Sunday morning, but there is usually plenty room for chocolate ones.

Chocolate Easter eggs can run from a few pennies each to hundreds of dollars. Pharmacies and dollar stores have plenty of the former but for amazing creations look to Montreal's growing corps of chocolate artisans. **Pâtisserie de Gascogne**, for example, has several stores in the Montreal area and a wonderful selection of chocolate eggs. They range from small foil-covered chocolate and praline eggs at about $6 a dozen to showstoppers like hand-built metre-high eggs covered with gold foil and filigreed creations including painted hens and chicks that look like porcelain and sell for hundreds of dollars each.

Most of the eggs that are sold for Easter, however, follow a simpler recipe. There is a coating, either sweet milk chocolate or the darker coloured and stronger tasting bittersweet variety. Inside is a soft fondant, essentially a flavoured and coloured sugar icing. The fondant can be as soft or hard as the candy requires.

Several stores bring in specialty chocolate eggs that are a

cut above those found in dollar stores and pharmacies. One worth looking at is **Euro-Plus**, a West Island delicatessen and importer which carries excellent candies, particularly from England, Holland and Germany. They have Walkers vanilla cream eggs with vanilla, mint and honeycomb soft fondant centres and Riegelein biscuits which are dipped in chocolate and have remarkably realistic yellow and white hard fondant "fried eggs" on top.

Empanadas

Everyone knows what an empanada is, even if everyone hasn't tasted one, yet. That's because the basic concept—stretching a little cooked meat or vegetables by chopping it up with seasoning and then wrapping it in a pastry crust that is enriched with eggs and butter or shortening—is common to many cuisines. Potato knishes in Eastern Europe, samosas in India, pupusas in El Salvador. Make the pastry less rich, just a simple sheet of pasta, and we have ravioli in Italy and steamed dumplings in China.

However, it is empanadas that we are going to see, and taste, more of. (Empanar means "to bake in pastry"). Montreal's Latin American population is growing and each owner of a small grocery store is sure to have a few empanadas warming and ready to serve. And they are sure to be the kind of empanadas they know from home.

Pupusas are similar but are made with corn flour and have less fat in the pastry. They can look like large stuffed tortillas. The meat and onions filling will have been marinated with vinegar and chilis. Pupusas filled with refried beans, topped with marinated cabbage and salsa, and served with yucca frita on the side, are a favourite treat. They can have sour cream and cheese mixed into the filling, too. One or two are enough for a meal.

In Northern Mexico, empanadas with fluted edges are made with wheat flour. The dough is rolled thin and surrounds a small bite of serrano-spiced shredded meat or chicken. A few of these fit comfortably into one hand. In the southern and central part of the country, they are usually made with corn flour. In Veracruz, on the gulf coast, they could be sweet and filled with plantains. In Oaxaca they might contain one of the famous mole sauces for which that state is famous.

Colombian empanadas are usually fried and can have a starchy filling like yucca. Chilean empanadas can be baked or fried and often have a seafood filling. Many Latino stores serve empanadas from several countries despite a name that indicates just one variety. A good place to sample them is **La**

51

Chilenita which has two small take-out places on the Plateau. **Marché Andes** has substantially enlarged the original grocery store and now has a cafeteria and take out section selling fresh empanadas, tamales, and simple hot meals. **La Peregrina**, a small market store in the east end of the city, has a lunch counter in the back with a few stools and serves food from the Dominican Republic.

Frankly, once the technique is mastered, almost anything works in an empanada. The Salon Mexico restaurant in New York City has a version that includes shiitake mushrooms, shredded duck meat laced with chipotle peppers, and Cognac sauce. I'd try that.

Dozens of colourful piñatas hang from the ceiling at Supermarché Andes on Bélanger East.

Epazote

Every cuisine has its little secrets, ingredients that, while not essential, nudge a dish closer to its essence. For Mexican cooking, epazote is one of those special flavours.

Epazote is often compared to cilantro (coriander leaf), another herb common to Mexican cooking but it looks and tastes quite different.

If cilantro were a person, she would be a slight, pretty Latina with an exotic perfume. Epazote would be the leathery guy, a little long in the saddle, who is just behind her watching your every move.

Epazote looks like a large, sprawling, extra-terrestrial parsley leaf with jagged edges. It is weed-like and can grow up to a metre high. Its flavour is muted and hard to place. Not quite parsley, not quite cilantro, epazote has a dusty edge. Unlike the herbs it is closest to, epazote is not chopped fresh and sprinkled on top of dishes. Instead, add it into the cooking of soups, stews bean dishes and sauces.

Epazote goes by other names, a few of which are more suggestive of its flavour, such as pigweed, goosefoot, worm tea and Mexican tea. The last two indicate this plant's medicinal functions. Epazote is cited as an effective anti-flatulent (hence its use in bean dishes) as well as a remedy for intestinal parasites.

Some people chew fresh parsley or cilantro; no one chews on raw epazote. In cooked dishes, however, it provides Mexican food with one of its distinctive flavours.

Latino markets may sell fresh epazote and often have it dried. If you buy dried epazote, ask for leaves. The stems are also sold but are used primarily as a tea. A teaspoon of crumbled epazote leaf equals a half-dozen fresh ones.

While epazote can easily be grown here, it has only been available fresh recently. Look for it at fresh herb stands at the **Jean-Talon** or **Atwater Markets**.

Falafel

Let's imagine you could have just one dish for the next week. What would it be? There are a few conditions. The dish would have to be tasty, since it would be the only food you would eat. It would have the essentials for a healthy diet, which might remove poutine and Irish coffee from the list. It would also have to be cheap.

While there are plenty of one-dish meals that could meet these requirements, the one I want would also have to be easy to find in Montreal and as portable as *un hot dog steamé*. With these limitations the field narrows. Consider falafel.

Originating in Egypt, falafel is a longstanding Middle Eastern snack or appetizer. At its most elemental, this is a fried patty made from dried beans, usually chick peas, but other versions call for fava or white beans. What we are looking for is a nutritious mash based on one key ingredient (the beans) into which other flavours, particularly garlic, are easily incorporated. This is formed into small rounds or patties and deep fried.

The favourite method of serving falafel is wrapped in pita, but if that was all there was to it, this would be a pretty boring sandwich.

What sets falafel apart from other sandwiches is that it forces us to make a commitment: the customer has to decide what he or she wants to eat. The choice can be enormous. Layers of tahini, sweet and vinegary condiments, chopped lettuce, slices of pickled turnip and hot sauce establish singularity. Am I a spicy kind of guy, adventurous, dutiful but lacklustre? I may have come for a quick meal but I end up with a defining argument in every bite.

Falafel made in many places can be almost too basic, however. This is particularly true at chain operations where a falafel can be a substantial, decent deal for $2.75. However chains often make bland patties ahead of time. They stack them and microwave them on the pita just before serving.

Far better are the freshly made falafel served at several kosher snack bars in the Victoria/Van Horne/Queen Mary triangle in the Snowdon-Côte-des-Neiges area. This is a part of the city with large Orthodox Jewish and Israeli communities. Here, at places such as **Foxy's** and **Benny's**, the falafel are freshly made, as they are at **Pizza Cachère Pita** and at **Jerusalem Express** in the food court at Cavendish Mall. They are crunchy and hot and served with enough toppings to satiate any appetite: home-made sauerkraut, morsels of fried eggplant, red cabbage, diced cucumber and tomato salad, hummus, tahini, pickles, a fiery pepper sauce, and even French fries all stuffed into the pita. The key is to layer the ingredients properly. A large spoonful of hummus is spread inside the pita before the falafel and veggies are added. This keeps the pita from collapsing as it is eaten. Then a layer of salad and a spoonful of toppings is put in to cushion the falafel and the rest is added on top.

Falafel is often called the Israeli hot dog although that doesn't do it justice. This is more of a complete and complex meal, a vegetarian salad plate stuffed into a sandwich. All the textures and flavours come together as you bite through it: soft and crunchy, spicy and bland, moist and dry.

A few falafel in a half-pita is plenty for most of us. A whole falafel—filled with 6 to 8 chick pea balls—is enough for dinner.

Fat

I made roast chicken the other day. There was nothing unusual in that, except that I have been looking for a simple recipe. I didn't want to baste. I didn't want to turn the chicken onto its side every 15 minutes as Julia Child recommends. I wanted to season the chicken with salt and pepper, preheat the oven to between 375° F and 400° F, put the bird in and come back an hour later and eat it.

After several experiments and a lot of reading, I realized that the best and easiest recipes all had a little something extra in common. They covered their birds with fat. "Horrors! Gasp!" Some recipes I looked at didn't call for this treatment but had an equivalent like first browning the bird in a pan of sizzling hot oil. Others advised putting large nuggets of butter under the breast skin, sort of an internal basting. Maybe this has become necessary because today's chickens have less fat than they used to.

I didn't want to drown my chicken in grease. All I wanted was something that would crisp the skin, moisten the meat, and add a little flavour.

The key was to find a fat that will melt slowly and not burn once it falls into the pan.

Fat raises the cooking temperature evenly. It helps brown vegetables and meat. Food develops a more complex taste and texture—firm on the outside, sweet and soft within. Diced carrots, sautéed in a little oil until they turn bright orange, give soups a heartier flavour. Pan-fried potatoes are crispy outside; asparagus coated with a little oil broils beautifully in the oven and is much sweeter, with a more concentrated flavour, than when it is steamed.

The trick is to use the right oil. Butter, unless it is clarified, burns at 350° F. Most animal fats and vegetable shortenings will smoke between 350° F and 400° F.

Vegetable oils cook foods at different temperatures. Olive oil burns at too low a temperature for most cooking. Corn oil and canola are better. Peanut oil heats to the highest temperature (450° F) before it starts to smoke. It is the best oil for stir-fries and sautées.

I like vegetable oils for cooking vegetables. As for the chicken, I flavour fowl with fowl. The logical fat is, of course, from the chicken itself; but a tastier match is to cover the bird with a sheen of fresh duck or goose fat, available at many butcher shops, particularly those at the city's public markets. Duck fat gives chicken a lovely, slightly gamy flavour. Cook the chicken on a roasting rack so that it is raised just a little off the bottom of the cooking pan. By the time the bird is cooked, the fat has dripped off the bird, the skin is crisp and nut-brown and the meat is succulent.

Fennel

I would love to be European but I am not. I would love to state that my profoundly sensuous love for food comes from the Italian side of my family and that the rational side, which has led me to experiment and sample an endless array of comestibles, is distinctly French, but this is also not true. Maybe in a past life, and perhaps in the future I will be European. But I know that I am not because I don't yet understand fennel.

Fennel is a vegetable that tastes strongly of anise, similar to alcoholic drinks such as Pernod or Sambuca.

Fennel has been around a long time. Prometheus is said to have used fennel's hollow stalks to hide the fire he stole from the gods. During the Middle Ages the plant was hung over doors to ward off witches. This is of interest because we have a small doll, a kitchen witch, hanging above the doorway. It ensures that the evil eye, bad vapours or something malicious from Hogwarts will not burn the toast or smash the soufflés. I am tempted to hang some fennel next to our kitchen witch and let them fight it out.

Fennel is a member of the carrot family. The plant has three main parts: feathery leaves, large stalks, and a thick bulbous centre. Although fennel can be bitter and taste similar to celery, the varieties usually available at market are sweeter and strongly licorice-flavoured. Fennel slices used as crudités are fresh-tasting and crunchy.

Fennel stalks can be dried and put on a fire to lend a subtle aroma to grilled meat and fish. The bulbs, quartered or halved, are also often served grilled, brushed with oil and cooked quickly. Or else they can be braised in a little liquid, cooked for a few minutes and dusted with a mixture of Parmesan cheese and bread crumbs and cooked for another 10 minutes in a hot oven. Tender young stalks are often cut like celery and served raw in salads. The leaves are used as a garnish or tossed into soups just before serving.

I like fennel in Indian dishes, so perhaps there is a yet-to-be-discovered Indian food gene residing in my soul.

Indian dishes frequently use fennel seeds. I find these have a more delicate flavour than the stalks or bulbs. The seeds are often roasted and added to other spices. A similar mix is often offered out at the end of Indian meals or upon leaving a restaurant. It is meant to be chewed slowly, and aids digestion as well as freshening the breath.

Fermented Black Beans

If the wonderful complexity that is Chinese cooking could be reduced to one essential flavour, I would choose fermented black beans. Soy sauce is common to many Asian cuisines including Vietnamese, Thai and Japanese. Other ingredients such as chili paste or oyster sauce are also not unique to Chinese dishes. Fermented black beans, however, appear to be one of the few ingredients that remain in the Middle Kingdom and should be on the shelf of every cook who makes Chinese food at home.

The beans themselves look like small black raisins. When you buy them, they should be resilient. They can be hard and wrinkled although more pliable ones are likely to be fresher. The smell varies from smoky to cheesy and they always have a strong salty soy taste. I like the Yang Jiang brand which is preserved with salt and ginger. Left covered in the cupboard, it keeps for months.

Fermented black beans could be made at home, although few would do so. Susanna Foo, in *Susanna Foo Chinese Cuisine*, writes about a neighbour in Taiwan who made her own. "She would mix black soybeans with salt, spices and ginger root and let them sit out to ferment. She then sun-dried this concoction in her backyard for many days. During that time the whole neighbourhood acquired a pronounced smell, and my mother would complain that the odour was offensive."

Since these are soy beans, they are nutritious, although they can be very salty. Some recipes recommend soaking them to remove the excess salt and then rinsing them before they are used. It may depend upon the brand. I usually add them, chopped coarsely, directly to a recipe, particularly in stir fries where they pair wonderfully with chopped garlic. They also work well with chicken or fish.

Sea Bass with Black Bean Sauce
Try this dish: Use a whole cleaned sea bass or trout. Sprinkle the fish with a little salt and put it on a plate that will fit into a microwave oven. Grate an inch of ginger, chop a couple of

garlic cloves and 2 tablespoons (40 ml) of fermented black beans. Shred two green onions or scallions. Mix these ingredients together and add 2 tablespoons (50 ml) of soy sauce and an equal amount of dry white wine or sherry and a teaspoon (5 ml) of sugar.

Let the fish marinate in this for a few minutes and then cover it with plastic wrap, or leave it in the refrigerator until you are ready to cook. Set the dish in the microwave and cook it at the highest setting for about 10 minutes, more or less. It depends upon the thickness of the fish. If your microwave platter does not rotate, turn the fish after five minutes. When the flesh comes away from the bone, the fish is done.

Chinatown.

Fiddleheads

Fiddleheads sing of Spring. They are one of the first local vegetables to come to market. The corn may be from Georgia, new potatoes from Florida, and tomatoes picked from hot-house vines, but dark green, tightly curled fiddleheads are plucked from local wetlands.

Here is a local edible that demands we eat it when it is ready, not when we are. This is a true food of the terroir, le goût de chez nous! We are fools not to enjoy it during the brief time that it is at its best.

Fiddleheads are ferns. The kind we harvest in Eastern Canada is usually the ostrich fern. These will be at least a metre tall during the summer. When the fiddleheads are picked, the plant has small, tightly curled knobs that look just like the scrollwork at the top of a violin. The stems should be short, no more than a few centimetres long. The curl must be tightly wound and dark green and covered with a papery chaff. The chaff is removed before fiddleheads come to market but if there is still some on the plant, it rubs off easily.

Fiddleheads are a great source of fibre and high in vitamins A and C. They can be eaten raw but this isn't advis-able as many people find that raw fiddleheads upset their stomachs. They also have a bitter taste before they are cooked.

Wash the fiddleheads well to remove extra chaff or dirt. Cook them quickly, as you would asparagus—steamed, boiled or broiled with a little oil. They may uncurl a little when they are ready. Fiddleheads don't keep more than a few days in the refrigerator so eat them soon after you buy them.

When cooked, the taste of this plant is very clean and grassy, a little nutty and very much like a mild asparagus. Fiddleheads can be canned or frozen once they are cooked. They can be pickled too. But I think they are at their most succulent when they are freshest, cooked quickly and served in an omelet or a salad or tossed with pasta, or, best of all, on their own, steamed until they are tender and served with a sprinkling of sea salt, a drizzle of melted, unsalted butter and a squeeze or two of fresh lemon juice.

Fines herbes

Early summer is an eager season. I am impatient for fresh corn to come to market, for local tomatoes and ripe fruit. I want to go into our garden and pick what isn't there.

Fortunately, despite my inept attempts at gardening, we have herbs. These thrive in a shallow border of earth at the base of a brick wall. The space is about a metre long and a hand's breadth wide, but the eternally dripping garden hose is on this wall, so this patch gets water and there is plenty of sun. I am always surprised that in late spring, there are thickets of thyme, oregano, and garlic chives, parsley and mint.

This is a wonderful urban bounty. We have fresh and pungent flavours to enliven our cooking. Chicken with a sauce of cream, demi-glace and fresh tarragon, a soft cheese laced with chives, an omelet dressed with fines herbes ...

"Fines herbes" is a catch-all term. Traditionally, fines herbes refers to finely chopped parsley. Most restaurants have a tub of chiffonaded parsley on hand for garnishes. However, fines herbes now includes most of the classic French cooking herbs, a mixture of the leaves of plants—in particular parsley, chervil, tarragon and chives. The quantity of each depends upon the cook's preference. Oregano and thyme can also be used, but these tend to overwhelm the others.

There are recipes calling for fines herbes that include chopped mushrooms or truffles, but these have very particular uses. The traditional fines herbes mixes in French cooking try to balance a slightly wild sense of the outdoors (thyme) with the edgy (chervil or tarragon tasting of licorice) and the commonplace (parsley). All of these herbs have a slight bitterness which is why they marry well with cream sauces and salad dressings.

Most recipes that call for fines herbes incorporate their freshness and spark into a more elemental dish such as a green salad with a simple dressing or an omelet or scrambled eggs.

If you can't get them fresh-picked, one teaspoon (5 ml) of dried herbs is equivalent to one tablespoon (15 ml) of fresh. Rehydrate them in a bowl of very hot water.

Shirred Eggs Aux Fines Herbes

Here is a favourite family recipe for shirred eggs that should serve three. These are more settled than scrambled eggs, but not quite an omelet.

Break three eggs into a mixing bowl, beat them until the colour is uniform. Stir in a tablespoon (15 ml) of fresh fines herbes, a pinch of salt and a few gratings of pepper. Heat a tablespoon of butter in a medium-sized pan. As soon as the butter starts to turn brown add the eggs. Let the bottom settle for a moment. Add a tablespoon (15 ml) of cream cheese broken into small chunks. Use a wooden or metal spatula to push the thickening mixture toward the centre. Lower the heat if the eggs are cooking too quickly. Keep moving the mixture into the centre until the eggs are cooked to the right consistency. Sprinkle a little fines herbes on top and serve with hot buttered toast.

Five-Spice Powder

Five-spice powder is as essential to the Chinese kitchen as soy sauce and sesame seed oil. It may not be called for often, but there is no substitute when it is needed.

The traditional blend consists of star anise pods, fennel seeds, cloves, cinnamon and Szechwan peppercorns. These are ground to a fine powder. The unusual flavour for most who first taste it comes from the anise. By itself, star anise has a bitter, medicinal tinge to its licorice flavour. Fennel, which also has a licorice edge, is a little mellower and gives the mixture some depth. The cloves and cinnamon broaden the flavour spectrum the way burning incense in a church focuses the soul. All of a sudden we are not too sure which spice is dominant. The Szechwan peppercorns give this mix its ultimate air of mystery. There is something sensual here, but we don't know what it is. The peppercorns are not as thick or pungent as ordinary black pepper or chili pods. These are aromatic and fragile.

How rich China must have appeared to Marco Polo and the earliest western traders! Spices were rare in Europe. Here was a cuisine that, like that of the Indies, blended them by handfuls.

Why five? Some sources allude to an ancient mystical orientation. There is a pentagram about the parts. Each helps balance the whole. Not one works as subtly on its own.

On the other hand, why not six or seven or more spices? Some cooks like to add dried orange peel. One recipe has a ten-spice powder that includes coriander seeds, ginger and turmeric.

In short, like curries, there is no reason why each kitchen shouldn't have a mixture that suits its taste. But be cautious with this seasoning. Too much easily overpowers food. If you don't care to blend your own, five-spice powder is available in many grocery stores. Five-spice powder is usually reserved for cooking stewed meat, fowl and smoked fish. It is seldom used in vegetable dishes or soups. However, it does add a nice zest to pears or apples. Here is a dessert which is easy to make and offers a good introduction to this flavour.

The following recipe is for one apple and is easily doubled or tripled.

Apple Slices with Five Spices Powder
For the apples, choose a firm variety like a Granny Smith.

Peel, core and cut an apple into 6 or 8 pieces. Rub the sides with a cut lemon. Set the pieces aside. Make a sauce with 1 cup (250 ml) water, ⅓ cup (75 ml) sugar, 1 tablespoon (15 ml) of fresh lemon juice, and ½ tablespoon (10 ml) each five-spice powder and butter. Bring this mixture to a boil. Stir until the sugar is dissolved. Add the apple slices, bring the sauce back to a boil, cover and reduce the heat to a simmer. Cook until the slices are done, but not too long or they will fall apart. Remove the slices with a slotted spoon. Bring the syrup back to a boil and reduce it to half the amount. Strain the sauce and let it cool a little before serving over the apple slices.

Fried Dough

Oh, for the fried dough man, the bitso-bitso stand, the churrería, the New Orleans beignet. Not for me the endless varieties of focus-group-formulated, over-sweetened, candy-crusted, cheaper-by-the-dozen doughnuts. What I crave is a tasty flour-and-egg-batter fried quickly in a little oil or fat, served hot and fresh with maybe a sprinkle of sugar or cinnamon. I'm easy to please.

We get close to authentic fried dough with recent innovations known as beaver tails and funnel cakes, I suppose, but these are fried in far too much oil and gunked up with apple sauce, maple syrup, caramel spread and so much other stuff that they look like pizzas that wandered over to the dessert stand and never made it back. A similar product, the Volcano, is made at **L'Esprit Carnival** on rue de la Commune just west of Place Jacques Cartier in Old Montreal. The Volcano is a fried dough ball topped with ice cream. Not bad, perhaps, but not the basic treat I have in mind. (Better to stick with their simple $2 version made with a light batter dusted with cinnamon and sugar.)

Remember the basic Dunkin' Donut dunking doughnut? That's the long one, crisp on the outside, chewy and tasty and it had no hole. It came close, too.

We fried-dough mavens have to scout around. There is a family which occasionally shows up at food festivals. They make Latin American churros, foot-long crisp crullers filled with a choice of chocolate or cream or lemon custard. I prefer them simple, dusted with sugar. Sometimes fresh ones pop up in Latin American grocery stores like **Marché Andes.**

Fresh and delicious Maghreb-style doughnuts, served with honey, can be had with authentic Moroccan mint tea at **Maison du Bedouin** in Le Faubourg Ste-Catherine.

This is not difficult food to make and is common to many cuisines. Lately, I have seen them in Filipino grocery stores. They are called bitso-bitso and come two to a bag. **Fiesta-Pilipino** makes them in their small bakery just south of Van Horne on Victoria.

Vietnamese and Chinese bakeries also make fried dough treats. These are delicious with a Vietnamese coffee, strong and sensuously layered over sweet condensed milk. Yow Chang Quai is Cantonese for fried bread. They are made fresh at **Vinh Hing**, a small pastry store and restaurant in Ville St-Laurent.

Garam Masala

Indian cooking may be the world's most complex. This is not because of the basic ingredients. The vegetables, rice, pulses like peas and beans, and meat and fish are in many recipes common to much of the world. However the ravishing use of spices and herbs has made Indian cooking one of the most difficult for the unwary to try at home. Freshness is key. Packaged curries and prepared spice mixtures fall flat.

While most of us can't expect to keep amchoor (dried mango powder), mustard seed oil, or fresh turmeric root around the house, it is worth making sure that the basics for a good masala—or spice mixture—are on hand. One of the easiest is garam masala.

"Garam" comes from the Persian word for "hot". Indian cooking classifies herbs and spices as to whether they have hot or cool reactions with the body. Hot, in the masala sense, doesn't always mean fiery. It is more akin to zesty. Some of the "hot" spices are cinnamon, cloves, black pepper and black cardamom. Cool spices might include coriander and cumin. In Northern Indian cooking the masalas are usually dried and ground. In the south they are often made into a paste.

There is no one recipe for garam masala. The mixture will vary according to the recipe and the chef's tastes. A simple version might be a teaspoon (15 ml) each of cardamom, cumin, black peppercorns, cloves, allspice and a little cinnamon bark. Grind this as finely as possible and keep it stored tightly out of the light. Use this in rice and vegetable dishes.

Here's an easy recipe. Peel a couple of potatoes, cut them into cubes and parboil them. Sauté a chopped onion in a little butter until it is soft and golden. Add ¼ teaspoon (1 ml) of salt, and one teaspoon (5 ml) each of powdered turmeric and the garam masala. Stir and cook this over low heat to warm, but not burn, the spice mixture. Add the drained potatoes and a cup (250 ml) of thawed frozen spinach or steamed fresh spinach. Mix well. Cover and cook everything together for about 15 minutes until the potatoes are tender.

Garlic

In the world of miracle foods, garlic—fresh or in capsules—is extolled as the appropriate medicine for the hyper-tense, arthritic, and generally dyspeptic. Crushed garlic, strewn throughout a garden, is purported to stop fungus and ward off parasites.

Conversely, there are claims that garlic does relatively little and is low in nutrients. But there is tremendous agreement that garlic is great in the kitchen. Everyone knows what it tastes like. More important than a first kiss is that first date in a restaurant when both are willing to eat the garlic. One of our city's great culinary memories is when Prince Charles (pre-Diana) was officiating at something in Montreal. He decided to dine at one of our most classic French restaurants, Chez la Mère Michel. Only the chef was told "no garlic" in the food. Quelle dommage! Diplomacy trumped the palate and garlic was pushed off the plate.

Why does garlic have such an unmistakeable effect? Garlic's components—allicin and mustard oil—pack a punch. The former gives garlic its signature taste and aroma. The latter gives fresh garlic its bite. This is a volatile oil. It dissipates rapidly. That is why powdered or dried garlic doesn't have the same sharp taste. It also disappears in cooking, even as the sugars in garlic slowly caramelize, which is why roasted or braised garlic can taste sweet.

Garlic is from the same family as onions, leeks and chives. Any of these can replace garlic in a pinch. Of course, since garlic can last for a long time, it's easy to keep several heads around. The long braided strands of garlic are meant to be stored through the fall and winter.

There are several kinds of garlic at market: a potent red tinged or Italian (sometimes called Mexican) garlic, the common silver-skinned, and even a very large one known as elephant toe garlic. While impressive, this variety has the least flavour. Early in the season, look for a darker, almost dirty garlic available at many stands. It has larger cloves, is slightly sweeter and very tasty fresh, but it does not keep its flavour during cooking as well as the later varieties.

Ail du Midi is the local name for a new variety. It has a less intense bite and a sweeter flavour than other garlics. It would be perfect for salad dressings or recipes in which the garlic is barely cooked. It is grown locally from bulbs imported from Provence. Look for it at **Cinq Saisons** stores and **Les Douceurs du Marché** at the Atwater market.

Well-cured garlic, if stored in mesh or paper bags, will last several months in a cool part of the kitchen where there is ventilation. Don't store garlic in a plastic bag. Refrigerators can be poor places to keep garlic if they are too dry. Don't separate the cloves from the bulbs until they will be used. If you have to substitute dried or powdered garlic for fresh, figure that 1/8 teaspoon (1 ml) of either is equivalent to one clove. When using garlic cloves, cut through them lengthwise and remove any bitter green shoots that may have started to grow.

My favourite garlic recipe is Chicken with 40 Cloves of Garlic. Most French cookbooks have a version. I confess to making this, savouring the intensely flavoured roasted garlic, soaking up the juices with hunks of baguette, and cheerfully ignoring the chicken. This is a dish best eaten among good friends.

Here is an easy version.

Cut up a 3-4-pound (1.5-2 kg) chicken into serving pieces. Separate the thighs and drumsticks. Mix salt and pepper with 2 teaspoons (10 ml) of fines herbes and rub this mixture into the pieces. Put the chicken in a casserole dish. Add about a ½ pound (225 g) of garlic—4 to 6 heads— separated into cloves, leaving the skins on (the garlic can be squeeze out easily as if from a small tube, when the dish is cooked). Pack the cloves around the chicken pieces. Add a half cup (125 ml) of olive oil, a stick of celery, a carrot, parsnip and a few bay leaves. Put a tight lid on the casserole. Cook it in a 350° F oven for 2 hours.

Gefilte fish

At a dinner party recently, we were trying to figure out what foods capture the flavour of a culture's cooking but might not be appreciated elsewhere. The Chinese like congee, a rice gruel few non-Sinophiles request. The Scots, and perhaps only the Scots, enjoy haggis. Québécois crave cretons. And, for Jews, there is gefilte fish.

It's gefilte, sometimes gefülte. To quote from Leo Rosten's *The Joys of Yiddish* "Pronounced ge-FILL-teh fish. From the German 'stuffed fish.' Fish cakes or fish loaf, made of various fishes which are chopped or ground and mixed with eggs, salt and lots of onions and pepper. Sometimes with sugar. The traditional Friday night fish, served at the Sabbath dinner... delicious, hot or cold ... with red or white chrayn (horseradish)." This is the flavour of Jewish cooking and it's not just for Friday night!

Chez nous, my mate, born in Poland, does not like chrayn with her fish. Her mother, also from Poland, used to make gefilte fish with lots of sugar. Her father, from a different part of Poland, hated it sweet. I like the carrots grated coarsely so the dish has more texture. And so it goes.

Once, in the days before Catholic dietary practices were liberalized in the mid-1960s, my teen-age friend Jean-Pierre was at our house for an erev shabbos (Friday night) meal. In those days good Catholics did not eat meat on Fridays and Jews traditionally ate plenty of it—a brisket of beef, a roast chicken, something carnal for feasting. We looked in the fridge for something for Jean-Pierre and came out with gefilte fish. He went home and raved about the meal. His mother called. "Where do you get this fish?" she asked. "He never eats fish at home." "Oh, it's easy," my mother said, "we get it from a jar."

Well, not quite, and certainly not in this book.

Real gefilte fish is traditionally made from several kinds of fish. Doré (pickerel), pike and whitefish are common but others could be used. The fish used to be chopped, mixed with seasonings à la Rosten and stuffed back into the skin of the largest of the fish and baked or steamed. The process took hours and the house stank of overcooked fish for days. Quite often the final product resembled Montagnard bowling balls. However, there is a better way.

This is a simple recipe for light, easy to make and authentic gefilte fish. It is prepared in a microwave oven in a glass or microwavable bundt pan. This is essential. The uniform shape of the pan and its open centre allows the fish to cook perfectly. Unmolded, the dish looks great plus there is an opening just the right size for placing a large mound of red chrayn.

Fresh horseradish is only available intermittently so buy a jar and keep it in the fridge. However, several fishmongers have the requisite ground fish mixture on hand. **New Victoria Fish** grinds it fresh to order.

Gefilte Fish
This recipe is based on a medium-sized microwaveable bundt pan. After you make this once, you can adjust the proportions and cooking time according to the size of your pan.

2 pounds (900 g) minced fish
2 onions, chopped
2 eggs, beaten
4-5 tablespoons (60-75 ml) matzoh meal
2 tablespoons (30 ml) sugar
1 tablespoon (15 ml) salt
1 teaspoon (5 ml) white pepper
1 carrot, finely grated
1 cup (250 ml) cold water (fish stock is better)

Combine all ingredients well. Place in an oiled microwaveable glass bundt pan. Smooth the fish so that it is even and shake the pan slightly to break up large air bubbles. Slowly pour a 1-inch layer of water or fish stock on top. This prevents a skin from forming as it cooks. Cover the dish with plastic wrap and poke a few pin holes in the wrap to vent the steam. Microwave on high for 20 minutes, turning the dish once after 10 minutes if you don't have a turntable in the oven.

Cool the fish, pour the liquid into another container and unmold gently. More liquid will drain from the fish as it cools. Siphon this with a turkey baster. Serve the liquid in a gravy boat or freeze it to use for the next batch of gefilte fish.

Gelato and Granita

Summer is the time for gelato and granita. There is regular ice cream of course, but even the high-octane, super-rich premiums like Ben & Jerry's or Häagen-Daz are meant to be eaten robustly. They are packed into cones, shakes and sundaes. The bigger the pile, the greater the enjoyment. At least that's the theory. This is American-style ice cream and it isn't meant to be savoured slowly. That perspective is reserved for the European cousins: gelato and granita. They are indulgences meant for small bites. Their deep, rich flavours fill the mouth. They are Italy's gift to a hot day.

Gelato is a milk-based product. It uses the same ingredients as ice cream but tends to be creamier, not quite as cold, and richer. For example, compare chocolate ice cream, even a Baskin-Robin's "world class chocolate," with a real Italian tartufo offered in many Italian restaurants. The best tartufos are intensely flavoured, almost like a frozen chocolate mousse.

Granita, likewise, could be tossed off as Italian sherbet or sorbet, but it is easy to stumble here. Sherbet is technically not the same as sorbet although the terms are often lumped together. A sherbet can contain milk, a sorbet never does. This leads us back to granita. Good granitas are satiny and oh-so-smooooth. In essence, they are ices, made from water, sugar and flavouring. Fruit juices, cold espresso, and even wine can be used.

Both granitas and gelati should have strong, intense flavours. A lemon granita, for example, pairs unbelievably brilliantly with just a drop of very old balsamic vinegar. Nuts and fresh fruit are particularly popular with both of these frozen delights. Torroncino (nougat), hazelnut, chocolate and sweet liquors are common.

Montreal's large Italian community ensures that fresh gelati and granitas are made regularly in small quantities in many parts of the city. Many sports bars and espresso cafés in Little Italy or in St-Leonard serve them during the summer. Look for a sign in the window or ask when you drop in for an espresso.

Ghee

Ghee is an intriguing food with a delicious buttery flavour—not surprising since ghee is either made from butter or made to taste like it. It is a common food in India, the Middle East and Africa, all these are places where milk products soon go bad without refrigeration.

However, butter will keep for a long time, months in fact, if it is clarified. This is unsalted butter that has been cooked slowly so that the water evaporates and the milk solids precipitate. The milk solids turn brown in the cooking and give the oil a nutty flavour. When the solids are strained out, the oil that remains is clear and golden. It solidifies as it cools, but becomes clear again when heated.

Clarified butter used to be common in kitchens. Western cooking has largely discarded it. We have easy access to refrigerators, and use more non-dairy cooking oils such as corn and canola. But clarified butter still exists in much of the world's cooking.

In India, ghee was once made only from the milk of the water buffalo but today any milk can be used. Ghee made from butter is often called usli ghee. It is a rich food given to kids as a food supplement, similar to a daily multi-vitamin pill.

More common, and less expensive, is ghee made from soy bean, palm and other vegetable oils. Vegetable ghee has artificial colour and flavour added to make it look and taste like butter; it is cholesterol-free, unlike butter-based ghee.

Ghee gives food a subtle buttery taste and, better than butter, it doesn't burn as easily. The smoking point of both vegetable- and butter-based ghee tends to be higher than most vegetable oils. A little ghee can take the place of a larger amount of oil for frying food and it works well in a wok where a high heat is necessary for stir-frying. A teaspoon (5 ml) of ghee in a small pan easily cooks a couple of cloves of minced garlic without turning acrid. You can also use it to make popcorn.

While recipes may state that vegetable oil can be used as

a substitute, ghee has a much stronger flavour and should be used when a dish calls for it.

Ghee is a fat and can be used the same way other cooking oils are used. A bottle or can will keep for weeks on the counter and several months in the fridge.

Almost every South Asian, Middle-Eastern, and Caribbean grocery store carries ghee.

Gravlax

Let's say you went fishing and ended up with too much salmon but had no place to put it. If you were in Sweden, you might consider digging a hole in the ground and burying the fish. After a few days the buried (grav) salmon (lax) would be cured and the flesh soft and edible.

As far as I know it is impossible to buy gravlax prepared this way, and probably a good thing too. Fortunately, there are plenty of supermarkets and fish stores selling gravlax made by more modern methods.

Gravlax, when it is well prepared, retains salmon's rich complex flavour. In this way it is similar to Japanese sashimi. However, sashimi is raw fish while gravlax is cured in brine. Gravlax looks similar to smoked salmon, which is often called laks or lox. However, the taste is different since gravlax is not smoked.

Those squeamish about sushi or sashimi are often at ease with gravlax. Those who find lox's smoked flavour overpowering, usually appreciate gravlax's milder taste. It is particularly tasty sliced thin and served atop small rounds of rye or pumpernickel bread with a dollop of a sweet dill mustard sauce.

To prepare gravlax, salmon is filleted and the bones removed. The skin is left on one side of the filet and the fish is marinated from one to three days in a mixture of salt and herbs, usually with fresh dill, and pressed down. The mixture can also include sugar, peppercorns, and even cognac or other spirits. The fish is usually frozen before it is cured to kill any parasites. By the way, most fish that is used for sashimi or salmon tartar is flash frozen for the same reason.

In the last few years gravlax has gone from being an obscure Scandinavian treat at the smorgasbord table to a commonly served appetizer. **Costco** and supermarkets sell it. **Poissonnerie N.D.G.**, **Poissonnerie René Marchand**, and **Saum-Mom** make their own.

Greek Cookies

I know it's not really Christmas until my neighbour, Mrs. Voyatzis, brings over a batch of kourabiedes and melo-macarona. These are Greek holiday treats. While they are available in most Greek pastry stores throughout the year they are traditional during the holiday season.

Kourabiedes are Greek shortbread cookies. They are usually infused with anise or almond flavouring. Covered with mounds of confectioners' sugar, they look like small mountains of snow in the bakery windows. They are light and quite sweet since confectioners' sugar is also added to the flour as the dough is mixed.

They are perfect for a festive season where everything is decked in white. I can only presume that whoever chose the images of "sugar plums dancing in their heads" or "chestnuts roasting by an open fire" never ate kourabiedes.

While these cookies are delicious, be warned: they demand to be eaten delicately. This is not my strong point. Either the inevitable quarter-inch of powdered sugar on top of the cookie drifts over my pants and jacket or I breathe in as I am about to eat one and the sugar racks my lungs before the cookie hits my tongue.

Melomacarona (just saying the word is fun) is the other seasonal Greek delicacy. They are dense and saturated with honey syrup after they are baked. Traditionally the flour should be semolina and the texture is grainier and coarser than cake. The flavourings here are traditional Christmas spices: cloves, cinnamon, orange peel and ginger. These cookies are covered with chopped walnuts.

Both melomacarona and kourabiedes are available during the holiday season at any Greek pastry store. There are several on Souvenir street in Chomedy as well as along Parc Avenue between Mont-Royal and Jean-Talon.

Ground Cherry

Search on the Internet for ground cherry and you're likely to come across fifty references to "weed control" for every mention that this large ripe berry is also a delicious fruit. Ground cherries look like miniature tomatoes (to which they are related). They grow wrapped in a papery husk.

The technical term is *Chamaesaracha coronopus* and, because of their unusual wrapping, they are part of a group of plants known as the Chinese lantern family. In Quebec, they are known as cerises-de-terre.

Ground cherries grow on low spreading perennials. The berry can be green or purple but is most commonly yellow. It gives off a sweet, slightly musky smell and tastes plummy or even a little bit like an apple. The plant grows easily along roads and cultivated land in many parts of North America. In Quebec, however, it is most often grown indoors and transplanted because it rarely survives our winters.

Since they grow so easily on farmland, they are frequently treated as a pest, particularly in the American southwest, where they are pernicious in cornfields. Most farmers treat them as a weed and control them with a combination of mechanical tillage and chemical herbicides.

This is unfortunate because the ripe fruit is delicious. It can be eaten fresh (peel off the papery covering), or made into compotes, preserves and jams like other berries. When not yet ripe (if the stem end is still green) ground cherries taste bland with a hint of tartness and look like tomatillos, a standard ingredient in Mexican salsas.

If you want to pick your own, Ken and Lorraine Taylor often have ground cherries available at two loonies for a pint at **Windmill Point Farm & Nursery** on Ile Perrot. Ken has recently grown ground cherries from a native-to-Quebec plant that he found on Mont St-Hilaire. He says the fruit has a citrus flavour and the skin is orange. He calls the plant "Arctic Orange."

Halvah

The word means "sweet" in Arabic. I was brought up to think it was "Jewish cement." The halvah I grew up with is a candy made primarily from ground sesame seeds. The paste is then sweetened with sugar syrup. Then the good stuff is added. Sometimes it has honey. Often there are ribbons of chocolate or pistachios or chopped almonds inside.

This is the halvah that is sold in delicatessens or kosher grocery stores near the intersection of Victoria Avenue and Van Horne. This kind of halvah is sweet and has a wonderful nutty flavour from the sesame oil. Resist the urge to munch it like a candy bar. Nibble away instead. This is in part because halvah is rich and dense and a small bite lasts a long time, but it is also because chomping on a piece can seize those back molars with a grip as fierce as toffee. Fillings beware. Hence the nickname "Jewish cement" in some quarters.

It was a long time before I realized that there are as many types of halvahs, or halwas, in the Middle East as there are kinds of candy. Each country has its own variety. Iranian and Lebanese halvah often uses toasted wheat flour and is frequently flavoured with rose water. Greek halvah is similar, but not as sweet.

It is in India, however, where halva appears to have the strongest hold. Sweet shops make a carrot halvah—Ganjar Ka Halva—that is more like a small, dense, highly textured cake. These are likely to include condensed milk, cardamom pods and raisins. Other varieties include semolina and possibly beets, melon, fruits, coconut, poppy seeds or saffron and other spices. For festivals, the candy may be molded into special shapes. In northern India there is a caste of candy makers called Pardeshi Halvas.

In Montreal, you can drop into almost any Middle Eastern supermarket such as **Adonis** and **Marché Istanbul** and find halvah. Most are imported, although Indian restaurants such as **Pushap** sell freshly-made varieties.

Hemp Seeds

It's here, it's legal, it's hemp seed. And no, it doesn't get you high. A half pound (¼ kg) of hemp seed sells for about $10 and the small white kernels pack about as big a psychedelic punch as a wad of Kleenex. But even a small amount has a ton of nutrition and that is why we will probably be hearing a lot more about hemp-based food products.

Growing hemp for commercial use is legal in much of Canada. Manitoba, in particular, has more than 25,000 acres under cultivation. This non-hallucinogenic variety of the hemp plant has a lot of uses. The fibers can be used for paper, rope, textiles and building materials. Hemp seed oil is used like many vegetable-based oils (such as linseed and cotton) to make paint and industrial products.

In fact, boosters of hemp claim it is so useful that they make this plant sound like the vegetable equivalent of the shmoos. These were lovable little creatures in the old comic strip Li'l Abner. A shmoo "gave milk, laid eggs, tasted like chicken and had eyes that made fine suspender buttons."

As foods, hemp seed and hemp seed oil do seem to offer quite a lot. The oil has a low burning point so it is not recommended for frying or cooking. It is dark green but not as pungent as many stronger tasting olive oils. Hemp seed oil is very high in fatty acids and polyunsaturated fats. It has a nutty taste and there, way at the back of the nose, is a very faint whiff of marijuana. (Ahh, les souvenirs des temps perdus.) But I digress … hemp oil works well in salad dressings, baking and homemade mayonnaise.

Hemp seeds are also high in amino acids and protein. As a food they are often compared with soybeans, but hemp seeds are much easier to digest. Without their hulls, they look like pudgy sesame seeds. They have a slightly mushy consistency with a taste similar to sunflower seeds. When lightly toasted they lose a little of their raw character and become much nuttier. They are a tasty substitute for pine nuts or walnuts in pasta sauces such as pesto and very good sprinkled over blander foods like baked potatoes or rice. I think they'd be super wrapped with rice in a strip of nori seaweed for sushi!

The list of foods that include hemp seeds is getting longer: flour, beer, cheese, hemp milk, hemp ice cream, butters, flour and tofu-style hemp burgers. Many of these are hard to find. Some can be ordered only from internet sources. The oil and seeds are sold at some health food stores and also at **Les Douceurs du Marché** in the Atwater Market.

Hoisin Sauce

The yin and yang of Chinese food, the interplay of colour and taste, the textures and smells—these can all be confusing to the home chef who wasn't raised with a wok.

Even if I can't get a Chinese recipe right every time, it doesn't stop me from trying. There is a captivating flavour to Chinese food that makes my taste buds jump. Sometimes all it takes is the right sauce.

Hoisin sauce has everything I like about Chinese food. The word "hoisin" is linked to the sea and this sauce could be translated as seafood sauce, but it is has no relation to the harsh horseradishy ketchup condiment that gets dished up with cold shrimp in the West.

Hoisin sauce is complex. It has a strong fruit flavour that usually comes from plums or prunes. Then there is salt and sugar, garlic and rice vinegar, sesame and chilis, soy bean, and corn starch for thickening. Sweet and sour, smoky and spicy, plus garlic. This is one great sauce.

There are several brands of hoisin sauce and each has a slightly different take on the concept. Lee Kum Kee is a good brand to start with. It has a smooth texture and is a little on the sweet side. You can add some chili sauce or a favourite hot sauce to make it spicier.

Hoisin sauce is good mixed into a stir-fry at the end of cooking. Spoon in a dollop and stir it through with a spatula or wooden spoon. It also makes an excellent dip for cooked noodles and vegetables when you add water to thin out the paste.

For outdoor cooking, hoisin is a natural all-purpose barbecue sauce. Combine ¼ cup (50 ml) with equal amounts of soy sauce, apple cider vinegar, Chinese rice wine or sherry, a tablespoon (15 ml) of honey and enough chicken stock or hot water to thin this mixture so that it is not too thick and pours easily. Brush it onto chops, chicken breast or tuna during grilling. It partners nicely with Chilean sea bass which is a terrific fish for the barbecue (have it cut into steaks with the skin on). This fish is rich-tasting but not oily and costs less than tuna. Because one of the ingredients in hoisin sauce is sugar, make sure grilling is several inches above the coals since the sauce can burn before the meat or fish is cooked.

Hoisin sauce can be found in large supermarkets and in many Chinese or Korean food stores such as **Marché Kim Hoa** or **Kim Phat**.

Kim Phat on Goyer (just off Côte-des-Neiges).

Horseradish

Horseradish has nothing to do with horses and it is not a radish. In English, the first syllable was originally hoarse and was related to the pungency of the root of this plant. The French word is "raifort" and that simply means strong root. Botanically, it is in the family of plants that includes cabbages and mustard.

The word I like best for horseradish is in Yiddish. It is "chrain". The "ch" sound sounds like a thick rasping H from the top of the throat. It is a word that sounds as caustic as what it describes. There is nothing subtle about chrain.

Horseradish is popular in French cooking. A little grated horseradish is particularly effective in a sauce. The sharpness of the root balances the richness of butter or cream. A *Larousse Gastronomique* recipe for a simple appetizer starts with butter mixed with hot English-style mustard and chives. Spread this thinly on black bread. Top the canapé with grated horseradish and add a border of finely chopped hard-boiled egg yolk.

Such refinement, however, rarely made it into the Lazar manse when I was young, although there was always a bottle of Mrs. Whyte's hot prepared horseradish on hand. It is made from horseradish, vinegar and a touch of salt and sugar. Red horseradish includes beets.

But fresh horseradish is likely to be on the table in most Jewish homes at Passover. This is the feast of freedom which is in the Spring, usually just before Easter.

The Passover celebration requires that a bitter herb be eaten in memory of Jewish slavery in Egypt. While any bitter herb, such as romaine lettuce, will do, most reach for the number one masochistic vegetable in the market—horseradish. Proud papas watch as their children munch their first bite of this ferociously strong root. And, with tears streaming from their eyes, someone is bound to say, "That's good, but it is not as strong as last year."

I remember my mother making horseradish sauce for the first time. No knuckle-scraping grater for her. She tossed the chopped roots into our new food processor. It ground away for a minute. Strong fumes filled the air. The machine seized. A horseradish so strong that it destroyed the food processor became part of family lore.

Here's the way Mom makes it today. Wash and peel one large horseradish root and one beet. Chop these into smaller chunks. Mix together ¾ cup (175 ml) of water, ¼ cup (50 ml) of vinegar, ½ teaspoon (2 ml) of salt and 3 tablespoons (45 ml) of sugar.

Put the vegetables into a food processor. Chop finely while slowly adding the liquid. This makes about two pints. Keep this covered until serving or it will lose pungency quickly. I like the rock-and-roll bursts of bitter and sweet of this recipe as it attacks the tongue; but for a stronger horseradish flavour use less sugar or none at all.

Fresh horseradish root is sold in most supermarkets or Jewish grocery stores a week or so preceding Passover. It is easy to grow in a Montreal garden but, like rhubarb or raspberry bushes, planting a little can be dangerous. It takes two years for the first plant to appear from the rhizome and by then it may have spread underground throughout the yard.

Italian Tomatoes

This is the vegetable that makes summer eating great. Yeah, I know the tomato is botanically a fruit, but that's irrelevant by the time it gets onto my plate, thickly sliced with a dash of sea salt, some good olive oil and a ripping of fresh basil leaves. My, how could anyone think of this sublime food as poisonous. Yet so it was.

Cultivated tomatoes originated in the Andes. Italian herbalists were the first to describe them. The fruit was often called "poma amoris" (love apple). In Europe, many people would not eat tomatoes because the plant is related to the poisonous nightshade family that includes belladonna and mandrake. A tip of the toque to those few courageous cooks who let their palates be their guide.

We usually get a bushel of Italian tomatoes when they are at their best price. We scout the markets a few weeks before to get a sense of what the conditions and prices will be. Then we get to work making a year's worth of sauce. Although any tomato can be used for cooking, the best are the dense, oblong Italian varieties known as San Marzano and Romanella or Roma.

They may look like each other but each has different strengths in the kitchen. Romanellas taste better fresh. San Marzanos are less juicy and denser. They are excellent for making "sun dried" tomatoes. Ideally this could be done outside if we were blessed with a few consistent days of sunny warm weather, but lacking any meteorological guarantee, we prepare them inside. We have used both gas and convection ovens. An electric oven would also work if the temperature can be kept constant at 180° F.

Wash and dry the San Marzanos. Line an oven rack with aluminum foil. Cut the tomatoes in half along their length. Place the tomatoes skin side down on the foil. Sprinkle a little salt over them and place them in the oven. Drying can take from five to 20 hours, depending upon the tomatoes and the oven. Check occasionally. They are done when they are firm but springy. Spray them with white vinegar when they are cool and store them in jars that have been washed in very hot water and dried. We also store them covered in olive oil. The oil helps keep them from spoiling and the tomato-flavoured oil is delightful on salads.

Romanellas are more acidic than San Marzanos and are better for sauces. Although finely chopped onions, garlic, celery and other vegetables can be added as the tomatoes cook, I like making the sauce simply.

Wash the Romanellas and immerse them in boiling water until the skin splits. Ladle the tomatoes into cold water and remove the skin with your hands. Then heat a little olive oil in a pot, add the tomatoes and mash them into the oil. Cover the pan and let them stew in their juice, just slightly bubbling for a half hour. Stir and mash occasionally. Salt to taste. This sauce is a little chunky. If you prefer it smoother, run the sauce through a blender or food processor before you store it. It will keep in the refrigerator for a few days or in the freezer for several months.

If you want them to keep that fresh taste longer, consider hot-packing them. Pack the tomatoes in glass Mason jars that have been sterilized (with their lids) in boiling water or in the oven for 30 minutes at 250° F. (But boil the covers.) Leave a little room at the top so that the tomatoes don't bubble out. Make sure that the top of the jars are clean. Screw the lids and covers on the jars, but do not over-tighten. Immerse the jars in a large pot of boiling water. Let the water return to a slow boil and cook the jars for 15 to 20 minutes. Remove the jars. Do not tighten the lids further. As they cool, the lids will pop and depress, creating the vacuum you need for storage. If they don't pop, pour the tomatoes into a new clean jar and reprocess them. When there are problems, it is almost always because the lid was dirty or there was a small piece of tomato wedged between the jar and the lid. We keep tomatoes for up to a year this way. A bushel and a half of tomatoes (with about eight tomatoes per jar) makes about four dozen jars.

Japanese Snacks

I admit to having some problems here. On one hand I detest over-packaged, artificially flavoured, malnutritious North American snack foods. On the other hand, I really like the double- and triple-layered foil packages, highly-coloured and creatively-named, exquisitely-textured and highly-seasoned Japanese and Korean snacks.

Who can resist packages with names like Two Cops (onion and potato flavoured biscuits that look like multi-coloured mini-shredded wheat), Home Run Ball (with a candy nugget in each bite), or Pocky's chocolate biscuits, as long and thin as a conductor's baton?

North American snacks overwhelmingly fall into two dominant but similar categories: stuff that looks like potato chips and stuff that looks like tortilla chips. Once these were tasty by themselves, but increasingly they are manufactured as edible salvers for stronger-tasting foods like dips and salsas.

Japanese snacks (and these include similar products made in Korea) stand on their own. They are minimalist orchestrations based on texture and flavour with a surprise hidden somewhere in each mouthful. It may be the zap of wasabi (Japanese horseradish), the sudden hit of a salt crystal or a wrapping of seaweed around a crab-flavoured crispy nugget created to look like a mini-serving of sushi. There is a fun factor to these snacks. It is promised on the package and gets delivered with the contents.

Almost all of these snacks are an intriguing combination of colours, textures and flavours. Although they are mass-produced, each appears a little different so that merely holding a few in your hand makes for different contrasts in smooth-ness, texture and shape. Unlike chips and such, I look at each piece before I pop it into my mouth. Hmm, have I tried that one before? Is that a sesame seed giving my taste buds a nudge? What is that fish flavour ... ahh, sardine!

Getting mildly obsessive on the subject, we can see in the world of Japanese snacks, a philosophical difference between American and Japanese design. From Haiku to Sony,

Japanese approaches bring us to the edge of the product, emphasizing the aesthetics as much as the content.

The American approach is a compelling argument for quantity—how much can we stuff into something for how little cost? The minimalism is in the marketing (from producer to consumer in as few steps as possible). We have big pockets and big products. Our snacks run to singular concepts: the buttery flavour of the popcorn, the sourness of the gum, the size of the soft drink. Oh yes, and double up for 5 cents more!

Japanese snacks balance proportion, texture and flavour. The emphasis is on the taste, the packaging, the smallness, the variety.

If the goal is to eat as much as possible, the American snack wins. If the goal is to make the snacking process last longer and be more satsifying and aesthetic, the Japanese way of snacking succeeds.

Many stores stock Japanese snacks. Three good ones are **Formosa** in Le Marché de l'Ouest, **Miyamoto**, an excellent Japanese food store in Westmount and **Korean & Japanese Food** in N.D.G.

Jerk

Montrealers love their barbecued chicken. At its best, it is subtly seasoned with a spicy sauce and cooked over charcoal. But over the years it seems to me that the taste of Montreal-style barbecued chicken has become pretty uniform, almost bland. I'm less concerned with Latino or Portuguese rotisseries which have their own style, but I long for the old-style barbecued chicken, eulogized by the late Nick Auf der Maur and others, the traditional home-grown variety that was grilled on a spit and came with a great tangy sauce. For the most part these days, there isn't much difference from one place to another and the sauce in particular seems as if it all comes from the same can: insipid, brown, and thickened with too much cornstarch.

Now imagine that the chicken is coated with a great mix of herbs and peppers for a long time and that the flavour permeates the meat. Then it is cooked slowly, like a traditional barbecue so that the meat is juicy and tender, practically falling off the bone. And as for the sauce, let's kick it up a few notches. Have it pack a real punch with cinnamon and allspice, Scotch bonnet peppers, shallots, tons of flavour and just enough heat to make you stand up and salute before tucking into another moist and tasty piece.

At this point we have left the feeble blandishments of debased caramel-coloured cornstarch and fowl cooking à la Montréalais. Now we are in Jamaica and eating a delicacy called jerk. Montreal's large Caribbean community ensures that there are lots of restaurants serving jerk chicken here. The motto of Jamaica is "Out of many, one people" and it could be applied to jerk cooking. Out of many spices, one wonderful flavour.

Jerk chicken, by the way, is related to jerky, a form of dried spiced beef. Traditionally jerky is cut into long thin strips, covered with a spicy marinade and dried for a long time over a smokey fire. The etymology comes from the Spanish "charqui".

The jerk we are talking about, once it gets through a

Jamaican kitchen, is a pungent salve of herbs and spices that is forced into the meat. Caribbean cooking excels at getting the most flavour from the toughest cuts of meat. Goat or pork is also cooked with jerk seasoning. Chicken, even if we no longer use an old hen, takes exceptionally well to jerk. Most of the heat stays on the skin so there is a quick sharp bite which seems to disappear as the meat is chewed, but wait a minute and it comes around again.

With all this heat and flavour, it isn't necessary to order half a chicken to feel full. A couple of pieces per person is usually enough. This is flavour that gets spread out with other parts of the meal. Rice will moderate the heat, with maybe a sweet fried plantain as a counterpoint, and, if you can get it, authentic Jamaican Red Stripe beer to wash it down.

Two spots that make great jerk are **Ma's Place**, a friendly hole-in-the-wall joint in the west end of Montreal (and their new location in Ville St-Laurent) and the larger, long established **Caribbean Curry House** in Côte-des-Neiges.

Jerky

Why don't we make our own beef jerky? I don't mean you and me, although it is almost as easy to make jerky at home as sun dried tomatoes. But why can't we buy locally made jerky the way we buy Quebec honey, maple syrup or other foods?

At its most basic, jerky is dried and flavoured meat. Like smoking salmon or dryingchilis, jerk cooking preserves food. Canada's Food Inspection Agency says jerky is "considered a fully dry shelf-stable product." That's another way of saying it is safe. The Agency requires that commercially sold jerky must be dried for over an hour at 70°C (160°F) followed by a second drying of several hours at a lower temperature. This reduces the amount of water and kills any pathogens.

Beef is the most common meat used although bison, pork and even salmon jerkies are common. I'm waiting for turkey jerky to come along just for the fun of asking for it.

Jerky has long been part of the diet of North American Indians. They cut long strips of game and dried the meat in the sun.

Other countries make similar products, such as the Swiss and Italian air-dried meats, but these are paper thin and unseasoned. Jerky is made from thicker strips of meat. It is usually marinated, with smoke added for extra flavour. Jerky can be very spicy or quite sweet. Unfortunately, it is usually sold as a highly seasoned tough piece of meat with the consistency of freeze-dried cardboard. My theory is that the jerky sold at gas bars and dépanneurs was really created for truckers on long-haul routes desperately trying to give up chewing tobacco.

There is great beef jerky tantalizingly close to Montreal. St. Albans and Swanton, Vermont, have several small jerky companies. One of the best is **Rosie's Vermont Beef Jerky** which takes long, lean strips of beef and marinates them in ingredients as varied as maple syrup, Worcestershire sauce, and soy sauce. Then they're cooked over corncobs. There are several varieties and the flavourings are subtle. Even their hot jerky—with peppers and chilis—isn't off the chart. The beef flavour comes through. Look for Rosie's when you travel through New England and hope that their jerky will be imported here soon.

Then there is **Stemmler's** "award-winning" beef jerky. It is a delicious smoked and dried beef snack made in Heidelberg, Ontario. It is rarely sold east of Cornwall and the company has no plans to bring it to Montreal. Pity.

We do get Canadian Rockies Bulkokee beef jerky. This is made in British Columbia for a Korean clientele. The Bulkokee gives it away. The word identifies Korean barbecued meats. However, this jerky is close in texture to traditional jerky despite the pronounced oriental flavours. The beef is marinated with soy sauce, sesame seeds and a little dehydrated apple. The result is sweet without being cloying, and chewy but not tough. **Amore**, a small Korean gift shop, sells Canadian Rockies jerky in regular and spicy varieties.

Another Korean-style brand is Soo Singapore Jerky from Richmond, B.C., which has recently become available here.

While Quebec doesn't seem to produce ordinary jerky, we do have gourmet varieties like Palme d'Or's magret de canard; it will never see a service station snack counter. This is a jerky made from thin slices of duck breast seasoned with salt, pepper and garlic powder. It is delicious in pastas or on salads. Another locally-made product is Atlantic salmon jerky. The fish is cut into thin strips and flavoured with sugar and wood smoke. Both of these are available in gourmet food shops such as **Saum-Mom**, a Mont-Royal store that specializes in all kinds of salmon products.

Kebab and Taouk

In summer, as the ol' joke goes, boys will be boys and grills will be grills. Steak is probably the number-one choice for barbecue meisters at home but good cuts are expensive and, frankly, there are only a few ways that a sirloin or rib steak can be served: rare, well done, or occasionally chez nous, Pittsburgh (burnt on the outside, raw within).

But walk into a Middle Eastern take-out restaurant and it is obvious that steak is the least common way to grill meat. Along Ste-Catherine Street downtown or in Park Extension, kebabs, tikkahs and taouks rule the grills.

Essentially, these are marinated meats that are cooked on skewers. Portions are small and the meat is usually accompanied by vegetables, bread, and rice or couscous.

The dishes originate in the Middle East and India. "Kebab" or "kabab" refers to cutting the meat into chunks. "Shish" or "sis" is the sword or skewer on which the meat is cooked. Tikkahs are Indian kebabs.

This method of cooking lends itself to cuts of meat that are flavourful but tough. Marinating first tenderizes the meat, and grilling seals in the juices and cooks it quickly.

Alan Davidson in *The Oxford Companion to Food* points out that agrarian European communities had plenty of firewood and farm animals. People would use a whole carcass and bake or roast it.

However, Middle Eastern and Asian countries were more urbanized and had less access to large amounts of fuel. It was (and still is) more efficient to use smaller pieces of meat and cook them quickly over small, hot fires.

The skewer, when it is metal, holds the pieces of meat and transmits heat quickly. Meat cooks internally almost as fast as its surface is grilled over the coals.

"Taouk", which means chicken, is another word that we commonly see when this kind of grilling is done. Shwarma and donair (or doner) are meats cooked another way. These are thin slices of meat, usually chicken, beef or lamb, marinated and stacked tightly on a large skewer. This is held vertically and turned slowly in front of an upright gas or charcoal grill. The meat is sliced in thin strips as the outside of the stack broils.

Many countries have similar ways of cooking. Souvlaki is essentially a Greek shish kebab, while shashlik is the term used in Armenia and Georgia. Kofta kebab is ground beef or lamb, highly seasoned, and rolled onto a skewer. Fish kebabs are also common in Indian and Turkish cooking.

Most Middle Eastern stores with butcher counters, such as **Marché Akhavan** and **Adonis**, sell prepared marinated meat for donairs or kebabs for grilling at home. **Marché Norouz** serves delicious Persian kebabs in a pita with a grilled tomato on the side. **Restaurant Shish-Kebab** on l'Acadie Boulevard grill their Lebanese and Armenian kebabs over real hardwood charcoal.

Preparing Persian kebabs at Marché Norouz on Sherbroooke Street West.

Kimchi

I am on kimchi alert these days. Most people think of kimchi as that spicy cabbage stuff that gets served alongside Korean cooking: eat rice, slurp noodles, munch kimchi.

For too long I shied away from Korean restaurants. I found them overly similar and the menus unfathomable. But with more Korean restaurants and grocery stores opening up, the variety of dishes on the menu has increased and the staff is often better at explaining to non-Korean clients what each dish is.

One of the delights of Korean dining is the attention paid to detail, particularly the balance of colours and tastes. A well-constructed dish is a delight to see and eat. Variety of colours is as important as flavour and texture and kimchi is the spark that makes the meal glow. It is as essential to Korean dining as rice or noodles.

Basic kimchi is fermented cabbage. This is an inexpensive condiment, low in fat, high in fibre and loaded with minerals and vitamins. One guide to Korean culture comments: "some kimchi a day keeps the doctor away."

In a way, kimchi is similar to that eastern European staple, sauerkraut. But that's a superficial comparison. No sauerkraut gets the attention and spices that kimchi is known for. To make kimchi, one starts by trimming and brining cabbages. The leaves are then packed with salt, garlic, ginger, red pepper and whatever extras the cook wants or can afford to add. These could include sliced radish, strips of marinated squid, and sliced green onions. This can be left to ferment for as little as a few days or up to several months. Traditionally kimchi is kept underground in urns, but, except for a few home brewers, we are unlikely to have it prepared for us this way.

But that doesn't mean that all kimchi is mass-produced. There is an artisanal approach to kimchi and it's easy to find in Montreal. Go to several Korean restaurants and you'll notice that each has its own approach. Some cabbage kimchis are sharp and sour, others hot, still others slightly sweet. Turnip kimchi is delicious and you often have to ask for it. Here the turnips are cut into small cubes and mixed with spices and chilies. First there is the heat on the surface, then the cool centre of the turnip cube. It is slippery and firm, red and white, savoury and sweet all at once.

Cabbage and turnip kimchis are considered winter condiments in Korea. They are made in late fall and traditionally stored outside in covered crocks. But in Korea there are many other kinds of kimchi. Carrots, pears, chestnuts, pine nuts and seafood can be incorporated into the mix. Our Korean community is growing and I am waiting to try these.

You can buy imported prepared kimchi in Korean grocery stores. **Korean and Japanese Food** in N.D.G. makes it fresh every day and sells a 500 ml (2 cup) container for $3.75.

Korean and Japanese Food (Épicerie Coréenne & Japonaise) in N.D.G.

Knafé

"Psst," said my friend Chuck as we scouted out some early morning pastry shops in the north end of Montreal. "Ever had one of these?" There was a crowd in front of an Armenian bakery early on a Sunday morning. There was freshly made lahmajoun (a thin Armenian pizza) and other goodies inside, but the wait was for the knafé.

Knafé (it rhymes with café) is made in many ways throughout the Middle East. It is essentially a kind of pancake, large and pliable. It can be served with something as sumptuous as a rich cheese and nut filling or as simple as butter and honey. It can be a thick leavened batter cooked on a well greased pan or dry and as thin as a crepe. The batter, more of a dough than a batter really, can even be made from a mix of shredded filo dough and plenty of butter. Trying to pin down exactly what knafé is, is hard. A lot depends upon the knafé maker and how it was made in the old country.

The one I was about to eat was a large, thin round pancake, maybe a metre 3 ft) in diameter and a couple of centimetres (one-inch) thick. It was made from semolina and covered with a thick sweet cheese similar to ricotta. Slices were pared away and this thin "cheese cake" was grilled until the cheese melted. Meanwhile someone was offering me a bagel, but it was unlike any made on St-Viateur Street. It was round but far less dense, almost as light as a croissant and covered with sesame seeds. The roll was sliced and the cheese-pastry filling put inside. It was doused with a sprinkling of rose-flavoured sugar syrup and served hot. Forget about croissants au chocolat (well, don't forget about them, but put them aside for one weekend). On a cool, sunny spring morning, knafé au fromage was the early morning brunch treat.

That was a few years ago and except for the occasional trip to that part of town, a good knafé became hard to find. Montreal's Middle Eastern community has grown since then and many stores make them fresh. One good place to get knafé, and not just on Sunday, is the **Adonis** supermarket at Sauvé and l'Acadie. It has a pastry section almost a block long. Many

Middle Eastern bakeries like **Haddad** on Laurentian Boulevard also make knafé. Ask for a knafé-au-fromage to go and it will be heated quickly in the microwave. It is served with as much syrup as you can handle. Unless you have quite the sweet tooth, be prudent. A sprinkling is sweet; more is cloying. Beyond that is for sugar junkies only.

Lahmajoun

Lahmajoun is an Armenian gift to flat-bread cooking. This is basic Middle Eastern yeast dough rolled thin to about the size of a dinner plate and spread with a thin layer of ground meat. Thick lahmajoun look like pitas, but the tastiest lahmajoun are rolled thin and baked crisp at the edges while remaining soft and pliable. They are often sold double-layered, folded over so that the filling stays in the middle. This makes it an easy snack to eat.

As Italian-style pizzas become increasingly overdressed and hard to handle, lahmajoun retain an essential simplicity. Don't ask for them with cheese, all dressed or extra pepperoni. The filling is almost always the same: ground lamb, tomato paste, onions and spices. Maybe there is a little green pepper or extra parsley, maybe it's a Syrian variety with a little pomegranate juice added to the mix, but these are subtle differences.

Lahmajoun are delicious as appetizers, sliced into quarters and served barely warm with plump salty Greek olives and pickled vegetables on the side. They are great for picnics and brown-bag lunches and they heat up equally well in a microwave or toaster oven.

Several local bakeries make lahmajoun and they are available in Middle Eastern stores. **Al-challal** is an excellent large Middle Eastern supermarket. It is open every day and prepares them fresh.

Good lahmajoun bakeries include **Boulangerie Arouche**, **Farhat**, **Haddad** and **Lahmadjoune Beyrouth-Yervan**. Authentic lahmajoun is made with ground lamb, but flatbreads without meat are also made at these bakeries.

Lassi

During the summer I like a lassi. No, not a wee Scottish lass, but one that's thick, tasty and Indian. Lassi is a yogurt-based drink that is better than beer or tea to douse the flames of a fiery curry. It is also refreshing in summer when even a small glass seems to quench thirst better than other beverages. Maybe it's the thickness of the yogurt which satisfies and makes me feel that I have enough or the richness of the taste which makes lassi seem more satisfying than soft drinks or soda water.

Yogurt-based drinks are common in much of the world. In Turkey they are called "ayran" and made from a blend of yogurt, water, and a little salt. When served in a restaurant, some crushed mint or finely chopped cucumber may be added. Ayran, which is called "doogh" in Iran, is produced locally and is available in most Middle Eastern stores.

Another similar drink, "kefir", originates in the Caucasus Mountains. This drink is slightly fermented and natives there claim that they live long lives in part because of this drink. You can find kefir in many eastern European groceries such as the **Bucharest Delicatessen** and **St. Petersbourg Russian Delicatessen.**

These drinks tend to be thin and watery. They are tasty if you like their slightly sour milk flavour. The taste is close to, but not quite as rich as, commercially produced "cultured" buttermilk. All of these milk beverages are very healthy and they are more digestible for people who have problems drinking milk. However, when given the choice, I'll reach for a lassi. Lassi is thicker and richer than the Asian or Middle Eastern varieties. The flavour lasts a long time. This is a drink for sipping, not gulping, and is refreshing with either spicy food or by itself as a hot weather drink. In India, lassi is popular for breakfast as well as a snack.

Lassi is available in almost any Indian restaurant in the city and the quality tends to be uniformly good, occasionally verging on the superb, if additional flavourings are added. Lassi should be made with yogurt and ice-cold water. The ingredients are put in a blender; the drink should be thick and frothy when served.

Lassi comes in two main varieties. Salt lassi has salt, and sometimes other spices. Cumin is popular and black pepper or chilis also work well. In sweet lassi, which can be as thick as a milk shake, sugar replaces the salt. Rosewater, mint or coriander leaves may also be included. Sweet lassi drinks such as mango lassis, popular in many Indian restaurants, can be rich enough for dessert.

Lemon Grass

Imagine the flavour of a fresh lemon without its acidic, mouth-puckering bite. Try to capture the scent of lemon geraniums in the air, the softness of a delicate citrus-like perfume on a warm summer day. That, to me, is what lemon grass conveys.

While lemon grass is common to many Asian cuisines, it has a dominant role in Thai dishes where its aroma and subtle flavour help achieve the balance of sweet, sour and pungent that makes Thai cooking distinctive.

Lemon grass, *Cymbopogon citrates*, originated in Sri Lanka and looks like a plant that would grow well on a PEI sand dune. It is an ornamental grass with a bulbous base and long, tapered, hard blades. It can grow several feet high in dry soil. If brought indoors during cold weather, there is no reason that it cannot grow here.

For a long time, lemon grass was one of those dried herbs tucked into cellophane packets and stapled to cardboard display sheets somewhere behind the cash register in "exotic" grocery stores. I bought it only when a recipe called for it. I made whatever dish I was cooking and didn't know what to do with the rest of the packet. It would go stale, if it wasn't already. Inevitably, I tossed it out.

The trick, for those of us who do not eat Thai food every day, is to learn to incorporate lemon grass into non-Asian cooking. Minced lemon grass is delicious in marinades, chicken soup, and added to salads. Lemon grass tea makes a refreshing tisane. Just stir a small amount of chopped fresh lemon grass into boiling water. Work in some honey or ginger for sweeter or spicier flavours.

Happily, with Montreal's growing Asian communities, fresh lemon grass is available in stores in Chinatown. It is also sold occasionally in supermarkets and in specialty grocery stores like **National Food**. At about 50 cents or so a stalk, it is far preferable to the dried variety. I buy fresh lemon grass when I see it. It is as easy to use as fresh garlic or ginger. Discard the dried covering around the base and for each helping finely chop an inch or so from the bottom of the stalk. Use about twice the amount in a recipe as you would dried lemon grass.

Also tasty, but without fresh lemon grass' herbal edge, is bottled lemon grass. These are shoots, packed in water and ready to use. The cost is less than for fresh. One brand to look for is Thai Kitchen. A small jar has about 20 shoots, more than enough for several meals. Also interesting is a summer drink made by the Bottle Green Drinks Company near Toronto. This is a non-alcoholic beverage that has lemon grass, ginger and sugar cane.

Fresh stalks and frozen chopped lemon grass are sold in Asian grocery stores like **Marché Mit Thai Lao**, **Kim Phat**, **National Food**, and **Marché Thai Hour**.

Marché Thai Hour at St-Denis and Jean-Talon.

Licorice

I went looking for candy and found health. That's not the way it is supposed to be; but then, I haven't much of a sweet tooth. Offered a really good dill pickle or a slice of pretty good (but not fantastic) chocolate cake, I pick the pickle every time. Maybe that's why I like licorice. Licorice root is naturally sweeter than sugar but it has an astringency that perks up the taste buds.

Licorice flavour is extracted from the perennial herb *Glycyrrhiza glabra*. "Glycyrrhiza" means "sweet root." The plant, which is a member of the same family as peas, is common around the Mediterranean. There it has been used medicinally for thousands of years. Recent citations promote it as a natural remedy in an amazingly broad range of illnesses from high cholesterol and arthritis to AIDS and coughing. In China, licorice is prescribed more often than ginseng. In Europe, licorice extract is added to drops and taken like cold lozenges.

On the negative side, licorice, even as a candy, can affect those susceptible to high blood pressure. Purer forms, such as licorice extracts, can upset the balance of salt and water in the body. Pure licorice is not recommended for people who suffer from diabetes or kidney disease or those who have had strokes.

That noted, I was after the taste of a candy, with just enough licorice for flavour but not enough to do serious damage. That also meant I was sticking to black, since what is called red licorice, with its cloying artificial strawberry or cherry flavour, does not have any of the natural herb in it. To taste the best licorice candy, I knew we would have to go to Holland or at least to **Euro-Plus**, a Dutch food specialty store in Pointe-Claire.

The Dutch excel at licorice candy making and this store stocks more than two dozen varieties. After a demanding afternoon of tasting, our panel (which consisted of a 50-year-old man and a ten-year-old child) decided that the best were creamy toffees, hard little cats, sweet red devils, moka flavoured striped licorice sticks, and salmich balls which have a hard outer shell covering a small mound of licorice powder. The cola bits (looks like licorice, tastes like cola) were also tasty and great for cleansing the palate.

Our choices were highly subjective. Neither of us liked the salted varieties favored by many Europeans. Salt and licorice must be an acquired taste, even for a confirmed pickle lover. The amount of saltiness can range from the barely perceptible in TV pastilles (button-shaped candies to be munched while watching television) to the diamond shaped soft zout (which means salt). Perhaps this combination of flavours can only come from a nation that pulled its land from the sea. However, everything we tasted, from the toffees and nibs to the the slap-in-the-face DZ (double salt) had a cleaner, stronger licorice flavour than generic dépanneur licorice whips and drops.

Lime Leaves

If food could be a season, a Montreal summer would be Thai, the sweetest and most pungent of cuisines. Sugar and sour, heat and salt, and a little bitter just on the periphery. This is complicated cooking. Hit the right balance and the dish is delicious. Go off a note or two and the edge is lost, the food tastes muddy, the flavours are blurred and the sun is gone.

The bitter is perhaps the hardest flavour to capture. One of the best ways to get this edginess into the cooking is with lime leaves. These are makrut limes, but are often sold as citrus leaves. They are important to the food of south-eastern Asia and can be found in many Asian and Chinese grocery stores. The fruit is rarely used. The leaves are sold separately. They feel tough and waxy and are a dark green. If chewed raw the bitter lime-lemony oil bites the tongue. It tastes like an overdose of citronella. Yech. But lime leaves have a lovely faint citrus fragrance and when you tear one slightly, a buttery perfume escapes that is both grassy and lemony, and that's how cooks use them.

These leaves are incorporated into recipes the same way as bay leaves are, but the lime leaf flavour is much stronger. Shred a few lime leaves and toss them into curries or stews near the end of cooking. (They easily come off the stem; but as they come off, they can leave small sharp thorns, so be careful using them.) Stick a couple of torn lime leaves into the cavity of a fish before cooking it. I occasionally add a sprig to a bottle of gin, perfect for a summer supply of gin and tonics.

Liquid Smoke

Winter and even early spring are frustrating seasons for barbecue fans. Sure, you can do it. Pierre down the block fires up his gas range all winter. But real barbecue, the slow, wood-burning, beer-sipping doesn't really happen until the snow melts. Fortunately, there is liquid smoke.

I can hear a collective gasp. There is no other comestible that provokes the alacrity and knee-jerk consternation of liquid smoke. Mentioning this around the manse gets weird reactions. "The stuff will kill you." "It's carcinogenic." No, it is a simple food flavouring. That's all. In Texas, I have been told, they pour liquid smoke onto ribs, into sauces, maybe some use it in coffee. Used copiously it is overpowering, but added prudently, a few drops at a time, liquid smoke does wonders for marinades, soups, even salad dressing. It will give the same taste as a hunk of smoky bacon and it is fat free.

Here are the ingredients: water and natural hickory smoke. The brand I am using these days is Woodland. It has no other ingredients, no added caramel colour or flavourings. There is a little residue around the neck. It's natural. The colour is red gold. The smell is of late night camp fires, more pungent than autumn, of old wood cabins and crushed leaves. Heaven.

The other week I brined a large chicken breast, with the skin still on. The brine was one cup (250 ml) of water, 2 tablespoons (25 ml) of brown sugar, a tablespoon (15 ml) of sea salt and ½ teaspoon (2 ml) of liquid smoke. I brought the water almost to a boil to dissolve the salt and sugar and then let it cool to room temperature. I poured it into a container, added the chicken and let it sit in the refrigerator for a few hours, turning it a few times. Then I drained the liquid, wrapped the breast loosely in foil and heated it, skin side up, at about 200°F in a toaster oven for 90 minutes (thermometer temperature 180 °F). I removed the chicken, unwrapped it and let it cool to room temperature. It was delicious. Everyone at the table grabbed a forkful. I told them I used liquid smoke. It didn't seem to bother them a bit.

Mahlab

This unusual spice is a favourite in Middle Eastern baking, particularly at Easter. Mahlab or mahleb are the seed kernels of a black cherry tree that may have first grown around the Mediterranean. The ancient Lebanese city of Mahalep is mentioned in the Bible.

The fruit of this plant is similar to sour cherry. The tree can grow to five metres (16½ feet) and is very hardy. It resists diseases and insects. Mahlab root stock is often used to graft less vigorous North American cherry trees.

Mahlab seeds have a slight bitter almond flavour. Many recipes suggest substituting almonds or even anise for them, but many bakers look for mahlab to add authentic flavour to Armenian cheoreg (coffee rolls), Greek lambropsomo (Easter bread), and Syrian ma'amoul (date- or nut-filled pastries).

The seeds should be ground just before adding their flavour to a recipe because the nutty aroma dissipates quickly. Don't buy mahlab powdered unless it smells fresh. An easy way to grind these seeds is by mixing in a little of the sugar or salt that is bound to be called for in the recipe. Use a mortar and pestle to grind the seeds into powder. **Anatol Spice** in Little Italy has mahlab in stock.

Here is a recipe for cheoreg based on one from a community cookbook called *Treasured Armenian Recipes*. Mix together one cup (250 ml) of warm milk with one cup (250 ml) of melted butter. Add two beaten eggs and one tablespoon (15 ml) of yeast. Mix well. Grind together a half teaspoon (2 ml) each of anise and mahleb with one teaspoon (5 ml) of salt. Add to the liquid. Then add 3 tablespoons (50 ml) of sugar. Slowly blend in enough flour, about 6 cups (1.5 litres), to make a soft dough. Knead it until smooth. Cover the dough and let it rise in a warm place until it doubles. Roll out finger-length pieces into strips about 8 inches (30 cm) long. Shape these into circles. Put them on an oiled cookie sheet. Brush the tops with beaten egg. Sprinkle sesame seeds or chopped nuts over each. Let them rest for two hours. Bake in a 350° F oven until golden brown (about 20 -25 minutes).

Maple Smoke

We are rich. I know this is true because an American told me so. He works in a well-known restaurant in Washington, D.C., and said that he could never afford to cook me the simple but intensely flavoured dish l ate recently at a friend's home in the Laurentians.

It was a simple meal—potatoes, a salad and steaks at their most primal. They had no sauce or special seasonings, not even salt and pepper, yet when the meat was brought to the table everyone oohed and ahhed. I had never had steaks served this way and now that I know the secret, I can never eat another without comparing it to these.

The secret was in the wood. The steaks were cooked in a fireplace over split maple logs. The wood had been stacked outdoors for a year or two. There was no charcoal, no briquettes. Instead of a barbecue on the balcony, there was a large wrought iron rack set into the living room fireplace.

A few well placed logs burned under the rack. "This is the way I cook," said our host, Ron Walker. He was in the kitchen cutting inch-thick steaks from a roast.

After a half-hour, the logs settled. Ron brought out the steaks and seared them over very hot coals with flames still licking up from the wood. The steaks cooked quickly, seared on the outside, rare within. He brought them to the table. The scent of maple permeated the meat. The flavour was ambrosial.

Not long after, we were in Washington and a friend took us to the **Capital Q**—a successful barbecue spot. Every legislator from the western states had his or her signed picture on the wall. Even Ken Starr, who hails from Texas and presumably knows a few things about grilling, had compliments for the place.

The Capital Q is famous for its smoked beef brisket. The man behind the counter gave me a sample slice. It was tasty but not as good as Ron's. "We use oak," he said serving some chopped beef sandwiches. " The wood is cheap and local but it doesn't give any special taste." I enthused about the maple-infused steaks we had enjoyed. The Q man licked his lips. He said, "We add a little hickory for flavour." I said offhandedly that some people I knew use apple wood too. The Q man frowned, "We couldn't afford to cook the way you do."

Ron Walker's elemental approach to cooking also solved another mystery for me. I always wondered about the Bible story of Cain and Abel. As you may remember, Cain's oblation of charred vegetables was not accepted at the highest levels. Instead the discerning deity pointed to the meat that Cain's brother was cooking. Now I understand. Abel was serving up maple-seared steaks and the aroma wafted into heaven.

Maple Syrup

Maple syrup must be the Quebec flavour: tangy and sweet, seasonal, with a pungent aroma of the outdoors. Any Quebecer, whether native-born or immigrant, who has not visited a cabane à sucre or tasted that first pull of thick, syrupy snow-taffy hasn't really arrived.

If you can't get to a sugaring-off party, try the **Atwater Market**. Several farmers' reps are at their stands during the season. That's the short time of year between winter and spring. The days have to be above freezing so that the sap will flow, but the nights must drop to below freezing as well. It's a tough balance and we always need a good few days in a row to get it right. But when the sap is running, so am I.

The Atwater Market usually has a few regulars with some specialty maple syrup products. Louis Chartier comes in from the Lanaudière to sell Vin d'érable, which makes for a very enjoyable aperitif, and at **Les Douceurs du Marché**, René Lavallée and his staff sell an upscale bottled syrup from Cleary's, a producer near Thetford Mines. Éloi Beauregard, from St-Hyacinthe, has a nice #1 clear grade.

Although many were worried that the ice storm a few winters back would seriously affect future harvests, the yield has been plentiful. Maple syrup is usually available in different grades depending upon when the sap emerged from the tree. The first run of sap is paler and not as strongly flavoured as the runs that come later in our short season. The medium grades are darker although preferred by many because of their stronger, maple taste. The final runs are much darker. They can have strong woody flavours and are usually bought by food manufacturers and used as flavourings.

With the help of the tasting panel—two kids and three parents—we decided to see if there were any real differences. We first tried Beauregard's clear and medium grades. Then we sampled some of Cleary's medium, and finally we poured a shot of a thick dark syrup that had been stored in our freezer and taken out for pancake breakfasts. This last one was a medium grade from last year and we had always thought it tasted great.

Comparing the syrups, it was striking how the colours and aromas changed, even from one region to another. The best of the four was Beauregard's #1 clear. It was only a few weeks old with a brilliant amber hue and subtle maple aroma. It was sweet but not cloying. The medium grade from Cleary's was a little darker and almost as good, while Beauregard's medium was sweeter with a definite smoky aroma. In comparison with these three, the batch from the freezer now tasted like brown sugar syrup. We'll save it for muffin mixes or barbecue sauce. It will never see a pancake again.

Traditionally, maple syrup tastings include munching on a piece of bread or even a pickle to refresh the palate. However, our crew of tasters, which included a graduate of McGill's Faculty of Agriculture, swabbed out their tasting glasses with their fingers, determined to get every last drop.

If you are keen to go to a cabane à sucre, look for *Les Sucres au Québec* at newsstands. This annual publication lists dozens of sugar shack restaurants throughout the province. Alternatively, check their web page at http://arcsq.qc.ca.

Matzoh

The flavour of matzoh is of scorched earth. The ingredients are simple: flour and water. The dough is made quickly. Thin slabs are pin-pricked in long furrows so that the bread won't puff when it bakes. The heat of the oven sears the top of each brittle piece with hundreds of charred scars. There is no yeast or fermented sourdough to soften the burnt flavour, no salt to sensualize the taste, no sugar to caramelize. Here is the most basic of breads: pure and unblemished. Even a small bite leaves my mouth parched.

More than a food, matzoh is a symbol. It is prescribed for the Jewish festival of Passover and is eaten first at the Passover Seder (the word "seder" means "order," as in the correct order of the service). This is a communal supper to which even strangers may be invited. The matzoh is broken, as all good bread is, at the beginning of the meal, and it is shared. There is ritual and joy. "Companion", after all, means "with bread."

"Matzohs," says a friend whose religion does not command her to eat them for eight days straight at Passover, "oh yeah, Jewish diet crackers. I love 'em."

I do not. This is flat bread but there are lots of great flat breads on the world's tables. You can buy matzohs made with salt and egg or onion but these are just feeble attempts to make the Bible's "bread of affliction" less afflictive. Matzoh no more belongs to the family of tortillas, na'ans and pitas than an ascetic does at a buffet.

Matzoh's virtue is its simplicity. The mere act of eating it makes one feel pious. As a bread, it is best juxtaposed with other, more flamboyant flavours—the sharp sting of horse-radish at the traditional Passover meal or as a foil for good strawberry jam the next morning. Best of all is matzoh-brei: soak several matzohs in very hot water for a few seconds to soften, then soak again in egg and milk, fry them in plenty of sizzling butter and serve with maple syrup. Matzoh's naked purity means that, when eaten with just about anything else, the surrounding taste is almost sinful in comparison.

(Aged) Meat

Meat is back. Of course, it never went away. It was herded out of town during the fear-of-food epidemic. This contagion is the curse of first-world countries whose consumers are satisfied with third-rate produce.

Food is cheap in our society. Almost everything is available any time of year because it can be shipped from anywhere. Transportability takes precedence over palatability. Voilà! Strawberries in February. Lucky us.

In North America, where this anti-gastronome trend is at its worse, foods such as fat-free yogurt, taste-free oat bran and imported water get prominence even as we gaze guiltily at French peasants who live long lives savouring triple-crême cheeses, foie gras and red wine.

Fortunately sanity is returning to the table and one of the surest signs that the anti-food fad may be ending is that meat is back. One only has to look at the proliferation of steak houses or the size of sirloins sent to the table. Gourmand and gourmet cross paths here. Big may not be not better in the flavour department. However, old is.

"Old", in the steak world means aged, ideally two to three weeks. Most butchers store their meat in large vacuum-sealed plastic pouches—the cryovac process. While sealing helps preserve it, the meat stops aging. The best aged meat is hung "on the bone," usually, a side or quarter of beef in the butcher's walk-in cooler.

The pink soft flesh of fresh meat is fine for hamburger but a great properly-aged steak should be firm and purplish. It will be an inch thick (2.5 cm) for a rib steak, more for a sirloin. It will be well-marbled, with streaks of fat fitting comfortably into the muscle, ensuring that the meat will be moist and flavourful when it cooks. It will smell fresh without that cloying cheesy smell that is often the mark of plastic-wrapped supermarket steaks. An aged steak should be cut from a roast in front of you. The butcher should trim it before it is weighed.

Aged meat is expensive, at least 25 percent more than

fresh to account for the shrinkage that naturally occurs. Eight dollars a pound ($20 a kilo) for rib steaks is not unusual. Three-week naturally aged filet mignons can be twice that. And the highest prices are around Christmas when the demand for this quality is greatest. By the way, if we find these prices hard to stomach, in New York City it is not unusual to find aged steaks selling in supermarkets for $30 a pound—that's $30 U.S.

Cooking a hand-cut inch-thick aged steak is marvelously easy to do on a grill or under a broiler. The meat should need nothing more than a light brushing of oil to ensure an even sear. Make sure the heat is hot and even and that the steaks are at room temperature. If using coals, they should have burnt down to a dull red and be slightly ash-covered and about four inches from the meat. A one-inch steak cooked medium-rare, as the steak gods intended, needs about four to five minutes on one side before turning and a couple of minutes on the other. Salt and pepper should be added just before you turn it over. Let the steak rest on a warmed platter for a couple of minutes before serving.

Butchers who air-dry and age beef in their coolers include **Boucherie de Tours** in the Atwater Market, **J&R Kosher Meat** in Cavendish Mall, and **Boucherie Westmount**. Several supermarkets, including some Métro stores, are also aging some cuts on the premises. Ask at the butcher counter to make sure.

Mole

What dish separates hombres from gringos? In Mexico, it's pronounced molé.

"But I don't eat chocolate on meat!" cry los flacos (the weak ones). Here is the first misconception. Not all moles have chocolate and moles that do are never mistaken for candy.

Mole means mixture. It is essential to all kinds of Mexican cooking. Most recognize it in the word guacamole, a cold appetizer whose main ingredient is avocado.

Mole as a sauce is different. It is strong and complex with layers of smoke and heat and a very subtle sweetness. The smoky taste comes from fresh or dried chilies. The nuttiness and silky smooth texture are from ground sesame seeds, peanuts or almonds. There might also be toasted stale bread, dry tortillas, herbs, raisins, garlic, onions and tomatoes. It's not uncommon for a mole recipe to have more than two dozen ingredients.

There are several varieties of mole but two major styles: green and red. The green has pumpkin seeds, fresh green chilies and tomatillos, which are also green.

In red mole, the greens are replaced by darker foods: tomatoes instead of tomatillos, red peppers, and chocolate. The chocolate is bitter and gives a dark mole a depth of aroma and taste that green mole cannot match. Green mole is great with fish and shrimp. But for turkey and beef, a dark red mole poblano or inky black oaxaceño is muy fabuloso.

We have brought back both powdered mole and plastic bags of mole sauce from Mexico. The sauce, which is closer in texture to a thick paste, keeps for a long time in the refrigerator, but I do admit we are a little gutsy in assuming that a bag of this pungent mash won't break in our luggage.

Fortunately, both red and green mole are available in jars in Latino food stores and some supermarkets. Look for Doña María or La Costeña brands.

Chicken with Mole

Here is a simple recipe. If you are cooking fish (a whole red snapper is good), go with green mole. If it's a chicken breast, either red or green would work.

Take a ½ cup (125 ml) of mole from the jar and mix it with 2 cups (500 ml) of chicken stock or water. I use a blender for this. Then cook it down until half the liquid is gone. While reducing the sauce, preheat the oven to 350° F. Put a little sauce in a baking pan. Place the fish or chicken in the pan and pour the rest of the sauce over it. Bake uncovered until done. This should be 20-30 minutes for the chicken and a little longer for the fish (depending upon its size). Serve with the sauce.

Montreal Steak Spice

There is a tasty bit of our city in cupboards around the world. It is the eponymous Montreal steak spice. This is flavour that gets packaged and shipped out. It is a biting combination strong on peppercorns, coriander and salt.

I have seen spice mixtures with "Montreal style" on the labels in grocery stores in New England and the Maritimes, as if these words would let eaters pretend they were at **Schwartz's**. Sometimes, however, the ingredients are off-base. There is a company based in Indiana that sells "Montreal Steak Seasoning" with "salt, onion, garlic and other Amish Pantry spices."

Maybe it's time to look closer to home.

There are as many kinds of mixtures of steak spices as there are ways to prepare meat. Each blend reflects a local flavour. For example, Asian versions likely have lemon grass or a curry combination leading their list of ingredients. Those from the Caribbean or southern U.S.A. might include cinnamon and allspice.

What makes Montreal steak spice stand out is the absence of these floral notes. Our spice mixture originated with eastern Europeans, primarily immigrants from Russia, Poland, and Rumania. They came at the turn of the century and brought us karnatzle (thin dry sausage), dill pickles and smoked meat. They used spices that flavoured tough cuts of meat as they helped preserve them. Cinnamon, mace, nutmeg and similar fragrant spices were rarely used with meat. They might be in the spice box for the honey cake, but they were too expensive for rubbing into the brisket.

This is why the essence of a good Montreal steak spice mixture captures the flavours of the deli counter. The mix should be a blend of heat and strong flavours. It should have pepper and garlic, chilies and onion, mustard seed and coriander. Many combinations are available although most of the mixtures sold in the Montreal area seem to be made by **E.D. Foods Ltd.** in Pointe Claire.

E.D. Foods has packed spices for fifty years. The company

claims to have over 500 recipes for Montreal-style steak spice blends and to make most of the private-label versions sold in our supermarkets. Their house brand, ED Inspiration, uses plenty of cracked peppercorns. Although this blend does have a little sugar, which can make slow-cooking meats like ribs char on the barbecue, the overall flavour is quite good. It is excellent sprinkled on steaks just before grilling or shaken over potatoes cut into thick wedges, drizzled with oil and oven-baked at 350° F until browned.

Mozzarella

Maybe it should be spelled mozzzzzarrrelllllllah! After all, most people like it because of the way it strings pizza and lasagna from plate to fork to mouth. Pizza ads are full of this stuff as if flavour could be measured by the span of cheese.

However, If stretchability were its only attribute we might as well be eating latex. Unfortunately, commercial pizza cheese is processed for texture, not taste. But authentic mozzarella has a great fresh-milk taste that most pizzas mask.

This is an enjoyable mild-tasting cheese. What is usually available here is made from cow's milk and has the sweet flavour of whole milk and a slightly chewy but not rubbery texture. Traditionally, however, mozzarella is made from water buffalo milk. In Italy about 400 years ago, water buffalo were introduced to work the rice fields and buffalo milk mozzarella began to be made. Today it is imported and sold in Italian grocery stores, gourmet food stores and cheese shops as uovos di bufala—buffalo eggs!

However, what we are more likely to eat is made in Canada from cow's milk—usually by the Saputo company or National Cheese under its Tre Stelle brand. Both make fresh mozzarella cheese in small white balls, bocconcini, which are packed in a weak brine. Tre Stelle has a richer flavour because it has more butterfat, 25 percent versus 18 percent for Saputo's.

Bocconcini should be eaten within a few days after it is bought. The cheese should taste fresh and sweet. It is delicious on a homemade pizza. Add a grating of Romano or other hard, salty cheese before you bake it to give the fresh mozzarella a bit of a tang. Bocconcini are also wonderful served uncooked. Slice and layer them with a ripe garden tomato. Add a few leaves of fresh basil and a drizzle of good olive oil.

The mozzarella most of us regularly buy, however, is not this fresh. It is a little older, with a pale yellow colour and is sold from a block of cheese. This is an excellent mild-tasting cheese. It is served in slices and is great on sandwiches or as part of an antipasto served with olives and cold cuts. Also look for smoked mozzarella and a dried version called scamorze which is occasionally available.

There is also mozzarella sold the old-fashioned way, in a ball. This has more butterfat and is superb shredded onto a lasagna or homemade pizza.

The tastiest and most expensive variety is mozzarella di bufala. The texture is both creamy and chewy and the flavour makes cow's milk mozzarella seem bland in comparison. Mozzarella di bufala is packaged in small containers. Warm the container in water (about 140° F) for 10 minutes before serving to enhance the flavour. Slice it thin and savour each bite.

Mulled Wine Spices

In Frank Capra's holiday film *It's A Wonderful Life*, a guardian angel walks into a bar and asks for mulled wine "heavy on the cinnamon, easy on the cloves." For many, hot wine, which would be unthinkable in any other season, is a heavenly drink around Christmas time.

It has been a wintry favourite for a long time with almost as many names as it has recipes: glögg in Scandinavia, Glühwein in Austria, and a bishop in England when made with port. (When served piping hot, call this a Smoking Bishop, as in Scrooge's decision to discuss Bob Cratchet's affairs "over a Christmas bowl of Smoking Bishop.") Then there were the medieval drinks of Clarrey which included honey and spices, Caudell which was thickened with eggs, and Ypocras which comes closest to the mulled wine or cider we know today.

However this drink is made, the spices always include the highly aromatic ones common in Britain and Northern Europe hundreds of years ago: cinnamon, nutmeg, ginger, allspice, mace, perhaps cardamom and a citrus peel. Honey or sugar is often added for a sweeter drink. What was once a common guzzle, now seems exotic. What is most galling is the fancy packaging for mulled wine spice sachets that makes this mixture seem esoteric and expensive, even though most of us probably have everything we need on our spice shelves.

You can experiment with the spices mentioned above, but a typical recipe for mulled wine would be a teaspoonful or two (5-10 ml) of honey or sugar, a stick of cinnamon, and a large pinch each of ginger, nutmeg, mace, cloves and cardamom for each cup of wine or cider or apple juice. The wine does not have to be expensive. Most red dépanneur plonk works quite nicely, thank you. For something with a richer taste, use one-third port and two-thirds red wine. Add a strip of orange peel.

To make the mulled wine heat the spices in the wine over low heat, stirring occasionally until the sugar or honey is completely dissolved. It is important not to boil the wine. For a clearer drink, strain the hot wine through a coffee filter before serving.

   As you raise a glass, you might consider proffering this heart-warming toast:

   Beaujolais, Beaujolais, appellation controlée
   Le vin est joli,
   Parfumé et chaud.
   Bon santé et cheerio.

Mustard (Classic)

There are times when it's grand to be bland. One of those times was in 1904 at the St. Louis World's Fair. Americans were introduced to both the hot dog in a bun and a bright yellow American mustard that was its perfect match.

There is a problem with mustards. There are too many of them: Cordon Bleu Wholegrain Dijon, Cottage Delight English Horseradish Mustard, Vermont Roasted Garlic Mustard, Mutchler's Dakota Gold Original and even Dr. Pete's Praline Mustard Glaze advertised as "hauntingly sweet with giant pecans—try it on ice cream!"

This is only a small sample of concocted condiments which, if not in local stores, are available from Internet purveyors. But, for a few moments, let's get back to the classic, American-style ballpark mustard. French's is the oldest brand and was the one that mated well with hot dogs in St. Louis. French's is made with vinegar, water, mustard seed, turmeric (which colours it deep yellow), and spices. Grey Poupon has more water, white wine, fewer spices and vinegar, and no turmeric.

Ballpark mustard has a mild, slightly astringent taste. This isn't stuff you want to spoon on its own. It doesn't work well in a mayonnaise or sauce. This is a great product with a limited palate. It is made to cut the fatty taste of hot dogs, German sausages and salamis. It is perfect for school lunches of baloney or cheese sandwiches. It is tasty on a soft pretzel. That's about it. No one gives French's as a housewarming gift. This stuff isn't nearly pretentious enough for up-market pricing and a gingham cover; but it won't get relegated to the back of the cupboard after it's opened like the Dr. Pete's or the Vermont Roasted Garlic.

If you should be in Ottawa, **The Marvellous Mustard Shop** carries 90 kinds of mustards.

While we are on the subject, here are a couple of comments on cooking hot dogs. The classic Montreal steamé is steamed, not boiled, so why do we boil them at home and wonder why the hot dog has burst its casing? If you cook them in water, bring the water to a boil and then reduce it to a simmer before you put the hot dogs in. This will take minute or so longer but you'll get a perfect frank every time.

If grilling, the fire should be hot and about 6 inches from the grill. Make a few shallow diagonal slashes in the hot dogs to prevent them from curling. If you want to grill some salami, slice it almost a ¼-inch (5 mm) thick. Ask the deli counter to slice it at number 8. That's thicker than you would like for a salami sandwich, but great for the grill. Make a couple of small cuts at the edge—and just a little toward the centre—again to prevent the meat from curling as it cooks. If the coals or the gas starts to flame, move the grill higher or shift the meat to a section that is not as hot. These should take several minutes to cook. The danger in cooking them too quickly is that the hot dogs either burn or burst and the salami catches fire. Spectacular? Yes! Tasty? No.

Nachos

Slowly, surreptitiously, nachos are taking over the world. Well, not the whole world, just the corner of our kitchen designated as snack heaven. That's where we keep the fruit, cookies, chips, and other basics of casual munching. Recently, however, I've noticed that there is more likely to be an open bag of nachos than anything else.

Nachos, which are made from corn flour, have even replaced the potato as the chip of choice. They are more resilient and have fewer calories and less oil and salt.

Although most of us assume that nachos are part of Mexican cooking, you won't find the word "nacho" in a Spanish dictionary. Technically it should probably be spelled "Nacho" with a capital "N". This is the diminutive for Ignacio, a common Spanish name.

According to several sources, Ignacio Anaya was a Mexican chef who lived in a small town just south of Texas. In the 1940s he made a dish of tortilla chips, melted cheese and jalapeño peppers as a snack for some visitors. As much as Melba toast is named for the soprano Nellie Melba and Caesar salad for the chef who created it, Caesar Cardini, nachos should properly be given the appellation of its creator, but "pass the Ignacios" doesn't quite make it.

At their most elemental, nachos are another variation on that constant theme—what to do with leftovers. Tortillas are flat and supple rounds of bread, with corn or wheat flour as the main ingredient. They are essential to the Mexican table. However, they dry out quickly. Wrapped around some chopped meat or vegetables, corn tortillas become tacos. Lightly fried and served flat with plenty of toppings, they are tostadas. Chopped into smaller pieces and fried or toasted, we have nachos.

While all forms of the tortilla are used extensively in Mexican cooking, only nachos have permeated North American snackdom. Perhaps it is because they are so versatile. They can be munched alone, used to scoop up salsa, or baked in layers with enough cheese, sauce and toppings to make a pizza look anemic.

Montreal's growing Mexican population ensures that we have freshly-made tortillas and nachos on hand. These are less likely to break and usually have fewer stabilizers and artificial ingredients than imported packaged products. **Tortilleria Maya** is a small tortilleria on the Main. They make fresh tortillas, tostadas and nachos daily. There is also a small lunch counter in the store with a variety of homemade Mexican salsas and take-out dishes.

There are now several Latino groceries on St-Laurent Boulevard between Marie-Anne and St-Viateur. Another Latino food haven is the neighbourhood near Belanger and St-Denis, and especially **Supermarché Andes** and the pupu-serias. Most of the stores stock Maya tortillas as well as other brands. Look for Charras, an imported brand, for tostadas and nachos in cebolla (onion), chipotle (the smoky hot pepper), and jalapeño (very spicy) flavours.

Nuoc Nam

Try a spoonful of nuoc nam and taste history. This fish sauce, an essential condiment in the Vietnamese kitchen, may be the closest food we have to what ancient Romans enjoyed at their tables.

Nuoc nam is made by layering anchovies, or other small fish, with salt and ageing this for a year in containers. The mixture ferments and the liquid is poured off and used. Like virgin olive oils, the first batch is considered the finest quality and may be labeled "nhi". Whether it is top grade or comes from later pressings, nuoc nam is always pungent. Some say the sauce reminds them of old socks. To others it is as succulent as a ripe Camembert. On the other hand, this really doesn't matter since this is a sauce that adds flavour to other dishes and is not meant to be consumed on its own.

The Romans had a similar sauce to enhance their meals. It was called "liquamen" or "garum" and was factory-produced in Pompeii and other towns. It was made almost the same way that nuoc mam is. Layers of salt and fish were placed in an earthenware jar and left to ferment. A golden clear liquid rose to the top. It added a fishy, salty, slightly cheesy flavour to any dish.

Nuoc nam (aka nam pla in Thailand and shottsuru in Japan) is sold in large bottles and will last over a year if stored out of direct light. Because of its salinity, extra salt is usually not necessary in recipes that call for nuoc nam. Because it is based on fish, nuoc nam is also high in vitamin B and protein. Here's a simple Vietnamese shrimp and rice dish to try: fry a finely chopped clove of garlic and an onion. Add a handful of small cooked shrimp. When the garlic is golden brown, stir in one tablespoon (15 ml) of nuoc nam and one tablespoon (15 ml) of tomato ketchup. Add one cup (250 ml) of cold cooked rice and heat through while stirring. Garnish with chopped coriander leaves and green onion and, if you want some heat, a little chopped fresh jalapeño chili.

Oatmeal

"... each boy had one porringer, and no more, except on occasions of great public rejoicing, when he had two ounces and a quarter of bread besides."
–*Oliver Twist*, Charles Dickens

Oliver Twist's porringer—his bowl for porridge—was filled three times a day with a thin oat gruel. This was the porridge I always thought of when I had it occasionally as a child. Not that mine was thinned with water, but that it was a tasteless poor food desperately needing lots of sugar and milk to give it any flavour.

I knew oatmeal was supposed to be wholesome, but this was like hot glue, as appetizing as medicine. It's only recently that I realized oatmeal has its own subtly mild taste, not quite as rich as rice or as nutty as wheat, but delicious on its own.

Like wheat and rice, oats are a cereal crop. Oats lack gluten so they make poor bread. However, they are high in protein and a good source of iron and phosphorus. Oat bran, which is often added to other dishes, has plenty of fibre.

There are several ways that oats are processed for food. The most basic form is called groats. These are the oats separated from their bran. This processing makes the kernels easier to eat and to digest.

Groats can be cooked on their own but they need at least an hour and they are similar in consistency to brown rice. Steel-cut oats are groats cut into small pieces. A third of a cup (75 ml) needs one cup (250 ml) water, and takes about 20 minutes to cook on the stove or about 10 minutes in the microwave at a medium setting. This is plenty for a single serving.

Rolled oats are partially cooked and then flattened with large rollers. They take from 5 to 10 minutes. Instant rolled oats are precooked.

Each stage of processing removes more of the flavour and texture of the oats. By the time the instant variety is served, it is a tasteless mush. This is why it is usually packaged with maple syrup flavour or dried fruit or cinnamon—we might as well enjoy something.

But let's talk about steel-cut oats. These have a remarkable taste and the texture bears no resemblance to the quick-cooked version. Steel-cut oats fill the belly and sustain the soul. I get to the bus stop feeling well fed and comfortable on the coldest days.

Even better, steel-cut oats stand up to repeated cooking. Try using a little of the porridge left over from breakfast to thicken soup. It can also serve as a rice substitute in the evening, mixed with cheese and broth like a risotto. You can even fry a wedge of porridge with some chopped garlic like an Italian polenta.

The most common brand of steel-cut oats is John McCann's Irish Oatmeal, which comes in a large can. Bulk food stores often have steel-cut oats in bins where you can buy as much as you want. Another tasty brand is Bob's Red Mill Organic Steel Cut Oats, available in many health food stores.

Steel-cut oats take longer to prepare than rolled oats. However, at least once a winter it is worthwhile to get up a little earlier and cook them, if only to remind ourselves of how delicious a simple cereal can be.

Old Food

It was a gift that only one old friend should give to another—half a wheel of Stilton brought with the carry-on luggage from Heathrow to Montreal, warmed to room temperature, and sitting in magnificent blue-veined semi-putrescense on the dining room table.

This was not a cheese for children. It was a cheese for those who appreciate that ripeness and maturity are things to which we should aspire. We cut a large, crusted wedge to serve after dinner with homemade walnut-sourdough bread and a 25-year-old bottle of port.

Old things, old flavours. The sourdough had fermented until its inherent yeasts developed a strong winy smell. The walnuts were culled from trees that may have taken so long to grow that the person who planted them died before tasting their fruit.

The port was something else. We opened it before supper to let it breathe and took a sip. It had a thin purplish cast and it tasted insipid and bitter. We blamed ourselves. We had stored it poorly and waited too long to drink it. It was too old, but we couldn't bring ourselves to throw it out, not yet. We left it, opened, in a corner of the kitchen for several hours while we made dinner.

Later, after our child was asleep, we unwrapped the Stilton, took the bread from the oven and tried the port again. It was magnificent. It had recovered, in a way that only old things sometimes do. Given time to wake up, it had a surprising strength and rich berry flavours. It wrapped around the tongue like velvet. For a long time, we did nothing else but sip port, savour aged Stilton, and nibble walnut bread.

The expression runs "Youth is wasted on the young." Well, so is age. Old flavours are complex. They require patience and prudence. A cheese this strong could clear a crowded bus in minutes. Old foods must be approached with a willingness to set aside time to enjoy them. They will not be rushed and we are the better for it.

Olive Oil

Are you ready to pay as much for a bottle of olive oil as you would for a good bottle of wine? Think about that the next time you see a fancy label claiming "extra virgin, cold pressed" and going for between $20 and $40 a bottle.

Although good olive oil comes from many Mediterranean countries, such as Italy, Southern France, Spain Tunisia, and Greece, the fruit of this tree has become a high-priced luxury commodity. There are at least 500 varieties of olives in Italy and maybe 700 kinds around the world. Unlike wines, olive oil is almost always a blend, rarely made exclusively from one kind of olive.

The flavour of olive oil flows along three spectrums: soft, bitter and spicy. The way to sample a good oil is to warm up a little in a small glass cupped in the hand. Inhale the aroma, then slurp a bit with lots of air, just like you'd do with a good wine. Then have a piece of bread and munch some green apple or a few grapes. The sharp fruit taste refreshes the mouth for another sip of oil.

A new outfit bringing their products to Montreal is an Italian association called Mastri Oleari. The "masters of oil" mark their bottles with an HS for "High Standard." Using English on an otherwise Italian label must mean that the Mastri are targeting the North American consumer. The best oils have a light, almost creamy flavour and a grassy or herbal aroma reminiscent of a sunlit pasture. These aren't meant for frying fish, although drizzling some over the fish just before it's brought to table is a great idea. Oils with such full flavour are primarily tasting oils. They are great on salads or splashed on grilled meats just before serving. Some are light enough to use in pastry.

No matter its quality, don't keep olive oil in the refrigerator. The oil will congeal, which is natural, but when it returns to a liquid state it loses some aroma and the quality deteriorates. Unlike good wine, olive oils do not improve with age. They should be consumed within a year or two of being processed.

Many producers consider "cold pressed olive oil" to be a myth. Many expensive oils are processed from olives at temperatures between 28-33° C.

Two interesting Italian olive oils now sold in Montreal are Eirena and Fattoria di Asciano. The first is the colour of light amber with a very simple fresh aroma and a nice buttery taste. The second is unfiltered; it has a complex herbal scent and a lovely peppery finish that seems to hit the back of the throat half a minute after tasting it.

Also worth trying is Alberto Cipolloni, although it is pretentiously packed in a wine bottle complete with numbered label, cork and punt (that's the large dent on the bottom of wine bottles). This is a richly-flavoured oil with just a hint of a sharp taste.

Marcinase is another label to look out for. It is part of Italy's organic farming movement called Agricoltura biologica and produces several levels of olive oils from fairly strong (intenso) to fresh tasting and slightly fruity (leggero).

Olive oil's "virginity" is a descriptive term for its acidity. Virgin olive oil should have about 1 percent acidity. Extra virgin is half that. Unfortunately, fraudulent producers use these terms without discrimination. Your best guarantee of good quality is still your nose and mouth. Frankly, if it smells off or tastes bad, dump it. Conversely, if you are in a restaurant that serves good olive oil, ask to see the bottle. It is probably available locally.

Good oils are delicious and are increasingly sold in impressive bottles. They make superb gifts. Look for them in Italian food stores such as **Fruiterie Milano** and **Boucherie Capitol**, and gourmet shops. They often have different types of olive oil out for tasting. This is particularly true in many of the food stores in the Atwater and Jean-Talon markets, where olive oil from Italy and North Africa are readily available.

It is also worth looking for stores that sell olive oil in bulk and where customers can bring in their own bottles and have them filled. Places that sell oil this way include the food importer **Tortarella & Fils** (see The Restaurant With No Name) in the north end of the city and the **Cavallaro** stores.

Panettone

"Don't come here Christmas eve," was the warning I received from the young cashier at **Fruiterie Milano**, one of the city's top Italian markets. "It is going to be packed. Everyone comes here at the last moment." Now Wal-Mart or Canadian Tire I could understand for last minute Christmas shopping, but an Italian supermarket?

Of course, there would be lots of people who had yet to lay out the traditional after-mass feast, but the big score here is panettone. This is a large, rich bread, closer to a brioche than to a plain loaf. It can be baked with essentials: flour, butter, eggs, yeast and raisins. Or it can be elaborate and sumptuous, filled with alternating ribbons of chocolate cream and custard, flavoured with marsala wine, baked with pistachio nuts and candied citrus and then crusted with confectioner's sugar. These are delicious and last for weeks. A slice toasted for breakfast is ambrosial.

"Panettone" is a diminutive of "pane", Italian for bread.

Pandoro is similar to panettone but it is star shaped and usually does not have fillings. Large panettones and pandoros weigh a kilo (2.2 pounds). Many are sold in beautifully decorated boxes. Not surprisingly, they make tasteful gifts.

Both panettone and pandoro are sold in Italian food stores all year round, but the peak is in the month before Christmas. It is common to see hundreds of boxes of panettone hanging from the ceiling and stacked four and five deep on shelves. Prices range from a couple of dollars for a small, 100 gram (3 oz.) panettoncino to over $35 for about 2 pounds (900 grams) of rich Galup panettone filled with a guaranteed 200 grams (6 oz.) of chocolate nougat in a gift box wrapped in gold foil and ribbon. A few stores stock an imported table-sized panettone that goes for hundreds of dollars!

With such abundance, it's hard to pick the right one. The Milano cashier who warned me not to come Christmas eve suggested a brand called Le Tre Marie. It sells for about $15 and is covered in chocolate. Her recommendation was persuasive: "That's the one I bring my grandmother."

Parmesan and Romano

There it is. The plate of pasta is on the table and the waiter hovers with a dish of powdered cheese. We always take some even before we taste the dish.

Most often, the dish is good to begin with and the cheese adds little to the flavour. After all, the pasta was prepared when it was ordered while the cheese may have been sitting around, sometimes for days, getting stale. Still, our intimidation level is low. We nod our heads and the obligatory spoonful is dusted over our food.

This unmindfulness is a shame because Parmesan is a wonderful cheese, one of Italy's oldest, and it should get much more respect in restaurants.

If you have tried only powdered cheese, you have yet to enjoy Parmesan's great variety of flavours and textures. This cheese can range from young and mild-tasting to several years old with a mellow nutty flavour. Good Parmesan, no matter its age, is quite firm and has a fresh milk taste that lingers at the back of the mouth. It is never bitter or excessively salty.

Older Parmesans, like good cheddars, have a sharper edge to their flavour. They develop crystals that melt on the tongue. These are great for finishing a meal with the last of the wine. They are a perfect match for apples and ripe pears, and nicely complement figs and grapes.

As its name indicates, once Parmesan only came from Parma. Today Parmigiano-Reggiano is considered the best of Parmesan. This appellation does not refer to one cheese manufacturer. It is given to cheeses made in several areas in Northern Italy.

Parmesan or Parmigiano as it is rightly called in Italian, is made from cow's milk. It is often confused with Romano, which refers to the city of Rome. A combination of what the cheese is made from and where it originally came from, gives it its name. Well-known cheeses include Pecorino Romano, made from sheep's milk and Provatura Romano which uses cow's milk. The flavour of a good Pecorino Romano is tangy and well-suited for pasta dishes. Most U.S. varieties that call themselves Romano use only cow's milk or add cow's milk to sheep or goat to achieve a milder taste.

Parmesan and Romano cheeses also make delicious coatings for veal or fish instead of bread crumbs. Dredge a firm white fish like haddock in seasoned flour (salt, pepper, garlic powder and paprika). Dip in beaten egg, then dredge with finely-grated cheese. Fry each side until golden in a few tablespoons of olive oil over medium heat. Serve with a spicy tomato sauce and lemon wedges.

Similar and worth trying is the Swiss cheese, Sbrinz. It has a rich flavour that is almost like Emmenthal (the Swiss cheese with the holes). Sbrinz is hard like Parmesan and is also made from cow's milk. It is excellent as a grating or eating cheese. Another good eating cheese is a crumbly, older Asiago, made from cow's milk.

Most cheese shops will let you taste several kinds until you find the one that you like best. Serve it at room temperature. Keep a small hard piece to bring next time you go to an Italian restaurant. Then, when the waiter brings out the bowl of powdered cheese and asks if you want some, say "Yes, and use this. I brought my own."

Pasta

Our family eats a lot of pasta. Fresh pasta is sold in most super-markets and in many Italian food stores. Eaten with a light sauce, these can be delicious as the flour is mixed with eggs instead of the water used in dried pasta. But, while fresh pasta is easily available, we usually cook with dried noodles. They store well and there is always some on hand.

Pasta is good basic food but it can be so expensive that it looks more at home in an art gallery than a supermarket. $6.99 for 500 grams (1 pound) is not unusual for handsomely boxed packages filled with imported, hand rolled and individually dried metre-length strands of designer spaghetti. Are we expected to actually boil and eat this or should we frame it? On the other hand, Primo and other brands produced in Canada can cost as little as 89 cents for 900 grams (2 pounds).

Amazingly, check the packages and you'll see that regard-less of the price, the ingredients are the same. Except for those made with eggs or flavourings, most pasta is made from semolina flour and water. That's it. This is as true for basic Catelli as for the extravagantly priced Pastaficio Azienza Agraria Latini made by the "artisanal pastification method."

Wheat is key to pasta and semolina is made from durum wheat. This is tough stuff. Unlike regular wheat flour, pasta made from semolina won't turn mushy when it is cooked in water.

So if the ingredients are the same, why the difference in price? Could it be that one brand actually tastes 10 times better than another; or could it be—horrors—that we are willing to pay more because the package looks great?

We wanted to see if there was a flavour difference. We made six kinds of pasta and pulled in a small crew of adults and kids to taste test it. Each person tried a bit of each. For toppings, there was freshly grated Romano cheese, a simple tomato sauce and some garlic oil. The pastas were Giardino (available at **Costco**), Primo, Altieri and Latini. We also tried two brands made with eggs: Delaverde and La Molisana.

Aside from La Molisana, which was judged too eggy, our

group felt there were very minor taste differences between the noodles. When we added a topping there was no difference at all. There was a difference in the texture. Many of the higher priced pastas, like the Latini, have a rough surface which holds sauce beautifully. For some, that may be enough to justify the cost. However, it may make more sense to have a variety of inexpensive pastas on hand and use the one that works best with your sauce. Generally speaking, the heavier the sauce, the wider the noodle. Spaghetti with pesto, for example, and tagliatelli with a creamy Alfredo. Short shapes or small hollow varieties like elbow macaroni, penne or farfalle are great for liquid sauces or pasta salads. These also work best in baking. Very small pastas, such as alphabet noodles or the star-shaped stelline, are used in soup.

It is also important to cook the pasta in a large amount of water, at least a gallon (5 litres). It takes much longer to bring the water to a boil than it does to cook the pasta (usually 8 to 10 minutes), so start the water as soon as you walk into the kitchen. If there is too little water, the pot will stop boiling when the noodles are put in. The pasta will clump together and may taste starchy or feel slimy.

The easiest way to know when pasta is ready is to bite into a piece. If there is still a little bit of white in the middle, it is firm—al dente. If you prefer it less chewy, cook the pasta a minute or so longer until the white spot has gone. Drain it but don't rinse it under water. If it must sit for a while before serving, toss the cooked pasta with a little olive oil and keep it covered in a warm oven.

Here is a simple sauce if you want to try a pasta test at home. Smash a clove of garlic flat and cook it in a pan in ¼ cup (50 ml) of olive oil. Remove the garlic when it is brown. This alone is quite tasty on pasta. You can go a step further by adding a can of crushed tomatoes, salt, pepper and oregano to taste. Let this simmer for a few minutes. Toss in the cooked and drained pasta. Grate hard Italian cheese (Asiago, Parmesan and Romano are all excellent) over the pasta at the table.

Pastéis de Nata

If there is any food that is close to perfection, it is the Portuguese custard tartlets called pastéis de nata. The filling is as succulent as a crème brûlée and is made from cream, egg yolks and sugar with maybe a touch of cinnamon. And they are small. The pastry fits into the palm of child's hand. The crust is buttery rich and crackling. When cooked just right, the centre is dense, soft and rich while the top has a thin caramelized skin from baking or being burnished under the broiler. Each bite finds a little resistance with the crust and a sensual burnt sugary skin and then the consistency becomes meltingly smooth.

Eating one is bliss. They are so rich that one is usually enough! As food goes, these are heavenly. Not surprisingly, like many sweet and rich delicacies, natas were first made in convents and monasteries where there was not only the time needed to create such succulence, but the desire—in lieu of other non-sanctioned pleasures—to consume them. Another name for pastéis de nata is pasteis de Belém, after the Belém district of Lisbon, home of the Jeronimos Monastery which likes to take credit for creating this pastry.

Montreal is fortunate is having a large and vibrant Portuguese community. It still flourishes in the area bounded by Avenue des Pins and Rachel, and St-Urbain and St-Denis. Within this neighbourhood are several bakeries that make excellent bread and pastries daily. Three good places are **Romados**, **Stella Estrela**, and **Bela Vista**. Romados is a bakery and butcher shop, also known for superb charcoal-grilled chicken. Stella Estela and Bela Vista are traditional patisseries that serve coffee and have a few tables.

Natas usually sell for about 80 or 90 cents each and are cheaper by the dozen. They are great for a snack and delicious with coffee or port after a meal. Buy them fresh, warm from the oven if possible, and eat them the same day.

Patties

Patties are Jamaican snack food. They are situated somewhere on the turnover trail between a Latin American empanada and a Cornish pasty. All of these hand-held savoury pies share common ideas about how to make a delicious snack out of a roll of pastry with some chopped meat or veggies inside.

However, it is as hard to find a good pasty as a hen's tooth in Montreal. While we do have plenty of empanadarias, the quality, filling and size of empanadas vary extensively depending upon the country and even the region of the country that makes them.

What's great about patties is that there are only a few basic ways of making them. Once you know what you like, you should be able to walk into any Jamaican or West Indian grocery store or restaurant and order one, having a pretty good idea of what you will get.

Patties start with a simple pastry crust. The main ingredients are flour, water and lard or shortening. Curry and turmeric are sometimes added. The crust is golden, crisp, light and flaky. It should almost melt in the mouth.

The fillings are predominately made from beef, chicken, or vegetables, and these can be mild or searingly spicy. Common additions to the fillings include thyme, onion, garlic, tomatoes and curry powder.

Although many Caribbean stores sell patties, this is really a Jamaican snack food. The giveaway is that there is invariably some degree of heat in the filling. This can range from comfortably mild to full-blown Scotch bonnet pepper. Ask how spicy a patty is before you buy it.

Many dépanneurs in communities with large Caribbean populations have a small glass warming case filled with patties. These can be good. It depends on where and when they were made. However, if there is a dép selling patties, there is probably a local place within a few blocks that is baking them daily. Well-made patties freeze well and heat up beautifully in a toaster oven.

There are several stores making and selling patties on

Victoria between Jean-Talon and Van Horne, such as **Mr. Spicee** and along Sherbrooke Street West between Decarie and Cavendish Boulevard, including **Ma's Place, Arawak,** and **Bonne Bouffe.**

The original Ma's Place on Sherbrooke Street West.

Peppercorns

Salt and pepper are as common to the table as knife, fork and spoon. But salt acts as adverb and adjective to a dish. It supports and embellishes a food's flavour. Pepper, however, is often our way of saying "I can't taste a thing. Pass the pepper, please. At least that has flavour."

But, what are we putting on our food? The pepper that is usually at hand is likely as appetizing as sawdust, perhaps with a dash of bitterness and pain. There is heat but no flavour. It is like having tears without emotion. Yet, we sprinkle it on, feel the bite, and think it has done some good. We savour the edginess, the small dose of agony offsetting the blandness of the food on the table.

Peppercorns, however, are a wonderful spice and deserve to be savoured for their pungency and aroma. Let's get back to the basics. Black pepper is the dried berry, the fruit of the *piper nigrum* plant. It is harvested before it's ripe. White pepper is the same berry left a little longer, but still not ripe. The black cap comes off as the berry is processed and the white seed is used.

The most versatile form, however, may be the green peppercorn. These are the least ripe, the most immature form of the berry. It is available dried as well as canned in a weak brine.

Dried green peppercorns can be blisteringly hot and should be used in the same way as black ones. They break into small granules more easily than black peppercorns. They are great for crusting a steak before it is grilled or broiled.

Brined green peppercorns are subtler. They have a surprising delicate taste with just a suggestion of peppery potency. Bite into these and there is a short intense burst of flavour with a clean finish with a quick hint of evergreen. Use them when cooking long simmering stews.

These pickled berries are also great in vinaigrettes, mayonnaise, or in any sauce that requires pepper without the bite. Try them in a homemade boursin-type cheese. Drain a tablespoon of green peppercorns and mash them into a ½cup

(125 ml) of cream cheese. Roll the cheese in your favourite herbs. Shape it into a ball or cylinder. Wrap it and chill it in the refrigerator before serving.

There are also some less common varieties of peppercorns that have recently been introduced here by Montreal caterer Philippe de Vienne. These are long peppers grown in India and grains of paradise from the Caribbean.

Long peppers are corns that have formed into thin rods and look like miniature pinecones. Break off a nugget and let it roll across the tongue. There is a sweet perfume and then, a long minute later, a bite that snaps us to attention with a short sharp shock. This is the pepper that was prized from Roman times through the Middle Ages. It was worth three times the price of black pepper back then and that ratio remains the same today.

Another delicious pepper is called grains of paradise. These are about the same size as black pepper corns. They have a reddish shell and are pure white inside. They taste heavily perfumed, similar to cardamom to which they are related. They have only a slight bite. They're expensive, $120 a kilo ($55/lb.), but a gram or two goes a long way.

Long peppers and grains of paradise are rarely used alone. Combine them with whole black pepper corns in a table grinder. This adds an aromatic swath to the singular sharpness of ordinary pepper. Or use them like cooks do in India and Ethiopia, mixing them with other spices such as nutmeg, cloves and turmeric to give substantial flavour to cooking. They can be found in gourmet stores such as **Les Douceurs du Marché**.

Pho

Is there anything at all wrong with Pho? These are the hearty, nutritious, tasty, cheap and huge portions of soup served in Vietnamese restaurants. They are cheap—a few dollars buys an enormous bowl. Forget about small and medium. The word may be on the menu but that is the translation. My experience has been that these words don't really exist in the Pho lexicon. And did I mention that this was a cheap meal?

"Pho" is pronounced like "full" but drop the "ll." It's a noodle soup packed with flavour. The word seems to be attached to almost every sign for a Vietnamese restaurant but it just means "soup."

While Montreal seems to have a glut of noodle shops these days, few of them offer the full flavour of good pho. That's because a real pho is a two-stage affair.

First there is the broth. It must have a rich meaty taste, particularly if the sign says that Pho Tonkin is served. This is soup common to northern Vietnam. Beef bones are simmered for a long time. There are other styles of pho and these are occasionally found in Montreal. Cochin is a southern style of fish soup, and pho ga is based on chicken stock.

Once the broth is ready—and this takes hours of slow cooking—pho is ready to be made as the customer orders. A basic bowl includes rice noodles, green onions, meat and a few vegetables. Condiments include brutally hot small chili peppers (which the wise remove), fresh coriander leaves, bean sprouts, and the essential Vietnamese fish sauce, nuoc nam. Use it instead of salt or soy sauce.

Pho is a delight because its textures change with every slurp. A good broth acts as the basso profundo of this dish. The deep, rolling, constant flavour is the base upon which everything else jumps. Meat is heated with the broth just before it is served. The selection of meats ranges from thinly sliced almost raw steak to thickly-sliced cooked brisket. Usually on the menu are the more exotic bo vien (small homemade meat balls), tripe and tendon. These may make the uninitiated squeamish but are favourites among Pho connoisseurs because they add to the soup's textures and flavours.

Photunately, there are lots of good Vietnamese soup restaurants in the Montreal area especially in Chinatown, along Côte-des-Neiges between Queen Mary and Jean-Talon, as well as within a block or two of the corner of St-Denis and Jean-Talon. One of the best is a small place called **Pho Rosemont**, opposite the Rosemont Métro station.

Vietnamese and Chinese restaurants and stores, east side of St-Laurent Boulevard in Chinatown.

Pickling spices

Sometimes, it's good to be in a pickle. It's certainly delicious to eat one. The word "pickling" is rooted in the pick, that acidic vinegary bite that attacks the tongue whenever we bite into pickled vegetables or fruit. Pickling was once the most common way to preserve food, particularly before there was refrigeration and quick trans-border transportation.

Canada's first cookbook, *The Cook Not Mad; Or Rational Cookery*, begins with pickling recipes for meat. "To pickle one hundred pounds of Beef to keep a year" with a list of ingredients that includes three quarts of salt, six ounces of salt petre and 1½ pints of molasses. Further along are recipes for producing lesser quantities of fruit and vegetables.

Today we are less likely to pickle to preserve a vegetable than to augment the taste that fresh food doesn't have. We like the difference between a pickled and fresh cucumber. Each has its use and delights the palate differently.

When we pickle at home we are less likely to use alum and syrups called for in early cookbooks. Instead, we reach for the vinegar and pickling spices.

While vinegar preserves the pickle, spices give it flavour. There is no one pickling spice, despite what the label on a bottle implies. Most brands combine several herbs and spices: bay leaf, coriander, chili peppers, and white pepper are common but there could also be dried juniper berries, pieces of cinnamon bark and cloves. For dilled pickles, of course, we add large sprigs of fresh or frozen dill.

Whole spices and herbs are used, never powdered. Powdered spices are effective but they have less taste and make the pickling liquid unappetizingly cloudy.

Cucumbers are everyone's favourite pickle, but carrots, cauliflower, pearl onions, and crabapples also make great pickles. Here is an easy recipe for pickled carrots.

For each pound (500 g) of carrots use 1½ cups (375 ml) of vinegar, ½ cup (125 ml) of water, ½ cup of sugar (125 ml), and 1½ tablespoons (20 ml) of pickling spices. For the spices, use a commercial blend or make a combination of those mentioned above. Add whatever extra flavours you like such as a couple of cloves of garlic or an extra chili pepper or two.

Mix all the ingredients except the carrots. Bring this to a boil, stirring so that the sugar dissolves into a vinegary syrup. Simmer this covered for about 15 minutes and then strain the liquid and set it aside.

Cover the carrots with water and boil for about 5 minutes. They should still be crunchy. Drain and peel them. Cut them into chunks that will fit into pint-sized canning jars. Boil the jars and lids in another pot to sterilize them.

Bring the syrup mixture to a boil. Add the the carrots and boil for 5 minutes. Tightly pack the carrots into the hot jars and cover with the syrup. Put the lids and covers on and hot pack them in boiling water for another 20 minutes. Remove the jars. As they cool the lids should depress slightly and you should hear a ping as the lids seal. These can be kept in a cupboard for over a year. If they don't seal keep them in the fridge. In either case, the pickling flavours will become stronger over time.

There are several good books on pickling but we still cling to an old standard, *The Joy of Cooking*. A significant lapse of *The All New Joy of Cooking* is that it has little on pickling and preserves. The old *Joy* had lots of recipes and suggestions. It remains an invaluable resource. If you don't have it, it is worth looking for in used bookstores.

Pierogies

Punch in the word pierogi on an internet browser and and a raft of commercial sites pop up promising ethnic cooking and accordion music. But pierogies aren't just for polka parties. And they aren't even specifically Polish.

Every cuisine that has flour and leftovers has its version of pierogies. Italy has ravioli. The southern United States offers dumplings. In Chinese restaurants the menu is likely to list Peking ravioli or pot stickers.

These are all useful for stretching basic ingredients such as chopped meat, mashed potatoes, and small amounts of onions or other vegetables. They add a flavour common to that cuisine (chive or ginger in Chinese cooking or oregano in Italian) and wrap it in a thin dough. The result is cheap, tasty and filling. They are tasty fried or boiled. They can be eaten plain, or served with a sauce (sour cream with eastern European dumplings, soy sauce and sesame oil for oriental ones). As tortellini, wontons, or the Russian dumpling called pelmeni, they are often served in a soup in a clear broth.

Pierogies are a tasty version of this treat. With slightly different spellings and pronunciations, pierogies are common to all eastern European cooking and they are made with an almost endless variety of sweet or savoury fillings. In Montreal it is easy to find pierogies stuffed with meat and sauerkraut, potato and cheese, mushrooms, onions and even blueberries or sour cherries. In some households, pierogies are traditionally split into two classifications. There are kreplach stuffed with meat and seasonings and there are verenikas with a non-meat filling. Sometimes, after being boiled, they are fried until one side is crisp and then served with a topping of crisply fried onions and sour cream on the side.

By the way, If you want to be precise, in Polish, it is one pierog, two pierogi, but "pierogies" has become the accepted plural in English and, anyway, no one can eat just one.

Many eastern European grocery stores sell both homemade and commercial varieties of pierogies. Supreme Pierogies is a common commercial brand made in Toronto.

It is available in several varieties including sauerkraut with pork and beef. However, many of Montreal's eastern European stores make their own pierogies and it is worth asking for them.

Décarie Boulevard, between Sherbrooke West and Jean-Talon has half a dozen food stores such as **Bucharest** and **Absolut** worth checking out. **Batory** on St-Viateur near St-Urbain is another good source.

If you want to try a plate of pierogies, walk into **Chopin** on Décarie near Monkland. This is an excellent Polish charcuterie and pastry store that looks like a small café. An order of home made pierogies followed by a piece of their scrumptious cheese or apple cake is a delicious, inexpensive lunch. The pierogies at **Mazurka**—fried or boiled—are also a good bet.

Pine Nuts

In late summer, the markets are full of basil and the cry goes around the kitchen, "It's time to make pesto."

Our recipe is simple. For a small quantity, I use a mortar and pestle and pound a few garlic cloves into a paste with a little coarse salt. Then I add a handful of basil leaves, a teaspoon (5 ml) or so each of toasted pine nuts, freshly grated Parmesan or Romano cheese, and enough olive oil to create a smooth sauce.

Basil and garlic are in season. Good cheese can often be found on sale. It is only when I have to buy the pine nuts that I pause. "The price has gone down this year," my corner grocer tells me. "Last year we paid $45 a kilo for pine nuts. This year it's $30." Still, that works out to about $4 for 150 grams. I taste one to make sure that it is nutty and slightly sweet. At that price I want to make sure that they are fresh.

Pine nuts (or pignolia nuts) are expensive because it takes a lot of work extract them. There can be a hundred or so nuts in a pine cone which must be heated, then cracked without damaging the kernels inside. Pine nuts, the edible seed of various species of pine trees, grow in China, Italy, Afghanistan, Mexico, North Africa and the southwestern United States. There are two main varieties. The Mediterranean or Italian kind come from the stone pine tree. It has a longer shape and a less intense flavour than the Chinese variety.

Pine nuts are higher in protein than most other nuts. Due to their high fat content they can turn rancid quickly. They keep for a year if stored tightly sealed in a freezer. I toast pine nuts to bring out the flavour before I use them. This is best done by putting them in a frying pan, a handful at a time, and browning them slightly over low heat, stirring often.

We tend to reserve pine nuts for pesto, but elsewhere they have other uses. They are incorporated into Catalan pastries or strewn across almond cakes. They are also tasty stuffed inside a roasting chicken. Afghanistan and Tibet are reputed to have particularly large and tasty kernels from the Chilgoza pine which are eaten as an aphrodisiac.

Pomegranate

It is the most carnal of fruits. First there is the hard, leathery skin, then the waxy intensely bitter interior; finally, bright-red juice spurts from sweet plump seeds. A clean slice reveals what the poet Elizabeth Barrett Browning called "a heart within blood-tinctured, of a veined humanity."

Known also as a Chinese apple or Granada, the pomegranate is an unusual six-sided fruit that grows on a bush or small tree. It was first cultivated thousands of years ago around the Mediterranean, but is now grown in Europe, Asia and the Americas, wherever there is rich soil, hot weather and a dry climate. King Solomon had pomegranate orchards. The prophet Mohammed recommended the fruit "to purge the system of greed and hatred." In the Punjab it is called anar and is used as fresh fruit or a powder in many vegetable and legume dishes. In Iranian cooking, fresh pomegranate seeds are sprinkled over rice or added to stews. Scattered like rubies, they make the simplest dishes festive.

When shopping for fresh fruit, look for ones that are heavy with a bright colour and a skin without blemishes. Pomegranate juice or syrup is high in vitamin C. It is an excellent meat tenderizer and adds a sharp-sweet taste to salad dressings. It tastes great over vanilla ice cream and makes fantastic sorbets. The syrup works well with club soda or dashed over fresh grapefruit, or mixed into various citrus and vodka sunrises to lend a blushing brilliance to the drink.

As a syrup, pomegranate juice is often sold as grenadine. Stores which specialize in European food products tend to carry well known brands such as Teissiere. These are tasty but rarely have pomegranate juice in them. Instead, they rely on a mix of several red berry fruits, particularly raspberry which comes closest in flavour but isn't the real thing. Real pomegranate juice (usually sold mixed with sugar and sometimes called pomegranate molasses) has a lovely bittersweet tang. Look for it in Middle Eastern stores.

Muhammara is a Syrian and Turkish appetizer that melds the pomegranate's sweet and sour flavour with roasted red peppers and walnuts to create rich, deeply-flavoured relish. It is great as a dip with raw vegetables and toasted pieces of pita. It also is a good accompaniment to stews, kebabs, grilled meats or fish. Some recipes add an onion to the garlic and pour on the hot-pepper sauce. Others suggest a garnish of toasted pine nuts. Many Middle-Eastern restaurants such as **Le Petit Alep** have this dish on the menu. Here is a great basic version as prepared by Montreal food lover Michael Dworkin.

Muhammara

Drain a 7-ounce (200 ml) jar of roasted peppers. Lightly toast ⅓ cup (75 ml) walnuts and chop them finely. Mash 4 large cloves of garlic to a paste with ½ teaspoon (2 ml) salt. Combine all of this in a blender or food processor with ⅔ cup (150 ml) of fine fresh bread crumbs, 2 teaspoons (10 ml) of pomegranate molasses, 1 teaspoon (5 ml) of ground cumin, ½ teaspoon (2 ml) or more (depending on how hot you want this) of red pepper flakes. Gradually add olive oil—up to ¾ cup (175 ml)—as it blends until it has a smooth consistency. Taste and add more molasses if you want, and maybe a squeeze of lemon juice. This will keep for several days in the refrigerator. Serve at room temperature.

Pork Rinds

When is the last time you had some good old-fashioned crackling? That's the roasted skin with most of the fat cooked out. Kosher butchers occasionally sell gribenes, which is made from goose or chicken skin that is fried with a bit of onion. Latino butcher shops have chicharrones (it rhymes with "macaronis") made from pork skin. Filipino grocery and video stores often sell packaged pork rind. And everyone knows that the best part of the Peking duck is the crisp skin served at the beginning of the meal.

During the maple syrup season grattons, more popularly known as "les oreilles de crisse" are served at cabanes à sucre during sugaring-off parties. The traditional recipe calls for a couple of hours of cooking salted fat back at a low temperature so that the fat is mostly cooked off and the skin is golden and crunchy. These are then drained on paper towels and served warm and salted.

Crackling is opulent eating. It has a fine flavour when it is properly prepared. There is a rich flavour from the meat that the fat and skin was pulled from, and it is not as greasy as might be expected. The flavour is so full that a little goes along way. This is particularly true of freshly made crackling, not the ersatz packaged product.

Crackling is great snack food with a bad rep. We are used to eating large amounts of meat: chops, roasts, hams or chickens. However, not too long ago this gourmand approach to getting our protein was a luxury. When meat was expensive we ate it occasionally, not daily. Every part of the animal was sold. In the case of the pig, the saying was "We eat everything but the squeal."

The fat of the animal was necessary, both for nutrition (it's high in calories and vitamins) and because it contributed a tremendous amount of flavour. Used judiciously, fat was barded into larger and tougher cuts of meats, such as roasts. It kept them moist as they cooked. The skins were served as choice bits to savour—the cook's treat.

There are still plenty of places that make fresh crackling.

The Italian butcher **Tranzo** in the west end of the city usually roasts a small pig every day. **Charcuterie Hongroise** on The Main always has fresh crackling too. Ben Top, owner and master barbecue chef at **Sun Ling Lung** in Chinatown, roasts several carcasses a day in his own oven. He also sells roast duck and chicken. Latino butchers such as **Supermarché Andes** serve warm chunks of chicharrones ready for munching.

Charcuterie Hongroise on The Main.

Poutine

"To be really authentic the potatoes must be old
The gravy must be hot and the cheese must be cold
With a *Journal de Montréal* wherever it is sold
Served with a roll in a bowl by a troll."
—Bowser & Blue, from *The Night They Invented Poutine*

"I make it for la famille," said Normand Laprise, of Montreal's famed restaurant Toqué. "La famille" is chef-talk for the restaurant's staff and the dish Laprise is talking about is not his famous foie gras. It is poutine. "I use a little goat cheese and some duck gravy. I prefer Yukon Gold potatoes for frying." It's not quite what they serve at the **Montreal Pool Room** but it does have the essential ingredients: cheese, gravy, and potatoes.

David MacMillan, the creative force behind two of the city's most creative kitchens—**Globe** and Rosalie—also takes pride in his poutine, which he has been known to serve on request. His version is made from thickly cut and freshly fried potatoes, a sauce derived from rendered duck skin, and Stilton.

And Gilles St-Hilaire, formerly of the Ritz-Carlton Hotel, says he makes poutine at home.

Poutine's climb into the exalted kitchens of our master chefs needs context. The word itself derives from pudding. According to Bill Casselman's *Canadian Food Words* "pudding" became "la poutina" in Southern France. Loosely translated, it meant stuff stuck in a mess of something else.

Acadian dishes include a *poutines rapées* that call for grated or sliced potatoes. Our local version seems to have originated in L'Estrie (Quebec's Eastern Townships). There, one day a truck driver with a load of cheddar cheese curds persuaded restaurant owner Fernand Lachance (often called "le père de la poutine") to mix the cheese into the French fries. Lachance added his wife's gravy. Voilà, la poutine de chez nous!

You might consider poutine as an all-in-one meal. There's protein and calcium in the cheese, fiber and vitamins in the potatoes, plenty of carbohydrates and enough calories to jump-start the Concordia Stingers offensive line.

Great poutine requires as much effort as any good cooking. The potatoes must be freshly cut and fried. They should be crunchy outside, soft within and firmer than standard fries. They have a heck of a load to bear.

The cheese should be cheddar curds. It should smell fresh and taste rich from the milk and salty from the processing. They need to melt satisfyingly onto the fries but still retain their consistency and flavour. Really fresh curds actually have a wee squeak when you bite into them.

Finally the sauce must have its own flavour and be a little tart to balance the richness of the cheese. It is usually the same gravy used for hot chicken or hamburger sandwiches at a good casse-croute.

The standard is high. Most of the chains cut their fries too thin to support the cheese and sauce. Worse, some places crush the curds into the fries and turn everything into mush. Not so at **Chez Clo**, an unpretentious "mets Québécois" snack bar/bistro in the city's east end.

At Chez Clo, the juke box is stacked with 45 rpm records and the poutine tastes great. The potatoes are hand cut, the cheese is fresh and the sauce is not starchy or cloying but spicy and beefy as good gravy should be. The ingredients are a secret. "It has a chef's love," said Isabel Ruel who makes it.

Great chefs know that simple food can make sublime dining. "Why shouldn't we serve it? It has good local ingredients," said Fred Morin of Globe. "We should take pride in poutine."

Here is how two top chefs make poutine:

Traditional *Poutine à la Ritz* (The Ritz-Carlton's Executive-Chef Gilles St-Hilaire serves this at home.)

¾ pound (350 g) French fries
6 ounces (200 g) canned poutine or barbecue sauce
½ pound (250 g) cheese curds
2 tomatoes, diced
½ teaspoon (2 ml) fresh tarragon, chopped
1 clove of garlic, minced

1 tablespoon (15 ml) olive oil
A dash each of chili, salt and fine ground pepper.

Preheat olive oil in a skillet. Add garlic, tomatoes and tarragon and simmer for 2 minutes. Once done, set it aside. To add flavour to the sauce, reduce it by half and add a few roasted chicken bones while it cooks. Strain before serving.

In a deep bowl, put 4 ounces (100 g) of cheese and all the French fries. Add the tomato mixture, then the rest of the cheese. Add the poutine or barbecue sauce. Sprinkle with a dash of chili, salt and finely ground pepper.

Poutine Pont-neuf

David McMillan builds a tower of poutine and cheese in a lagoon of rich duck gravy or a reduced red wine sauce. This version is based on what he serves.

Make the sauce first and set it aside. The sauce could be as simple as the one in the previous recipe. Better yet, save the pan drippings the next time you roast meat or fowl. Pour off the fat. Add enough chicken stock and a dash of good red wine to make a cup (250 ml) of thin sauce. Boil this slowly to reduce the amount by as much as half or until it thickens. Add salt and pepper to taste. You can thicken it further by adding one teaspoon (5 ml) of cornstarch. To keep the sauce from being lumpy, first add enough liquid to the cornstarch to make a runny paste and then stir this back into the sauce. Remove from heat and keep warm.

Cut two large potatoes Pont-Neuf style. These will look like small square logs about ⅓ of an inch thick and 2½ inches long. Fry them golden brown. Drain them well. Stack them to build a small square tower 4-6 inches high. Fill the centre with your favourite cheese. Stilton, fresh mozzarella or cheddar curds all work well. Top with some finely chopped fresh chives. Pour the sauce around the base of the tower.

At **Chez Clo** poutine is always on the menu and starts at $3.75. At **Globe** poutine must be requested, and, if available, starts at around $10.

Quatre Épices

The mark of a great cuisine is probably that a signature blend of spices has evolved with it. One of the most fragrant and commonly used is quatre épices, the blend of basic spices that is used in many recipes from France. On one level, this is a mix of fragrant spices that the cook kept at home. Basic versions usually had cloves, ginger, nutmeg, and white pepper. The blends can vary considerably and include herbs as fragrant as bay leaf and thyme. Julia Child and Simone Beck in their ground-breaking book *Mastering the Art of French Cooking* have a deliciously complex mixture with a dozen ingredients. In other words, this is not a blend of spices to buy from a store. It is something to create at home to match the cook's profile. If you are a spicy kind of person, why not add some allspice and mace? A little bit more subtle? Start with the basic four. A comfortable balance might consist of one teaspoon (5 ml) each of the first three ingredients (cloves, ginger and nutmeg) with two tablespoons (25 ml) of pepper. If you are mixing them fresh leave out ginger as it will be too wet. Instead, grind together one teaspoon (5 ml) each of cloves and nutmeg, a ¼ cup (50 ml) of white peppercorns and a thumbnail-sized piece of cinnamon bark.

This is a tasty spice mixture to add to simple cake recipes, cookie dough, custards, crepes and omelets. It also goes well mixed in with ground chicken or pork.

Quatre épices dates back to the Middle Ages when relatively few spices reached the European courts. Even after a few months, it retains a robust refreshing fragrance. It must have been a wonderful mixture to dispel the rather funky smells that were integral to life back then or to be wrapped in a handkerchief to cover the mouth and nose during the plague as potential pestilential protection.

Over the centuries, as living standards improved, herbs gradually replaced imported spices. However, quatre épices remains a fragrant echo from a period long ago when the spice trade was still essential to the flavours of the kitchen.

Root Beers

Hot weather requires cold drinks. For most that means beer or soft drinks. But I find that the former has too much alcohol and carbonation for continual quaffing, and the latter is too sweet. The best summer drinks are refreshing but not cloying.

The hotter the weather, the more I reach for my roots. These are the roots that soft drinks come from: ginger, birch, mauby and spruce come to mind. Today's popular colas were once touted as stimulating tonics. They were made from herbs, carbonated water and syrups. Consider the kola nuts in Pepsi-Cola or the coca leaf originally used in Coke. Root beer is traditionally made from the root of several plants such as burdock, dandelion and sarsaparilla.

While mainstream beverages are very similar (how many of us would pass the Pepsi/Coke test?) root beers have unique flavours and a refreshing bitter-sweet balance that often comes from citric acid or quinine.

Many places once featured a local root beer. Our own home-brewed variety is spruce beer, which technically isn't a "root" beer. The flavour comes from the twigs and bark of the spruce fir. This was once a common drink throughout eastern North America. An 18th-century New England officer recommended spruce beer as healthier for seamen than the prescribed daily tot of rum.

Spruce beer is still produced and is found in many stores (look for Marko, a new brand on the market). It's really a Quebec taste and is rarely sold outside the province. To taste this unique drink at its best, drop by **Émile Bertrand**, a snack bar on Notre Dame Street. A deliciously tart, sparkling spruce beer is brewed on the premises.

For those of us who want more variety, try drinks common in the Caribbean. They have mellifluous names like Velvet Falernum Liquer, Sweet and Dandy Mauby syrup, and Aunt May's Ginger Beer Syrup. I confess I go for the appellations as much as the essence. These and similar brands are sold in many Caribbean grocery stores.

Velvet Falernum is a lime-based syrup with hints of

almond and clove. It is traditionally served like a lime cordial, over crushed ice with a shot of rum. I find it refreshing mixed in ice water; although served this way, there is a strong medicinal undercurrent to the flavour that rum easily masks.

Mauby syrup also has a slightly bitter medicinal edge, as do other vegetal-based beverages like the Italian Brio. Mauby Syrup is made from sugar and water and mauby bark and has become my favourite drink. It is similar to root beer but without the cloying quality of commercial brands. I like my drinks not too sweet and less syrupy than the one part syrup to four parts water that the bottler recommends. Conversely, I can make a sweeter drink if others prefer.

Then there is ginger beer, truly one of the great drinks of summer. Aunt May's version consists of ginger concentrate, water and sugar. It's tasty with club soda, iced tea, or fruit juices; but for a real treat try making a drink often called a shandy or shandygaff. Mix one part ginger beer syrup with four parts club soda and an equal amount of ale. Add a slice of lemon or orange. The ginger gives the drink a sassy kick and the beer, now diluted, is refreshing but not heavy.

If you find these Caribbean island flavours too strong, try some from a closer locale, Prince Edward Island. A company called Seaman's Beverages produces what may be the tastiest soft drinks in North America. Seaman's was recently taken over by Pepsi-Cola but the family recipes, which date back sixty years, are still used. Several supermarkets now carry their products in Montreal. They make many flavours including birch beer, root beer and a zesty ginger ale.

Finally, there are several regional soft drinks that rarely make it to Montreal. If you are travelling north of Quebec City look for Kiri, Ideal Sport, and Saguenay Dry GingerAle (maybe it was considered politically incorrect to stock Canada Dry here) as well as a sweet, non-alcoholic drink called Red Champagne. In the Eastern Townships ask for the local favourite with a great label—Bullshead GingerAle.

Roti

Imagine a stew you can eat with one hand. A delicious ladle of curried chicken or a scoop of spicy potato and peas, wrapped in a large thin bread and folded perfectly so that nothing drips out. That's roti. It's a Caribbean treat and if this was a perfect world, there would be a roti stand on every corner of this city.

The Caribbean is a wonderfully multicultural area where Latin, African, Chinese and Indian cultures have blended for over a century. The result, certainly in food, is a real melting-pot. The dishes seem familiar and at the same time somewhat different. Plantains, sliced thin and fried, are munched like potato chips; fish cakes turn into dumplings; and long-simmering stews get wrapped in an Indian flat bread called a roti.

While the word roti comes from India, Caribbean cooking uses it to describe both the 15-inch-round crepe or skin that enfolds the stew as well as the dish itself.

The roti skin is a flat bread. It is made of whole wheat flour, cornmeal, and ground chickpeas. Although eventually rolled quite thin, it is made with yeast or baking powder and rises substantially before it is finally baked on a large griddle. Packaged roti skins can be purchased at Indian and Caribbean food stores. They are tastier, larger and more pliable for wrap-style sandwiches that the ersatz pesto and sun-dried tomato tortilla "wraps" that have cropped up everywhere.

The best rotis, however, are made fresh in Caribbean restaurants and snack bars. Popular fillings include chicken, potato and vegetable, goat, and ox tail. These last two are succulent meats that demand slow cooking to make them tender. And few kitchens cook them better than those of the Antilles.

A roti sandwich costs between $4 and $6 and one is sufficient for lunch. Fillings are often available with or without bones. I find that the meat still on the bones has the most flavour. It's worth the extra time to chew each morsel carefully. Generally, roti fillings are tasty but not overly spicy. If you like curried food with that extra tang, ask for more hot sauce, but be cautious. Some places make their own sauces and take pride in how much heat they can pack into a few drops.

Three areas of the city for fresh rotis are Côte-des-Neiges, Mile End and LaSalle. In Côte-des-Neiges, the section of Victoria Avenue north of Van Horne Avenue, has several Caribbean restaurants and bakeries such as **Mr. Spicee** and **Caribbean Curry House**. In Mile End, rotis are the main event at **Jardin du Cari**. In the West End try rotis at **Bonne Bouffe** and **Ma's Place**.

Salicorne

Every summer, I need to taste the sea. When we go on vacation and finally hit the beach, the first thing I do is run to the water and bring a few delicious drops to my mouth. The slightly salty, complex ocean flavour is close to our own sweat and saliva, to the taste of life. And when we return home, it is the taste of the sea that I miss the most. But it doesn't have to be that way thanks to a delicious briny plant called salicorne.

Salicorne is the taste of summer by the sea. It is slightly salty with a fresh, not overpowering, herbal taste. It grows exceptionally well in salt marshes and can sometimes be harvested under wharves. Although salicorne is a weed and does grow by the sea, it does not look like seaweed. It is more like a sprig off a tree with small dark green fleshy branches.

Salicorne is also known as samphire. Some call it sea asparagus and it does have a little of the sweet flavour of that vegetable. It is also known as seabean and slender glasswort but that sounds too much like a botanical from a Dickensian apothecary.

Chez Louis, the vegetable and fruit stand (the choice of many chefs) on the southern edge of the Jean-Talon Market carries fresh green salicorne from Brittany through February, and a slightly more fibrous, red variety from the Gaspé through November.

The plant is also pickled and occasionally sold in cans, but the fresh variety is worth looking for. At $3.50 for 100 grams (4 oz.), it is not too expensive. Cut into small pieces when fresh, salicorne is great in a salad.

Some restaurants serve it steamed under fish. While quite nice cooked this way, I find salicorne tastiest when fried for a minute or two in olive oil or butter. This caramelizes the slender branches slightly and makes the flesh a little less salty and sweeter. Serve it on its own or toss it with a little garlic and oil over pasta.

Salt

The taste of salt is the taste of life. The word salt and saliva come from the same Latin root. Salt helps control our internal electric circuitry. It is in our blood, our sweat, our tears. It is the flavour of our essence. It is the only rock we savour.

For most of human history, salt has been a valuable commodity. It was once a rare and prized mineral, extracted from mines with slave labour or slowly and painstakingly harvested from the sea. It was brought over the Arabian peninsula on the backs of camels. It was a treasure kept in salt boxes and used sparingly at the table. Romans paid their soldiers with it. They received salt money, a salarium, and we still get a salary.

Now we have too much salt. We throw it on roads to melt snow. A table without a salt shaker isn't quite ready for dinner. There is hardly a recipe that doesn't call for the stuff. We are addicted to it. Salt is the most elemental of foods but its flavour is hard to describe.

Salt tastes, well, salty. But that isn't quite so. In front of me, as I write, are samples of four salts. There is Diamond Crystal, chemically pure salt—a little sodium, a little chlorine and voilà! sodium chloride. Add a dash of sodium silico-aluminate to keep it running free, a hint of dextrose to sweeten it and a touch of potassium iodide to return some of the iodine to us that we would normally get from sea salt. This is ordinary table salt but it is the taste my tongue is used to. The tongue says "Right. Salt. So what? Put it on some celery, put it on my meat. Everything tastes better because this is how I eat." This is the salt of habit. It pours easily from saltshakers. It is a technological marvel completely devoid of the funkiness of the sea.

Then there is a generic sea salt from a "health food" store. Surprisingly, this tastes just like the Diamond Crystal only with a stronger saltiness. This is the salt I have been using because it seemed more natural, more virtuous. But now that I compare it with the Diamond Crystal I feel that it hasn't been worth the difference in price. Tasting either leaves my tongue parched.

Next is Le Paludier, a sea salt from Brittany. It looks like fine sand under a gray sky. The crystals glint silver in the room light. This salt tastes different. It is fresher tasting, with a slight earthiness. It is complex, made from what the sea offered and what the stones that ground it left as residue. I can touch the salt to my tongue and not feel desiccation set in. My saliva increases to wash the sea away. It is a good taste.

And then there is La Baleine—large crystals of naturally evaporated sea salt from France. It crunches satisfyingly between my teeth and dissolves quickly in my mouth. It grinds beautifully in an inexpensive mill. The flavour is savory but the level of saltiness feels normal. It is not overpowering. Within a few seconds the brininess has moved to the back of my mouth. A moment later it is as tasty a memory as being washed by a warm wave.

Until recently, La Baleine and similar natural sea salts were hard to find. However most supermarkets now carry them.

Another salt to consider is coarse or kosher—it has no additives and is excellent for cooking and brining.

Salt Cod

Mention salt cod and most of us will probably turn up our noses. Fresh is the order of the day, every day. So we ask for the salmon, the sole, the haddock and the snapper. We look over the tuna and the swordfish. On the rare chance that there is fresh cod at the fishmonger's, we might take it home and cook it for dinner. But that dried slab in the corner with the salty crust and the strong fishy smell—why buy that when there is so much fresh around?

Ahh, but those from Africa, the Caribbean and particularly from southern European countries, they know better.

Salt cod was essential to people from the Mediterranean basin for almost a millennium. Meat was forbidden on Fridays and other days of abstinence on the Catholic calendar, especially during Lent. For many centuries dried fish, called stock fish, was imported from Scandinavia because there was not a constant supply of fresh fish in the Mediterranean or in that part of the Atlantic bordering Europe.

The oceans of cod that Cabot and Cartier sailed through off Newfoundland brought fleets of boats from Europe. But the voyage was too long to bring the fish back fresh and the weather was too wet in Newfoundland to dry it like stock fish. Gutting, laying the fish flat and salting it was the best way to preserve it. When it was fairly dry it was stacked and brought back to Europe. The same ships that brought slaves to North America returned to Europe with salt cod. Later the trade route included trips to the Caribbean. Ships introduced salt cod to these islands and came back with rum.

To merely think of salt cod as dried fish is to miss the point. This is not a lower quality of fish; it is completely different. It is like comparing fresh salmon with smoked salmon. Or pork with cured ham. There is a place for each on our plate and choosing one does not denigrate the other.

The flavour of salt cod is intense and not salty when it is well-prepared. The texture is meaty and firm, not unlike swordfish or even chicken. It is chewy and toothsome.

Properly prepared salt cod is soaked and rinsed over and

over again for up to two days, depending upon the thickness of the fish. Then the ethnic angle kicks in. Salt cod is common in Caribbean cooking, for example, where it is often served with akee. This is a fruit that, when cooked, has a taste and texture akin to scrambled eggs. Many Caribbean restaurants serve salt fish and akee for breakfast or on weekends.

In Greek restaurants, look for bakaliaro tiganito. Here, the cod is fried in a light batter and usually served with skordalia—cold garlicky mashed potatoes. In France a favourite dish is brandade de morue—a salt cod and potato purée. In Portugal, its bacalhau. In Spain, try bacalao with tomatoes, onions and garlic.

Although salt cod is sold in many fish shops, hydrating it and cooking it can be a long process. When you do buy it, remember that it will double in size as you repeatedly soak and rinse it.

Many restaurants have salt cod on the menu. Two excellent ones, with very different approaches to this meaty but meatless dish are **Café Ferreira**, the extravagantly wonderful downtown Portuguese restaurant, and **Rotisserie Panama**, an inexpensive Greek family-style rotisserie in the "Little Greece" section of Park Extension on Jean-Talon West.

Samosas

Every cuisine asks itself the same question: how can we stretch a little bit of meat or vegetables and make it more filling? The easiest way is to wrap it in dough. In this way we get verenikas, pierogies, ravioli, dumplings and empanadas. Whether the end result is fried, baked, steamed, or boiled, the answer is delicious.

One of the tastiest forms is samosas. These are common throughout India and much of southern Asia and eastern Africa. The pastry is a mixture of oil and ghee or butter, a little salt, water and flour. The oil and butter enable the pastry to flake as it fries. The result is crispy and slightly salty on the outside, soft and strongly flavoured within.

If filled with meat, they may be called kheema samosas. The filling consists of ground lamb, onion, tomato, peas and lots of spices. Vegetable samosas commonly have chick peas, potato, and green peas. They can be fairly spicy depending upon how much chili is used.

Samosas are best warm and crisp. They reheat nicely in a toaster oven but keep the heat low. The oil in the the pastry will cause it to burn if the oven is too hot. They should be served with a tamarind sauce or a chutney. If they are very spicy, have some yogurt on the side for a dip.

To make your own tamarind sauce buy a package of tamarind pulp without the seeds. Take a heaping tablespoon (15-20 ml) and mash it with your fingers or a fork to make sure no seeds are left. Mix this well in a blender with ⅓ cup (75 ml) of water, and a pinch of salt plus ¼ teaspoon (1 ml) each of curry powder, ground pepper, and sugar. Add a little more water if it is too thick. Add some chopped fresh coriander leaf on top before serving.

All Indian restaurants will sell samosas to go. Many Asian grocery stores also make their own and sell them at the counter. The vegetarian restaurant **Pushap**, near the Namur Métro, has a large variety of Indian sweets and appetizers ready to go. They can make vegetable samosas in large or small sizes on request. Small ones are great as hors d'oeuvres. A couple of larger ones are almost enough for a meal, especially a channa samosa—a samosa covered with chickpea curry and yogurt. Another good place is **D.A.D.'s Bagel** in N.D.G. This store is owned by a family that came from India. It is open 24 hours a day, great if you have a late-night urge for samosas. There is also a large selection of good homemade Indian takeout in the refrigerators—right next to the lox and cream cheese.

Schnitzel

Sometimes all I want is a good piece of meat tucked inside a sandwich. I don't want cheese slices, pickles, special sauce or any sort of onghepochket (a marvellous Yiddish word that means "something all messed up"). I just want a tasty chunk of meat in a fresh roll. That's enough to satiate my inner carnivore.

Fortunately, central Europeans understand this craving and created the schnitzel sandwich. The word "schnitzel" comes from the German and technically it means a shaving of something. This may be because meat for schnitzels (usually a veal or pork cutlet or a slice of chicken or turkey breast) is pounded thin before it is cooked. It may be slightly flavoured with salt, pepper, perhaps a little garlic, but usually it just has a thick covering of fine bread crumbs and is quickly fried. The crumbs provide a coating that keeps the meat from drying out as it cooks. Done correctly, a schnitzel is tasty but not oily. Served as a main course it can be more refined with successive coatings of flour, an egg wash and then bread crumbs. This creates a crisp, succulent crust. The schnitzel can be further augmented by truffles or artichokes or even served with an egg on top as a regal Schnitzel Holstein, but by now we have left the realm of sandwichdom for the blue-plate special.

A schnitzel sandwich is a simple dish. It might have a little mustard or mayo, even a slice of lettuce or tomato but it shouldn't go further than that. Quite frankly, with a fresh crunchy roll it is a satisfying meal by itself. If you want a pickle, get it on the side.

Bucharest Delicatessen on Décarie Boulevard and **Slovenia Meat Products** on Clark Street serve a delicious schnitzel sandwich. Ask for the schnitzel sandwich (with warm, seasoned saurkraut) at **Charcuterie Hongroise** on St-Laurent Boulevard. They also have sausages and ham smoked on the premises and prepared without chemicals. There is a counter for in-store eating, but why stay inside? Enjoy your sandwich while ambling down The Main.

Seville Oranges

Nothing puts the bite into winter like Seville oranges. Fragrant, pungent, inedible. Traders brought them from China to Spain almost a millennium ago. At first, they were treasured for their aroma. Maidens would cup them in their hands to release the heady smell and orange blossoms are still part of a Spanish bride's bouquet.

Rich in Vitamin C, they were one of the treasured "spring grasses" which helped combat scurvy. Although too bitter to be readily eaten, Sevilles were often served sprinkled with sugar. A traditional medieval treat involved splashing a little rum or gin on sweetened orange halves and grilling them. In Britain, Seville oranges are a key ingredient in the potent Edwardian punch called a Smoking Bishop.

Unlike the Navel, Valencia, Jaffa or other similar sweet-tasting oranges, Sevilles are only available for a few weeks in late winter or early spring. Most of this fruit still comes from Spain and most is sold in bulk to Britain where it is made into marmalade. This is a shame because the flavour and high acid content can work so well in many dishes. In Ecuador the oranges are used instead of limes for ceviche. In any dessert calling for oranges, Sevilles will give much more flavour than sweet varieties. And as for Canard à l'orange—wow!

I still like these oranges best in marmalade. The word "marmalade", by the way, is Portuguese and means "quince jam" since quinces were commonly used. Now Seville oranges have replaced them. Here is our recipe. It makes about six one-pint (575 ml) containers.

Seville Orange Marmalade

Wash seven Seville oranges and two lemons. Slice them as thinly as possible. Remove the seeds and put these in a bag made from a clean piece of J Cloth or cheesecloth. Soak the sliced fruit and the seed bag in 16 cups (4 litres) of cold water for 24 hours. Simmer everything in an open pot until the peel is tender and the mixture is reduced to 11 cups (3.75 litres). (An easy way to do this is to first fill the pot with 11 cups (3.75 litres) of water and make a mark on the outside of the pot. Then add the rest of the water, oranges and seeds. When the water has evaporated and the level is back to the mark, it is ready.) Remove the seed bag and squeeze the bag so that the liquid drains into the pot. Discard the bag. Add 9 cups (2 kg) of sugar to the pot. Turn up the heat a little and slowly boil the syrup to a gel stage (220° F). It should take at least 30 minutes to reach this temperature.

For a smaller quantity, decide how many oranges you want to use. For each one add a 1 cup (250 ml) of sugar and 1½ cups (375 ml) of water. Simmer this until it reduces by half to 1¼ cups (300 ml).

Shiitake

Shiitakes are dark, umbrella-shaped mushrooms with large caps and thin stems. When fresh, they have a light woodsy aroma and a very mild taste. Shiitake are commercially grown in North America. Many supermarkets such as Métro and Cinq Saisons stock them. They can be eaten raw like ordinary white or brown mushrooms. They can also be grilled like portabellos or oyster mushrooms. The caps are better fresh. The stems are tough but they have a good flavour and make good additions to soups or stews.

Fresh shiitakes are expensive. We are more likely to encounter them reconstituted in Oriental cooking where they have a particular affinity for strong flavours such as soy and chili sauces, oyster sauce, star anise, and sesame oil. Research on shiitakes has found that they may be helpful in lowering cholesterol.

Dried shiitakes taste of smoke and earth and have a meaty texture. Their rich full flavour belies their humble beginnings as spores on rotting oak and other dead trees. "Take" means mushroom in Japanese and "shii" is one kind of tree where this mushroom is found.

There are several grades of dried shiitakes. The most expensive can be as large as the palm of a hand and has a thick fleshy cap. These are best by themselves. Wash them and leave them covered in water overnight. (If you are in a rush, you can add them to very hot water and let them sit for about 20 minutes. They will become fleshy and supple but the flavour won't be as good). Any silt from the mushrooms will be left on the bottom of the container. Remove the mushrooms without stirring up the liquid, pat them dry and then sauté them in a little oil, or, better yet, chicken fat. Sprinkle soy sauce on them before serving. The liquid can be filtered through a paper towel or a coffee filter and used in other dishes. This grade of shiitake is hard to find outside of Asian food stores and Chinatown.

The next grade is a little thinner. The preparation is the same but these are best served in dishes, as an ingredient, rather than by themselves. These are great in a wine sauce served over grilled meats. Sauté a chopped shallot and a diced clove of garlic in a little butter, add a squeeze of lemon juice or a little rice wine vinegar, a few dashes of soy sauce and a pinch of sugar. Stir while pouring in just enough red wine to cover the bottom of the pan. Bring this to a boil, add a half-dozen dried mushrooms. Simmer these, tightly covered, over low heat for about 20 minutes.

Finally there are very thin and inexpensive shiitakes. These are often broken in their bags. The flavour is excellent but they aren't very attractive served by themselves. Rehydrate them, slice them thin and add them to soups, fried rice or noodles.

Shiitaki mushrooms are available almost anywhere in Chinatown, also at **Miyamoto**, **Formosa**, and **Korean & Japanese Food** and **Chez Louis**.

Chez Louis, Jean-Talon Market.

Smoked Meat

Remember that old song, "You say pastrami, I say binden-fleisch; you say corned beef, I say old fashioned ...." Of course in Quebec we just say "smoked meat" and everyone sings the same tune.

Smoked meat is one of the defining flavours of Montreal. The delicious blend of smoke, brine and spices permeates one of the tougher cuts of beef and makes it meltingly delectable.

Those from other cities may argue that there is little difference between Montreal smoked meat, actually created by Romanian immigrants, and similar cuts served elsewhere. But subtleties are important. There is a reason the Montreal version tastes so good.

Before refrigeration, meat had to be cured to be kept. The easiest method was to smoke it or cover it in salt. The liquid from the meat seeped out and created a brine. Today, brines are created to add flavour and they combine salt, sugar, water and flavourings. There may also be a dash of nitrite or other chemical to give the meat a colour and help ward off bacteria. The brine works well on a tough portion such as the brisket. The solution breaks down the protein and displaces other fluids in the meat and the meat emerges pink and juicy. At this stage it can be slowly simmered and sold as corned beef. "Corn" is an old English term for grain and in this case refers to the large grains, or corns, of salt that were used to prepare the beef.

Done properly, corned beef is juicy and flavourful. Unfortunately, a lot of processors inject extra liquid and smoke flavouring into the meat. This increases the weight, and the profits, but it turns decent beef into bright pink rubber.

But brining the brisket doesn't make it smoked meat. The next step is, of course, to smoke it. In Montreal, each processor has its own method. Montreal's best known smoked-meat emporium, **Schwartz's Hebrew Delicatessan** packs briskets in pickling spices for ten days, and then smokes them for about seven hours. **Quebec Smoked Meat**, which sells an excellent product used by many delis in Montreal, smokes for about 70 hours. Both producers sell what is called an old-fashioned style. This is heavily peppered and spiced before smoking. The finished brisket is tender and covered with a thick coating of black peppercorns. The brisket is a full, tapered muscle with more fat at one end than the other. A request for a lean or medium sandwich determines where the portions are sliced.

Pastrami, the favourite deli meat of New Yorkers, is prepared similarly but is often made with a leaner cut of meat than the brisket and isn't brined. Instead it is rubbed with salt, garlic and seasonings and dry cured in a refrigerator. After that, it is smoked and cooked.

Of course, meat could be cured without extensive brining. Then it is usually cut into long strips and air-dried (bindenfleisch in Switzerland, brési in France, bresaola in Italy) or dried even further as a beef jerky. However none of these would make a sumptuous Montreal-style deli-sandwich.

As a treat, ask a deli counter for end cuts. These are small slabs of meat that remain after most of the brisket has been sliced. The texture and fat content will vary and they are likely to be in uneven sizes and more heavily spiced than sliced smoked meat; however, end cuts are usually quite inexpensive and great eating. Dice a bit of this and add it to pea soup, or chop some into a really delicious corned beef hash, or fry a little and add it to scrambled eggs. The flavour of Montreal always comes through.

Solomon Gundy

"Solomon Gundy" is high on my list of words that are just fun to say. It rolls from the back of the mouth, twists the tongue around shifting vowels and then spits over the teeth in an exhalant last syllable.

Solomon Gundy, the Jamaican condiment, packs a similar kind of wrap-around-the-taste-buds punch. It is a mixture of mashed pickled herring, scallions and hot peppers. It has a long, almost smoky flavour that works wonderfully well in cheese balls, sour cream and yogurt dips, pasta sauces, or dabbed onto a cheese and tomato pizza. Calling Solomon Gundy simply a fish paste is akin to saying that Dijon and French's are both mustards and giving no further explanation.

This is a condiment with baggage. It is not a coincidence that it comes from Jamaica, an island country with a more diverse population, and a cuisine with a broader range of ethnic influences, than either of its larger neighbours—Cuba and Hispaniola. At its best, Jamaican cooking is a wonderful international pastiche. The Spanish planted oranges and sugar cane, Africans introduced ackee and yams, East Indians brought in curry, the British gave it custard, etc. One of the oldest waves of immigrants were Jews fleeing the Spanish Inquisition. They arrived in the Caribbean with Columbus. Among their recipes were several ways of preserving food with salt. One popular method of preserving fish became known as Solomon Gundy.

I'd like to believe that Solomon Gundy was a real person, maybe a Jewish immigrant who was the first to mix Jamaica's hot peppers with northern European pickled herring. That's a good story, but it's wrong. The etymology is equivocal but there is strong speculation that the phrase comes from "salame conditi", which is Italian for "pickled meat". This was a common way of preserving food in medieval Europe. By the time the words and the process reached Britain, the phrase was garbled into Solomon Gundy. It later became famous in the children's nonsense rhyme that begins "Solomon Grundy, born on a Monday..."

At that time, a Solomon Gundy was likely to be a plate of pickled meats or fish with onions and condiments. In fact, this is the way it is still served in some restaurants in Atlantic Canada: a piece of pickled herring and cocktail sauce. Real Jamaican Solomon Gundy, such as the Walker's Wood brand, comes in a jar. It is common in grocery stores like **Arawak** that feature Caribbean foods.

Arawak in N.D.G.

Soufganiot

The Jewish festival of Chanukah usually falls in December. It celebrates a Jewish revolt against the Greeks over 2000 years ago. When it came time to light the Temple lamp only a small vial of oil was found. Miraculously this oil lasted eight days and so candles are lit for eight days. Oil is important to this festival. Many of the traditional candelabra, called Hanukiah, still use oil instead of candles.

Foods fried in oil are also traditional for this festival. One of the best known is latkes or potato pancakes but there are lots of other delicious snacks that are just as appropriate.

A favourite is soufganiot, Israeli doughnuts. These are originally a European delicacy and came to Israel with the pastry chefs and bakers who emigrated from Austria and Hungary. They are similar to the Polish donuts called ponchkes, which are traditionally fried in butter and sold throughout the year in Polish bakeries. Both soufganiot and ponchkes are made without holes.

These are also similar to jelly doughnuts but the dough is yeastier and the flavour of the dough is stronger and often tastier than the filling inside. Extravagant and usually home-made, soufganiot may incorporate sour cream into the batter. Most doughs, however, aren't quite this rich. They are usually filled with jam or caramel cream and rolled in confectioner's sugar.

Almost all Jewish bakeries and grocery stores sell soufganiot. Remember that kosher stores are closed Friday night and Saturday. Two bakeries worth visiting are **Kosher Quality** in Côte-des-Neiges and **Adar** in Côte-St-Luc. Occasionally these bakeries make a scrumptious version which is a little larger than a golf ball. Two bites and it's gone.

Sourdough bread

My bread tastes great. Everyone tells me so. It's an old-fashioned sourdough so different from standard white bread that it might as well be from another world, or at least an older one. It takes days to make. The crust is hard. The crumb is dense. Chewing a piece is gratifying. But I don't bake bread just for the taste.

A dozen bakers in this town pull a more consistently delicious loaf from their commercial brick ovens than I get from my small gas stove. At Montreal's markets I am seduced by the fragrance from the wood-fired ovens of **Première Moisson**. I can't resist. Damn, we make great bread in this city.

However, their loaves can't give me a home filled with the heady aromas of toasted flour and natural yeasts. No bakery can recreate that wonderful feeling I get when I walk through the front door and smell my loaf, just out of the oven.

Even a lousy loaf, one that lacks conviction because it doesn't rise well or has too much salt or is undercooked, even a lousy loaf smells great. The truth is that I turn out enough loaves that lack conviction to convince me that I'll never master the baker's art. Instead, I approach my bread making with the diligence of a pilgrim divining Mecca and I look for small epiphanies along the way.

My bread has three ingredients: flour, water and salt. The first step is to let the dough create its own yeasts and become sour. Mix one cup (250 ml) of flour with the same amount of water and let this paste ferment for several days. I do this by leaving it in a small bowl and covering it with a damp cloth. The yeasts are there when the glop has a strong winey smell. If you are fortunate, you will only have to do this step once.

This unattractive mess is then mixed with a ½ cup (125 ml) of water and more flour. It is briefly kneaded as damp dough to the consistency of putty. This is placed into a bowl, covered with a plastic wrap, and put aside in the kitchen for a day or two until the dough bubbles up. I find leaving it on top of the refrigerator works well.

Sometimes the dough rises in the middle of the night and sinks back to the bottom of the bowl by morning. Sometimes I just trust that it didn't die.

The longer I leave it, the sourer the dough gets, but certainly after two days it is ready to be made into bread. A tablespoon (15 ml) of sea salt is mixed into this pudding with another 1½ cups (375 ml) of water. Flour is progressively added until the dough can be turned out and kneaded, adding more flour to keep it from sticking to the board.

I do not use a bread machine and I keep my utensils basic. There are a couple of ceramic bowls, a wooden spatula, and a favourite split-ash basket for that final rise. I enjoy using these tools. Good bread is a complex food that starts simply. Working this way, slowly and methodically, forces me to appreciate each step.

I knead by hand, pulling the dough out and rolling it over. Kneading ends when I start to perspire. I put the dough into a large bowl and cover it. When the dough doubles, I knead it briefly and then I pull off a piece the size of an egg. I dust this piece with flour, put it in a tightly covered container, and stash it in the refrigerator. This nugget will replace the gruel of fermented flour and water next time I make bread.

I punch the rest of the dough down, knead it for another minute and flour it. I put the loaf in the basket, cover it with a thick dry cloth, and let it double again. Near the end of the rising, I preheat the oven to 450° F. When the oven is ready, I turn the bread onto a hot stone in a preheated oven (barring the stone, I use a clay cooker or a Dutch oven or even a cast-iron frying pan). I slash the middle of the top of the dough and hope it will rise evenly. I turn the oven down to 375° F. The bread bakes for about 40 minutes or until the bottom sounds hollow when thumped.

If you are like me, telling you all this is worthless. There are chefs and there are cooks. Cooks can read recipes. Chefs create them. I could no more figure out how to boil an egg from a recipe than I could tell you how Moses parted the Red Sea. In both cases, I'd like to watch someone do it. That's the way I learn.

Three days of work for a loaf of bread may seem ridiculous, but it was three years until I got the first one right.

For three years, I read books about making sourdough bread. I diligently fermented water and flour. I put loaves into the oven and took out unleavened bricks. I religiously saved a portion of the dough and made something equally inedible the following week. I was convinced that sheer orneriness would make the damn things rise.

Then we went to Paris. I had been to Paris before, of course, but I had never visited Paris with a subliminal need to bake bread. I wandered through boulangeries with the fervour of an art student at the Louvre. I ate baguettes and croissants. I nosed the baskets of bread vendors at the outdoor market in our local arrondissement. On almost the last day of our visit, I happened by 8, rue de Cherche-Midi, the home of Pain Poilâne.

Lionel Poilâne, who died recently, practically on his own revived country-style homemade bread baking in France. His thick round loaves are dense, chewy and invariably inconsistent. The weather, the moisture content of the flour, the temperature in the kitchen, all of these affect the rise of the loaf and its final taste and texture, but the smell of this wonderful bread is always the same. At Poilâne, I stood surrounded by shelves of dark brown wheels of bread and the aroma of sourdough enveloped me.

A typical Poilâne loaf is about 14 inches round. I know this because we brought two home. One was bread. The other was a Poilâne pillow that is next to me now and still looks exactly like a loaf. We kept the two of them side by side for a couple of days after we came back from Paris. Then we ate the loaf. Then I baked my own. At last I knew what I was trying to do.

Here was bread with a thick crust and a heavy dark body with large, irregular air holes. After several days, it was still moist and chewy. The flavour was slightly acid and nutty.

It was like biting into the genus of bread, from which all future species would eventually emerge. From this coarse peasant loaf, they would all come: the French baguette, the English muffin, the Romanian bagel, the Viennese croissant, the pumpernickel, the rye, the biscuit, the bun, even air-

184

injected North American supermarket white sandwich bread perfect for sopping up gravy.

To eat a chunk torn from this impossibly large loaf was to taste the essence of that first primal bread, the staff of life, and the one for which all of us yearn, at least once.

My bread does not come cheap. So far it has cost me the price of several books on baking and a trip to Paris. However, with each loaf, I come a little bit closer to un vrai pain Poilâne. Even on those days when both myself and my bread fall by the wayside, the evanescent aroma from a homemade sourdough loaf lifts me toward the sublime.

Much of my technique, in bread and otherwise, is inspired by John Thorne. *Serious Pig* and the superb *Outlaw Cook* are two of his wonderful food books. Both are required reading for all who are trying to make sense of their lives, never mind dinner. He and his partner Matt produce the newsletter Simple Cooking. It and they can found at www.outlawcook.com.

Sour Salt

Looking for a little pucker power but out of fresh lemon? Try sour salt. This was once a staple in eastern European cupboards because lemons and limes were not often available.

Sour salt is citric acid, a powder extracted from acidic fruits, and fermented glucose. The flavour is acutely sour. It is inexpensive and a small jar lasts for years. A few grains or crystals has as much tartness as a couple of squeezes from a lemon or lime but the salt doesn't have a strong fruit flavour. Use it when a recipe calls for lemon juice and there isn't any in the house or when using lemon juice in a cake or muffin recipe would change the balance of dry to wet ingredients

Sour salt works best in recipes that include sugar and the goal is to balance between the sweet and sour flavours. Examples are cold beet borscht or lemony cheese cake. Using sour salt, you can find the balance of sweet and sour that you like. A good ratio to start with is 1 part sweet (usually sugar) to ½ part sour salt, than adjust the proportions as you wish. You can use this to make a sweet and sour syrup to flavour drinks such as margaritas or plain soda water. While I prefer fresh limes or lemons, if they aren't available, I would use sour salt. It tastes fresher than bottled or concentrated lemon or lime juice, which often has an unpleasant aftertaste.

Another good use for sour salt is in making acidulated water. Use one teaspoon (5 ml) of sour salt for a half gallon of water. Dipping freshly cut fruit and vegetables such as apples, pears or artichokes in this prevents their cut surfaces from turning brown. This also works with potatoes. Grated potatoes, in particular, can turn grey before they are cooked. Let them sit in acidulated water and then drain them well before you cook them and they will stay white. A half-cup (125 ml) of an acidic liquid such as white wine, lemon juice or white vinegar could be used instead of the sour salt but the sour salt is apt to leave the freshest taste and be less expensive.

Look for sour salt in the kosher sections of supermarkets and in Jewish grocery stores.

Soy Sauce

In front of me are 10 bottles of soy sauce. Behind me is a family wondering what I am going to do with them.

One bottle is Pearl River Light from China. It has a strong salty taste at first but the soy and wheat flavours increase pleasantly as saliva washes the salt away and the sauce flows to the back of the tongue. Then there is Kikkoman's standard brand, made in the U.S.A., slightly sweeter and not quite as strong as the Pearl River. Beside that is a bottle of Kikkoman whole bean soy sauce, brewed in Japan and available in a few Asian specialty shops. This is at least twice the price of regular soy sauce. It is supposed to be milder because it has been brewed longer and has less salt. I find it has a wonderful flavour that its American-brewed cousins don't quite match.

There are other brands as well but what I find remarkable is that each bottle lists the same ingredients: water, soybeans, wheat and salt. Yet each tastes different. Why haven't I noticed this before? Why do we pay so little attention to soy sauce, one of the world's oldest condiments, yet are prepared to spend small fortunes on balsamic vinegar, virgin olive oils and premium coffees?

"Once it was common to find aged soy sauce but people don't want to spend a lot of money for it these days," said Ben Top, my Chinatown purveyor, as he ladled out a pint of his own stock. "This comes from a barrel downstairs. It's thirty years old. Use it for dipping, not cooking."

This soy sauce is remarkable. It throws off sediment like old wine, but, like a vintage port, the flavour is not for everyone. There is a metallic tinge which disappears with a strong salty edge after the first taste. It leaves a rich, almost meaty flavour in the mouth. This is a sauce that cries to be mated with rice or a platter of steamed Chinese dumplings.

This aged sauce shows what we have lost to mass production. It indicates how far we have drifted, even from the late 1960s, when one book on Chinese cooking described how it was commonly made: "... (soy sauce) starts as a dough made of soy beans and wheat flour that is first allowed to ferment. Then salt and water are added, and the fermented liquid is placed in open earthenware urns, which are placed outdoors for several weeks while the sun's heat works on the mixture. It is said that the best grades of soy sauce can take as much as six to seven years of aging to reach perfection."

Compare this with how the world's largest soy sauce manufacturer describes the process today. "Kikkoman's proprietary microorganism is added as an enzyme to change starch from the wheat into sugars and protein from the soybeans into amino acids. All Kikkoman soy sauce is naturally brewed in the four-to-six months process that is often compared to the making of fine wine."

Then there is unbrewed soy sauce, very cheap stuff ($2 for a litre isn't uncommon) with sugar added. The fermentation is speeded up artificially and the word "hydrolysed" is somewhere on the label.

Within each process, there are generally three kinds of soy sauce sold: light or "lite" (with less salt and, I find, a fruitier flavour), regular, and dark (with sugar or molasses). I like lighter soy sauces for dipping and marinating and the others for cooking.

I asked a Kikkoman publicist if there were any special blends hidden away and was told that the company "does not have a private stock of specially brewed soy sauce aging in oak barrels in a cavern below Mount Fuji." But having tasted Ben Top's private blend, my search for full flavoured aged soy sauces has only begun.

Somewhere out there is a bottle of single-barrel, aged Pearl River Bridge. It has fermented naturally for many years. Its colour will be black, tinged rust at the meniscus. I will pour a few drops into a small white porcelain cup. I will taste the sauce and close my eyes. That night I will dream of honourable men and lies and blood.

Stevia

Sugar and spice and everything nice. That's what stevia seems made of. Stevia isn't the name of a little girl. It's as simple and potent a sweetener as nature ever created.

The leaves come from a bushy green plant, in the same family as asters and chrysanthemums. It is native to South America but is now grown in many countries. It is available here mainly in health food stores. In the U.S.A. and Canada, unprocessed stevia can be sold, but processed stevia, while not banned, has not received federal approval and cannot be used in food products. This does not mean that it can't be used, only that processed food cannot include it. Confusingly, however, dietary supplements do permit the use of stevia. A spokesman for the Canadian Food Inspection Agency said, "It hasn't gone through the formal process."

While not commonly used in Canada, stevia is a popular sweetener. It is grown and used commercially in many countries.

The essence of stevia's sweetness comes from stevioside which is a glycoside, a naturally occurring compound that makes things taste sweet. Stevia leaves are dark green and plain stevia leaf powder is the same colour. The flavour, when it is bought in this form, is very sweet with a slightly bitter licorice aftertaste. It is wonderful when added to brewed tea instead of sugar, and particularly good with fresh mint tea or sprinkled on ripe berries.

Stevia is also sold as a liquid and as a white powder. It is usually more expensive in these forms but but the bitterness and after-tastes are removed.

This plant makes an exceptional sweetener and it has no calories. It's sweetness varies depending upon how it is processed. A good test is to try as little as a pinch of plain stevia in one cup (250 ml) of water. Stir it up well and then taste it. I find at this level green stevia leaf powder is pleasantly sweet without being cloying with as much flavour as eight times the amount of sugar!

Sugar Cane

The dish at the next table looked enticing—shrimp paste grilled on thick skewers of sugar cane.

Much of the raw sugar that we eat comes from sugar cane. Although it is an important crop in the U.S.A., we rarely see fresh cane in stores or on menus.

I have enjoyed chewing sugar cane ever since I wandered down a road in Kumming, a city in southwestern China, and saw a young man on a bicycle selling yard-long lengths. The cane was heavy with syrup and delightful to eat. It was as subtly sweet as a top grade of maple syrup.

Despite its woody appearance, sugar cane is soft. It mashes up easily as you chew it. There is something that is fun and childish about walking down the street chomping on a long, thin chunk of wood and spitting out the pulp.

Fresh sugar cane is often available in West Indian and Asian food stores in the Montreal area such as **Arawak, Aliments Exotiques,** and **Kim Phat. Sami Fruits** in the Jean-Talon Market always has it, as do many places in Chinatown.

Make sure the cane feels heavy and dense. Light stalks mean that there is little liquid inside. These stores may also have cans of sugar cane sticks about the length and width of a middle finger. This is what is used in Vietnamese restaurants for dishes like Barbecued Shrimp Paste on Sugar Cane (Chao Tom) and Duck with Sugar Cane (Vit Tiem Mia).

Although these Vietnamese recipes are complicated, there is no reason that sugar cane won't work as skewers for a grilling shrimp or chicken and vegetable kabobs. Here is barbecue that lets you eat the skewer too.

Take a large chicken breast and cut it into long strips wide enough to easily fit onto the cane. Cut the canes in half lengthwise if they are too thick. Thread chicken strips onto the cane. You can intersperse the chicken with vegetables such as red or green peppers, water chestnuts or mushrooms.

Make a marinade of ½ cup (125 ml) each of white wine and soy sauce, one teaspoon (5 ml) of sesame oil, and ¼ teaspoon (1 ml) each of chili sauce and sugar. Add a finely chopped clove of garlic and one teaspoon (5 ml) of grated ginger to the marinade. Mix it well. Leave the chicken in this for at least an hour in the refrigerator, turning the meat occasionally.

Grill over hot coals or under a broiler for a few minutes on each side or until the cane starts to blister.

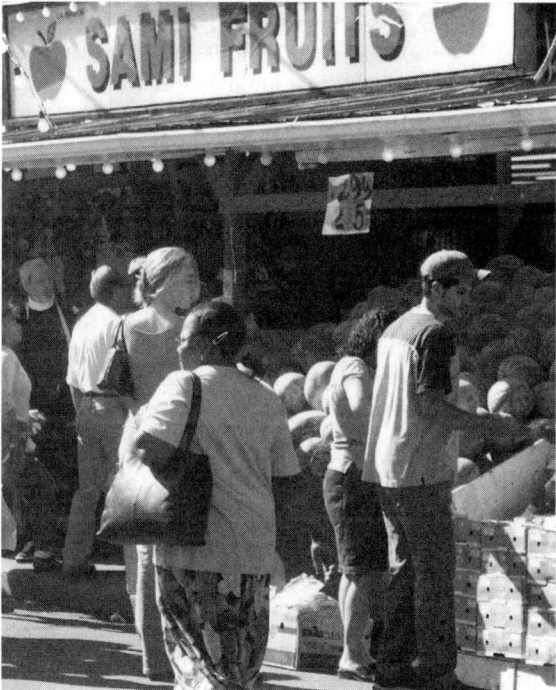

Sami Fruits, one of the largest fruit and vegetable vendors in the Jean-Talon Market.

Sushi and Sashimi

We should call it purple gold. I mean if oil is black gold, why not call a sliver of fresh tuna that can cost several hundred dollars a kilo—by the time it gets to our plates—something with a little more oomph than just sushi. There it sits: dark purple, glistening, mouth-watering, exorbitant. No wonder restaurants sell it by the piece, and a thumb-sized one at that.

Sushi isn't even the correct term. Raw fish is sashimi. It is served with a little wasabi (Japanese horseradish), a soy-based dipping sauce and a little pickled ginger. Most of what we get has been flash frozen to kill any parasites, but that fresh sea taste should still be there. Traditionally, sashimi has been served with vinegar. The tang of the vinegar or the sear of the wasabi are zippy counterpoints to fresh fish and particularly effective with oily morsels such as mackerel, tuna and salmon.

There are more exotic versions, too. Ikizukuri involves slicing a live fish presented on a plate in its original form. More rare is a serving of fugu. This is a fish whose liver and ovaries are highly poisonous. Only chefs with a special diploma are licensed to serve it in Japan.

Even when mundane salmon and snapper are offered, sashimi is too expensive for most of us to eat regularly. So we order sushi. This is similar, but the raw fish (or cooked seafood which might be shrimp, octopus or smoked eel) is served on a small mound of rice.

Not too long ago, sushi was just a way of preserving food and sashimi was rarely eaten. For centuries, fish was packed with rice, salt and vinegar. This would ferment a little before it was eaten. However by the end of the 19th century, quick sushi (hayazushi) became popular in Japan. This was raw fish served with vinegary rice, similar to what we enjoy today.

Almost any kind of fish or seafood can be served as sushi or sashimi and at many restaurants, the rule is the more exotic the better. Raw sea urchin, smoked salmon, caviar and spider rolls (which are made with deep-fried soft shell crab) are common at sushi bars. However these dishes are rarely made at home in Japan. A much more common way of serving sushi for the home chef is makisushi. These take a filling of sliced raw vegetables, mushrooms, a cold omelet, or simply a little cucumber and wasabi. This is layered over the rice and rolled in dried seaweed.

Several kinds of maki are available in sushi restaurants and take-out counters. One of the most popular is the California roll with crab (invariably processed fish that tastes like crab), avocado and cucumber. Futomaki (fat roll) is another version and often includes bamboo shoots, cooked eel and shiitaki mushrooms. Less cumbersome is oshisushi (pressed sushi) with layers of rice, mushrooms and thinly sliced vegetables, and often shrimp, a thin omelet or sliced ham on top. This is pressed and served in small squares.

It is not hard to find any of these in Montreal but the quality can vary. Good fresh fish of the calibre needed for sushi or sashimi is not always easy to get here. More to the point, great sushi chefs are rare. Very few in Montreal are from Japan, and in Japan it can take several years of apprenticeship before the budding Itamae-San is allowed to touch fish or even roll the rice before a customer.

Sushi has become a popular take-home dish in Montreal. It is sold in chains such as **Soto Express** and **Katsura Express** as well as supermarkets including Métro and Provigo.

However, eating sushi is more a ritual than a meal. There is the artistic flair which a good sushi chef cuts the fish and prepares each morsel. Great sushi chefs are not only artists with knives, they are as compassionate as your favourite bartender. A meal of sashimi or sushi should combine ambience and supremely fresh food. When those few morsels of maguro (the rich, flavourful filet of the tuna) are set before you, consider that this purple gold is your admission to a finely crafted show.

Soto in Old Montreal and **Kaizen Treehouse** in Westmount are favoured by Montreal's sushi cognoscenti.

Tabasco

"You know the marriage has lasted when they buy the second bottle of Tabasco," goes the 1950s wisecrack. That was, of course, before white, bored North Americans discovered there was a world beyond macaroni and cheese and when TV dinners were considered exotic. Way back then, a drop or two of Tabasco would be used ceremoniously to embellish the requisite Sunday brunch Bloody Mary. A bottle of Tabasco in the cupboard, a clove of garlic in the fridge—my, weren't we adventurous!

These days there are hundreds of hot sauces on the market. Many are packed with papaya, sugar, tomato purée and even concentrated capsaicin, the peppery ingredient that gives these sauces their masochistic punch.

Hot flavours are measured in Scolville units and Tabasco measures 40,000 on the Scolville scale. This may sound hot but many high-octane products with super-saturated capsaicin have Scolville units of more than a million. Does the world really need Dave's Insanity or Blair's After Death sauces?

Tabasco was where it started for most of us and, after venturing into the million-Scolville nuclear wasteland, it is worth getting back to. The sauce has been made by the McIlhenny family on Louisiana's Avery Island since the end of the American Civil War. Made of red tabasco peppers, salt and vinegar, the flavour is salty and earthy with a sweetness that emerges under the heat.

You can make a similar sauce at home. I use ¼ cup (50 ml) of mashed fresh hot peppers, ½ teaspoon (2 ml) of sea salt, and a ½ cup (125 ml) of vinegar. It's a decent table sauce and it brings out a bead of sweat on my forehead, but it will never have Tabasco's depth of flavour, colour and fiery sweetness, and it won't age for three years in oak barrels, as Tabasco does, before it gets served.

Tamales

The first tamale I ever had was served in the kitchen of a small house in a Mexican village. It was New Year's day. This, I was informed, was a traditional way to start the year. The abuela, the grandmother of the family, had made them. She had ground the spices and chilies by hand for the sauce. The chicken for the filling had come from the market. The masa— a limed corn mash—was made from corn stored on the roof of the house. The corn leaves that wrapped all of this together were, of course, from the family fields.

I know I should say that every tamale I have eaten since just hasn't been the same, but that is not true. Each one I have eaten since not only reminds me of how good it was, but that the one I am enjoying is great too. In truth, I've never met a tamale that I didn't like.

Each part of Mexico and every central American country has its own version of this treat. In most of Mexico the fillings (seafood, pork, chicken, beef) change but the basic idea stays the same. Take a corn leaf and spread a layer of masa. On top of that add some shredded meat or refried black beans or both, spoon over the sauce and roll it all into a tight bundle for steaming.

In southern Mexico they often use banana leaves. In Oaxaca we had sweet tamales with a ribbon of jam for dessert. In Guatemala they make tamales de arroz and use rice instead of corn. In San Salvador there is a special tamale for fiestas that can include just about everything: chickpeas, potatoes, olives—all enfolded in foot-long cylinders of banana leaves.

And they're all as tasty as that first steaming savoury tamale I was served on a cold Mexican morning.

With a growing Latino population, we are fortunate to have many restaurants and grocery stores serving fresh tamales daily. Two well-stocked and friendly stores which usually have a few varieties steaming away are **Marché Andes** and **La Peregrina**.

Terroir

One of the latest foodie buzz-words is "terroir." You can't go to the store and buy it, yet it is increasingly a part of our lexicon. The word means "of the soil". It speaks to a sustenance that comes from the farm and not from the lab.

Terroir is a concept rather than a reality. The word has roots in the vineyard. It articulates the flavour that makes an area distinct: the purity of the air, the richness of the soil, the nearness of a sea or river all impart their essence to terroir. We think of terroir when we try to imagine the taste of gravel that is said to seep through French cabernet or the peat in a single-malt scotch.

Terroir is the antithesis of engineered food, of genetically modified products, of hard tasteless tomatoes in January. Terroir speaks of honesty, hard work and meaningfulness. If terroir were a song it would be sung by the McGarrigle Sisters and it would touch the heart.

Early spring is the first season of terroir, when the earth yields its stink and we put on boots to go into the garden. It is the season when the first batch of maple syrup comes to market tasting sweet and the smell of the woods is just out of reach.

We are not famous for our wines but the taste of terroir is strong in Quebec, maybe strongest in our public markets. In the winter, last fall's root vegetable crops and bushels of apples are still at the stands. There are stalls which sell only Quebec products like blueberry vinegars and raw-milk cheeses and duck foie gras. This is terroir.

When I go to the market, do I seriously care where my food comes from? Well, think of the ramifications. Eating locally produced foods helps the economy, sure, but more than that it strengthens our connection to the soil. It removes thousands of kilometres and a slew of middlemen between those who grow the food and us. We are indeed fortunate. We can still go to market and meet the farmer who boiled down the syrup or the finisher who aged the brie. It is becoming more common to go to restaurants and see on the menu that the cheese or lamb or vegetables we are about to eat is from Oka or St. Jean or Marieville.

If I am what I eat, then perhaps it is terroir that makes me a Québécois.

Many gourmet stores, cheese shops and bakeries feature regional foods. **Le Marché des Saveurs du Québec** is a wonderful privately-owned store in the Jean-Talon Market which specializes in Quebec products.

By the way, while our wines are not yet receiving plaudits from the *Wine Spectator*, we do have a terroir-style of ice wine that is worth checking out at this store—it is often sold at SAQs, particularly the branch in the Atwater Market. It is a wine-lover's apple cider known as cidre de glace and it has a wonderful syrupy kick with a level of alcohol between 11% and 13%. Some producers mix other fruit with the cider. Labels include Domaine Pinnacle, Du Minot des Glaces, and La Grande Glace. Serve these very chilled as an aperitif. Here is a world-class drink that is only just starting to get the attention it deserves.

Tonka Beans

Every once in a while there is a new flavour for the tongue to trip over. Right now, it's tonka beans. These are thumb-size pods with a soft-wrinkled flesh and a thick almond-like seed. Botanically, they are members of the legume family, but tonka beans (*Dipteryx odorata*) are as different from a lima or a fava as Halle Berry is from Dame Edna.

Tonka beans smell of vanilla with strong hints of cinnamon, cloves and almonds. Cheaper than vanilla pods, they were commonly used as a vanilla substitute and are often added to perfumes, soaps and pipe tobaccos. Tonka beans are grown in the Caribbean and harvested after they have matured for about a year. They are reputed to prevent blood clotting. In witchcraft they are said to foster courage.

The aroma is sublime. It is best released by warming a bean or two in a liquid before the liquid is added to a recipe. You could also leave one or two beans in a light rum and then use the alcohol to flavour a dish. The caterer Phillipe de Vienne has imported some for his own use and sells them through **Les Douceurs du Marché**.

We haven't heard much of tonka beans because they are illegal in the U.S.A. Tonka contains coumarin, which gives this bean its vanilla-like odour. As an oil, coumarin is toxic. But this is also true of the pure oils and extracts of many foods and edible plants. Don't try eating pure chili oil or orange oil essence. Both burn the mouth and can do serious damage if more than a few drops are ingested, but that doesn't stop us from using raw chilies or orange rind in our cooking and both chili oil and orange extract are sold commercially.

Similarly, used as a simple bean to flavour dishes, tonka beans are not harmful. I keep a small jar of them in the cupboard and use them to flavour custards and cakes. Their aroma is much richer than vanilla, almost rum-like in its intensity, even before I let them sit in any spirits.

Tourtière

Few topics are as divisive at the Québécois dinner table as the matter of tourtière. This classic *canadienne* meat pie seems to be made differently in every village in the province. Some swear by pheasant and game birds, others use pork, mashed potato and plenty of seasonings.

In fact, the original recipe may be impossible to replicate. One version of the etymology of tourtière is that les tourtes had to be included. These were tiny game birds that were once common in the gulf of the St. Lawrence River. Other versions of this word have it rooted in the name for the pie pan used for baking tourtes.

Tourtière is a great winter dish. Ideally the meat is flavourful without being overly spiced. Spices like cloves or ginger and a few herbs such as savory are blended into finely chopped onions and ground meat. The meat may be lean pork, veal or beef or a combination of all three. The pastry should be simple, flaky and tasty. A homemade tomato sauce, or more often an ordinary ketchup, is served with it.

While tourtière is made throughout the year here and is easily available, it remains a traditional New Year dish.

Most supermarkets carry frozen tourtière. Pastry stores with charcuterie sections often make them fresh. They may even be able to make one to suit special requests, without pork for example, or with extra spices.

Several stores and small restaurants make their own. **La Binerie** has been serving them up for decades on Mont-Royal near St-Denis. Their 8-inch pie is good for four people and costs $6.05. Further west, try **La Foumagerie** in Westmount. It stocks an excellent frozen tourtière made by Aux Bricoles Culinaires, a small catering company in St- Timothée. This is a 9-inch pie good for six to eight people and costs $7.99. Bake it in a 350°F oven for about an hour or until the top is golden brown.

Truffles

Winter is harsh. The pocketbook is empty. We need some small opulence, a flavour that is warm and earthy and pungent. Dare we suggest truffles? In Italy truffle varieties have distinct seasons. I didn't make it in time for the harvest of the famed white truffle, *Tuber magnatum* Pico, perhaps the most prized, luscious and fully flavoured of the species. Of course the market price alone is prohibitive. Good specimens fetch hundreds of dollars. All this for a chunk of buried fungus that is smaller than my fist.

Still, lovers of good food have been indulging in truffles since Roman times. In Europe, until relatively recently, old virgin women were reputed to posses the uncanny ability to unearth these hidden treasures. (In passing, I would suggest that this presents an obvious dilemma since truffles are also reputed to be a powerful aphrodisiac.) In any case, when we think of truffle hunters we usually imagine old men with berets and staves following a pig or truffle hound. Dogs are preferable, since they are trained to find these mushrooms but don't really like them. Pigs, however, are pigs and will eat them whole-hog. The staves are used to push the pigs away once they have snuffled them out.

There are truffles in North America, just as there is caviar in Great Lakes' sturgeon, but they don't compare with the real thing—the black truffles of France or the white truffles of Italy. A few Italian companies make truffle oil and Urbani is considered the best. A thumb-sized bottle sells for $4, just enough to savour a taste.

Sprinkle a few drops on pasta that has been tossed with a simple sauce of warmed olive oil and and a little chopped garlic. For a sensational spread, mix a capful of truffle oil with a tablespoon (15 ml) of freshly grated Parmesan and beat this into a half cup (125 ml) of unsalted butter. Serve at room temperature. The flavour of truffle is both powerful and intimate and there should be just enough for two.

Fresh truffles are often available at specialty food stores such as **Chez Louis** and **Tortarella & Fils.**

Tsatsiki

It's spelled tsatsiki or tzatzki (and pronounced tzah-ZEE-kee) and it is often the first contact many of us have with Greek cooking. This is the wonderful garlicky yogurt sauce spread over souvlaki. But tsatsiki is more than a sauce. With a few thick slices of Greek bread and a glass of retsina or white wine, a dish of tsatsiki makes for a delicious summery lunch. Or, for a great combination, try it as a cold thick dip with thin slices of fried eggplant or zucchini. It also pairs so superbly with French fries that you may never ask for mayo or ketchup again.

The recipe for tsatsiki is deceptively simple: usually just yogurt, salt, garlic and cucumber. Some recipes call for a little mint or pepper; others suggest adding grated onion. But these can give tsatsiki too much of a kick.

There is a balance between the rich but not sweet taste of a good thick Greek-style yogurt, the freshness of grated cucumber and the pungency of garlic. All three of the ingredients need to be fresh. Try making this with a thin yogurt, let's say one having 2% or less butterfat, and the tsatsiki tastes bitter. The garlic and salt overpower the dish.

Good tsatsiki is so thick you could eat it with a fork. A thinner version would be a sauce and this does work as a meat or chicken marinade but it isn't as satisfying a side dish as tsatsiki.

There are proximate dishes in Turkish or Indian cooking. Compare, for example, raita. This may be tsatsiki's younger, less worldly cousin. Raita is a yogurt and cucumber dip with spices and flavours attuned to Indian cooking. Raita recipes often call for roasted cumin, freshly ground black pepper or a pinch of cayenne. Raita is meant to be served as a side dish. It is made for spicy curries. This cool, refreshing sauce breaks the heat of many Indian dishes. But, as tasty as it is, at its heart, raita is not a substantial dish. It is a condiment without the fortitude of a good tsatsiki.

Tsatsiki is easy enough to make at home, except that most of us don't want to keep large quantities of thick Mediterranean-style of yogurt on hand—this stuff is too good, too rich and has too many calories to be left alone. It is great with honey and it gets eaten quickly.

Fortunately, good tsatsiki is sold in most supermarkets. The brands taste pretty much the same and, since Montreal is blessed with a substantial and discerning Greek community, the quality is fairly good. However, store-bought brands don't compare with the pungency of freshly-made tsatsiki that is on the menu in Greek restaurants, any of which should be willing to sell a half-litre or so to go. The fish market **Poissonerie N.D.G.** on Sherbrooke near Victoria Avenue has excellent homemade Greek appetizers including a superb tsatsiki. **Marché Akhavan**, the fabulous Iranian store on Sherbrooke near Grand Boulevard, is always pleased to help you make up your mind by allowing you to taste samples from their selection of homemade tsatsiki.

Turkish Delight

The Queen knew . . . though Edmund did not, that this was enchanted Turkish Delight and that anyone who had tasted it would want more and more of it, and would even, if they were allowed, go on eating it till they killed themselves.

–C.S. Lewis, *The Lion, the Witch and the Wardrobe*

Well, this is what good candy is supposed to be: inherently, magically delicious. I have always been intrigued by Turkish Delight.

First there is the idea of things Turkish. To a small child in 1950s Montreal, a city that had yet to develop its multi-ethnic character, anything Turkish hinted at an exotic land of flying carpets and sultans. Then there is the word delight, a synonym for the essence of the confectioner's arts. So for me, Turkish Delight was more than a rare treat of an unusual candy. It was a taste of an enticing world.

In Turkish, the word for this sweet is "lokum" and that is how it is known in most Middle Eastern stores here. The basic ingredients are sugar, water, and cornstarch which are boiled together. Flavourings such as vanilla, lemon juice, rose water or crème de menthe are added along with food colouring. The syrup cools in pans and the translucent sheets are cut into squares. Chopped nuts such as pistachios or toasted almonds may also be added and, before it is packaged, the candy is thickly dusted with confectioner's sugar.

Turkish delight does not age well. Packages left on the shelves too long become stale. The texture should be chewy and not rubbery and the flavour delicate. This candy is usually sold in gift boxes; however, you can usually buy it by the piece as well. Look for Turkish delight in Middle Eastern stores at the dessert counters. **Bassé** and **Marché Istanbul** have good selections.

TVP

TVP tastes like nothing. This is a non-flavour. Think of it as the colour white in the taste spectrum. That means it goes great with everything.

TVP might stand for "tastes very plain" but the letters stand for texturized vegetable protein. TVP is made from soybeans or vegetable protein. If soybeans, these are cracked, dehulled, flaked, cleaned, dried and defatted, and extruded into almost any size or shape. This is serious processed food. TVP comes in chunks as large as Swedish meatballs or as small granules that bear an unfortunate resemblance to dried cat food.

On one level, this is just crunchy tofu. On another it is similar to Alaskan pollack, a bland meaty fish that easily absorbs the flavours of expensive seafood like lobster or crab and usually supplants them in cold dishes and salads.

Like pollack, TVP is nutritious and inexpensive. Its siblings are HVP, hydrolyzed vegetable protein and TPP, texturized plant protein. What they have in common is they are tasteless, they have good texture and they are able to absorb the stronger flavours of other ingredients. They are good partners where the intention is to replace some or all of the meat in a dish while retaining flavour and protein.

TVP hydrates easily. Boil one cup of water and pour it over one cup (250 ml) of TVP. Let it sit for about 10 minutes. You should have 2 cups (500 ml) of TVP. If the TVP is too wet, squeeze out some water. It should feel firm and a little spongy. Use it in chilies, stews, lasagna, or soups by substituting from a quarter to all of a recipe's ground meat.

TVP has been hard to find but it is increasingly available in health food stores and bulk food stores. Check the ingredients on packages of TVP since a few brands contain MSG—monosodium glutamate—to which some people are allergic.

Here is a vegetarian chili recipe my wife Celina regularly makes at home with TVP. See if your family can tell that it doesn't have meat.

Celina's Vegetarian Chili

Soak a cup of TVP in 2 cups (500 ml) of water that has been brought to boiling and taken off the heat. Leave this for a half-hour. While it is soaking finely chop 3 stalks of celery, 4 onions and 4 cloves of garlic and sauté in a little oil in a hot frying pan until they are soft and the onions are just starting to brown.

Take the TVP and mix in 3 bay leaves, 6 tablespoons (90 ml) of chili powder, 2 teaspoons (5 ml) of ground cumin, 1 teaspoon (5 ml) of salt and a few dashes of cayenne (to taste). Combine this with the onion, celery and garlic and sauté briefly until everything is hot.

In a large pot combine the sautéed mix and add a chopped green pepper, 3 ounces (75 ml) of tomato paste, 4 cups (900 ml) of tomato puree or canned crushed tomatoes, 4 cups (900 ml) canned kidney beans and 2½ cups (625 ml) of canned corn.

Stir everything well and cook covered over very low heat for a few hours, or put the pot into a 225° F oven to bake overnight. Check regularly to make sure the bottom doesn't stick. Some liquid may evaporate and you might add as much as a cup (250 ml) of water while it cooks. Serve with cornbread or bake a cornbread topping on the chili before serving. This serves eight to ten hungry people.

Verjus

Verjus has been cropping up in recipes recently. It's often recommended as an assist to wine or vinegar. It's great in rich sauces such as hollandaise. You might assume that verjus is a new product, another "do we really need this?" item, as necessary to cooking as a left-handed spatula.

Verjus (or verjuice) has been around a long time. The name comes from "vert jus" (green juice). It is the slightly acid liquid pressed from young fruit, usually grapes, before they are harvested for wine, but verjus can also be made from crab apples and other unripe fruit.

Verjus has a complex taste. There is the intense fruity flavour we associate with wine, but with a medicinal undertone and a bite. While it is acidic, verjus is not as strong as vinegar. Because of these in-between qualities—not quite wine, not quite vinegar—verjus is an intriguing substitute for both of these cooking staples. It works particularly well when the oil or butter in a dish needs to be balanced with a little acid while retaining a delicate edge.

Verjus was once used a lot in western cooking, especially in the Middle Ages. It is still common to Middle Eastern recipes, particularly in Iranian dishes.

I knew that verjus was becoming fashionable when I saw a California wine grower advertising red, white, and Chardonnay "verjuice" at exalted prices on the Internet.

Nevertheless, verjus doesn't have to be expensive. A half-litre bottle costs only a few dollars in local Middle Eastern grocery stores.

Some recipes suggest replacing verjus with lemon juice but even that can be too strong. Verjus is subtle. Play around with this stuff. Try it in salad dressings or to deglaze a roasting pan. Sprinkle a few drops over rice just before serving. Splash it over grilled fish. It's good to have on hand.

Vietnamese Coffee

Vietnam is at Asia's culinary crossroads. The food is unmistakably Asian, but there are strong differences. Vietnamese cooking has a strong French influence unlike any of its neighbours. This is part of the country's legacy as a French colony. French is still a common language in that country—one reason that Montreal has such a strong Vietnamese community.

If you think of Vietnamese cooking as only another Asian cuisine, you'll be surprised to see coffee featured on the menu. Vietnam is also a coffee-growing country. In fact, it is the world's fourth largest coffee-exporting nation.

The Vietnamese approach to coffee making, however, is unique. For those on the run who slurp an extra-large double double from a litre-sized cup, this kind of coffee is a throwback to a more leisurely era. Ordering a cup of Vietnamese coffee can make a Japanese tea ceremony look speedy.

The coffee is brought to the table in a glass—but there is no coffee in it. Instead, a metal container is perched on top and the glass is one-third filled with thick milk. This is condensed milk and it hearkens to a time when there was no refrigeration and stored milk was only sold in cans. It was condensed to make shipping more efficient and, once opened, was thinned with water for drinking or cooking.

The milk served with Vietnamese coffee, however, is undiluted, thick, sweet and rich. The metal container sitting on top of the glass has two parts. The bottom half is filled with dark-roasted finely ground coffee. Although two to three tablespoons (50-75 ml) of ground coffee per cup (250 ml) is common, it does not seem that this much coffee is used because it is compressed between two filters. Hot water is poured into the top half and it slowly seeps through the coffee and drips onto the milk. This takes a while. This is not a drink to gulp. You can get through a couple of sections of the Saturday paper while waiting for the coffee to drip through.

Loosening the lid a little will let the water run through the coffee more quickly, but the flavour will be weaker. As the coffee drips, it hardly disturbs the milk. There is a thick layer of white, another of black, and a little froth at the top. When the coffee has completely dripped through, remove the metal filter and stir the layers together. This has the texture of a good espresso and a caramel sweetness with a flavour similar to coffee ice cream. This coffee may actually be too strong for some people and it is not unusual to ask for a carafe of hot water to dilute the drink.

The marriage of sweet thick milk and intense bitter coffee is sublime. Each, by itself, is too intense to be enjoyed. The milk is too cloying, the coffee too strong. There is a classic yin and yang vying for attention and needing just a stir of the spoon to create an extraordinary taste.

Sip it slowly. The wait is worth it, particularly if you are nibbling a Vietnamese pastry. Vietnamese coffee may also be served over ice and is deliciously refreshing on a hot day.

If you want to make Vietnamese coffee at home, look for a strong, dark roast of coffee and have it ground a little less fine than for espresso. Both the coffee and the carafe for making it are available at Vietnamese markets.

Wasabi

Wasabi is that astringent mustardy-tasting dollop molded into a small green peak and served with a similar mound of pickled ginger alongside raw fish (sashimi) in Japanese restaurants and sushi bars. It is the thin green layer served between raw fish and rice patties (sushi) and is as natural an accompaniment to these Japanese foods as mustard is to a hot dog.

Wasabi is one of the few flavours that have resisted migrating to other cuisines. It is authentically natural to Japan where it grows in swampy ground by mountain streams. The root, which is the part of the plant we eat, looks like ginger and is usually about 4 or 5 inches long.

In Japan, wasabi is served freshly grated or in thin slices as a condiment. It is rarely available fresh outside Japan . Here, it is sold pickled or powdered, usually in small 1-2-ounce (30-60 ml) cans. Larger cans are available to restaurants but this kind of wasabi may be diluted with powdered mustard to increase the heat while cutting the cost. Not surprisingly, the wasabi offered in most sushi bars is more bitter and less aromatic than what you might make at home. In fact, in some sushi bars wasabi is referred to as "namida" which means "tears". Good wasabi has a nice herbal smell and makes a tasty substitute for an English-style hot mustard such as Keen's. **Miyamoto**, the city's best Japanese food store, has several varieties.

Wasabi is usually served as a paste. A tablespoon (15 ml) of powder is mixed with one teaspoon of water and left to stand covered for about 15 minutes. Mix a little of this paste with soy sauce to make a tasty dipping sauce. A small tin of wasabi will last about six months after it is opened. After that it loses its taste and bite. Wasabi is also sold as a paste and is much stronger than the powdered variety. Use the tiniest of dabs at first. It packs a wollop!

Pacific Coast Wasabi will FedEx fresh wasabi to Montreal at a cost of $120 for 500 grams. The taste is crisp and clean as cucumber, with a sharp horseradish bite that quickly disappears.

Worcestershire Sauce

Why don't I use Worcestershire sauce more often? My small bottle has been on the shelf for years. I open it rarely, usually when I think that a couple of shakes will add vigour to a glass of tomato juice. Yet I could be using it for its own flavour, just as I would other seasonings. For example, Worcestershire sauce is an excellent dipping sauce for squid or vegetables fried in a light batter or for small slices of pan-fried beef or chicken. It's as common as soy sauce in Japanese homes.

Worcestershire sauce is one of those condiments that have changed little over the years. It was created by accident over 150 years ago: a man who had recently returned to England asked two chemists in Worcester, John Lea and William Perrins, to mix him up a batch of a sauce that he had enjoyed in India. The chemists thought it smelled awful and left it in the basement of their store. According to legend, either the man never came back or it took years for him to remember to pick up his sauce. By this time it had fermented and developed a lovely rich taste. The druggists bottled it under their name and Lea & Perrins has been the standard ever since.

The ingredients are simple—vinegar, molasses, sugar, anchovies, salt, tamarind, shallots, onions and garlic—but the process is complicated. Lea & Perrins claims it only uses fresh ingredients and never cooks them. The sauce ferments naturally over a long time in wooden casks. Other versions, such as one made by Heinz, include caramel and soy powder. The products certainly taste different. I find that the Lea & Perrins is lighter and fruitier, but this is a matter of taste not a judgment as to which is better.

This sauce is also quite different from a brown sauce such as HP (which stands for Houses of Parliament) which is closer to ketchup, while Worcestershire sauce is thinner and less sweet. It is nearer, in consistency and taste, to a fruity vinegar. When I consider how much time I spend creating a meat marinade or a dipping sauce, with basically the same ingredients, I wonder why I haven't used Worcestershire sauce more often. Probably it is because even a small bottle is expensive when it comes to slathering the stuff on. Still, there is room for this flavour in stews, chilies, soups, and almost any dish when a complex sweet-and-sour flavour is called for. I am moving my bottle from the back of the cupboard to the front row.

Zatar

Zatar is to the flavour world what the Spice Girls were to music. Each was an unusual but intrinsically familiar combination of individual elements that technically might work on their own but go best together. Maybe Ginger Spice can make it without the rest of the group and maybe sumac or hyssop should get their own container on the spice shelf, but I think not.

Zatar, which rhymes with "batter", is Arabic for wild thyme and is common to Middle Eastern cooking. It is also spelled za'tar, zaatar, and zahtar.

Rarely sold as a single herb, it is usually packaged as a combination of several herbs and flavours with thyme and sumac dominant. The thyme gives it a loamy perfume and the sumac a slightly bitter, woody edge. The flavours work well with each other. Iranian and Lebanese grocery stores often sell zatar in a mix with sesame seeds and salt. Other mixtures might contain paprika, hyssop (an aromatic anise-like herb), olive wood, marjoram or oregano.

Traditionally, zatar is served with pita bread and olive oil. Dip the bread in the oil and then the herb mix, or make a paste of the oil and herbs, brush it over bread or pita and grill for a few minutes. Pita bread already baked with a zatar topping is available in Middle Eastern stores throughout the Montreal area. Many people also enjoy zatar sprinkled on ripe tomatoes or dusted over thick Lebanese yogurt or added to a yogurty mayonnaise for a vegetable dip. Zatar also makes for a wonderful alternative to the European herbes de Provence in recipes for dishes like roasted chicken or lamb stew.

Zershk

The Iranian dish came to the table with a side plate of white long-grain rice sprinkled with dried red berries. I knew that pomegranate berries are often added to Middle Eastern cooking, but these tasted different. They were tart and plump and were perfect counterpoints to the rice's flavour and colour.

"They are called 'zershk'," said the chef. A little research revealed that zershk—or zereshk—are dried red barberries. Barberries are too sour to eat fresh. They are often made into syrups or, as Iranians do, dried and then rehydrated by soaking them in water for about 15 minutes and then draining and cooking them in a little butter or ghee. If they are very hard they may need to be soaked for up to an hour. Boil the water, remove the pot from the heat and add the berries. Drain them as soon as they plump up but are not too soft.

The fruit is similar to red currants and comes to market here as a fresh ripe fruit in mid-summer. Zershk seems to be unique to Iranian cooking but it shouldn't be. It has a zesty flavour that would work well with many dishes in the same way that ripe currants are used in puddings and jelly. Barberries are high in vitamin C. In large quantities, they are used as a purgative. The bark and roots are used to make a brilliant yellow dye.

While zershk was served to me in a rice dish, as they do at **Quartier Perse**, it is often added to an Iranian soufflé called "kookoo sabbi" which is a kind of thick vegetable omelet. Zershk can also be used in stuffings for fowl or fish. The sourness of these berries makes for a lovely bitter-sweet sauce. Mix a little saffron into a couple of ounces (25 ml) of boiling water. Remove from heat and let the rich colour develop. Add ¼ cup (50 ml) of rehydrated and drained zershk berries, 2 tablespoons (25 ml) of sugar (more if you like a sweeter sauce), and a dash of lemon juice. Fry this mixture in one tablespoon (15 ml) of very hot oil until the sugar dissolves. Spread over rice when it is served or on any food that calls for a sweet and sour sauce. Or try it with Chinese eggrolls or as a tart topping on vanilla ice cream.

Freshly-picked produce at Montreal's public markets are magnets for foodlovers. The fall display above is part of Eric and Pendy L'Écuyer's stall at the Jean-Talon Market.

Montreal's Public Markets

There are three main public markets in Montreal and almost twenty neighbourhood green markets with fresh flowers, fruits and vegetables. There is plenty of basic information about all the city markets at www.marchespublics-mtl.com. This site includes the hours the shops are open as well as the merchants and their products. It is a little out of date and stores do change. Call ahead if you are looking for something particular at a specific market.

The main markets are wonderful places for wandering and serendipity. Taste a little here, walk a little there.

Marché Jean-Talon (Jean-Talon Market)
7075 Casgrain Ave.
Métro: Jean-Talon or de Castelnau, or bus 55, or bus 92
514.277.1588

The city's largest market is also the geographical centre of Montreal. It's prime influence is Italian which is not surprising since this is also the heart of Montreal's Little Italy. This part of the city was farmland until shortly before Word War I. Then two things happened. The Italian community that was established just north of Old Montreal became too big and needed new areas of the city to settle in. At the same time, electric streetcar lines were extended into this area making it only about a half hour ride from downtown. Soon the area was thriving with a substantial Italian community. The local church, la Madonna Della Difesa (at the corner of Dante and Alma) dates from 1910.

The site of the present-day market was once known as the Shamrock Athletic Field, testifying to the Irish community that moved into this area in the 19th century. There is still a Shamrock Street leading to the market.

The central market area has fruit and vegetable stands with most of the farmers bringing in local produce picked in the early hours of the morning. On summer weekends, and during fall harvest, the market proper, and the parking lot, can be packed.

Take time for a long stroll. Bring along a shopping cart. There are stands with double-yolked eggs, fresh flowers, herbs, organic vegetables, maple syrup and apple cider. Few can leave without at least a bag or two of goodies.

The market is open year-round although many farmers only set up stands during the growing season. Many of the producers offer tastings of produce such as locally grown melons, tomatoes, pears and apples during late summer and fall. Look for **Pierre Gingras'** artisanal cider vinegars and the **Michaca Farm** which brings in organic produce from their farm near the U.S. border every day.

The northern edge of the market includes a huge fruit and vegetable emporium called **Sami Fruit**, **Fromagerie Hamel**, an excellent cheese store, a **SAQ** (provincial liquor and wine store), and good Italian restaurants.

The southern periphery has become trendier in the last few years with several gourmet and ethnic food stores. **Dima** is an upscale food importer and "en vrac" (bulk food) store. There is also **Le Marché des Saveurs du Québec**, a great store with a spectacular selection of regional Quebec products including duck confit, potted Arctic char, pickled fiddleheads, many kinds of Quebec ciders and fruit wines, mead, locally produced raw milk cheeses and gift items. **Chez Louis**, the greengrocer to the best restaurants in the city, is also here. **Boucherie du Marché** is usually crowded and for a good reason: lots of wonderful gourmet specialties from France, an experienced butcher and fresh sausages. **Capitol** is a wonderful Italian butcher store with everything you'll need for a great antipasto (you'll see great appetizers being prepared at the back of the store), unusual imported buffalo ricotta as well as well-priced Quebec cheeses.

To take a break, check out **Première Moisson** in the central building at the western edge of the market. It has a large wood-fired oven, and substantial Paris-style pastry, bread, and charcuterie counters. There is also a pleasant terraced eating area. The building offers wheelchair-accessible public restrooms.

Marché Atwater (Atwater Market)
138 Atwater Ave.
Métro: Lionel-Groulx
514.937.7754

This is a picnic-lover's paradise—not as sprawling or ethnic as Jean-Talon Market, and much bigger than the older Maisonneuve Market. The Atwater Market is on the Lachine Canal, an easy bike ride from downtown Montreal.

The market was built as a make-work project during the Depression in the early 1930s. The clock tower is visible from much of the city. Renovations have made this the city's most fashionable market and the many butcher stalls on the second floor are renowned for selling cuts to order, aging meat, and many varieties of freshly-made sausage. While everyone seems to have their favourite, I have found that all the butchers willingly offer cooking tips so there is no need to be intimidated. This is a great place to discuss how to grill bavette (an inexpensive, very tasty steak) or get the filet cut just the way you want it for a Swiss fondue.

The market is arranged for easy browsing. On the ground level you'll find gourmet food stores, a fish store with a nice selection of caviar, scallops, fresh lobster and several kinds of smoked salmon, a pizza bakery, a sushi shop, and two very good cheese shops. The **SAQ** specializes in hard-to-find local wines (yes, we do have Quebec wineries!). **Les Douceurs du Marché** is one of the best places in the city for gourmet products and fine cooking utensils.

This is all on the east side of the market (there are no stores on the west side) and here is also where you will find flowers and seasonal plants (stacks of pumpkins in the fall, Christmas trees shortly after) and local fruit and vegetables. When you are finished, climb the stairs for the butchers, the bakers, and, during the Christmas season, a candlestick maker. The sausage chain **William J. Walter Saucissier** has a stand here (ask for a slice of their kielbasa). **Le Vrac du Marché** has grains, candy sold in bulk, olive oils, and bakers supplies.

On the second floor you'll also find a good pet supply store, freshly-made pasta, a cheese shop and charcuterie, a newspaper stand with a wide selection of both Quebec and international newspapers, a branch of the bakery **Première Moisson** and several places to sit and have a coffee and watch the crowds walk by.

Maisonneuve Market
4445 Ontario East (corner Pie IX)
Métro: Pie IX
514.937.7754

This is the smallest and oldest of the main markets and is a few blocks away from the Olympic stadium. The original building is a magnificent architectural monument to the empire period. According to *Montreal Architecture: A Guide to Styles and Buildings* (Meridian Press, 1990) this building was inspired by the Louvre and the Paris Opéra.

The market was built in 1914 and at one time attracted thousands of farmers a year. Its glory days ended in the 1960s and the market closed. It was reopened a few years ago in a building next to the original building. A half-dozen or so food merchants keep stands open year-round and farmers occasionally come in the summer with produce.

The market is open daily. The largest merchant is the ever-expanding **Première Moisson** with freshly-made bread, salads, sandwiches and charcuterie.

There is also a good cheese store which also makes baklava and other Middle Eastern pastries on site, a flower store, **Dima**, a bulk food store with another branch at the Jean-Talon Market, a fruit and vegetable store, and congenial butchers at **Boucherie du Marché**, who cut steaks and roasts to order and make their own sausages, as well as stellar meat, chicken and salmon pies.

Marché Public 440
3535 Autoroute 440
Chomedy, Laval
450.682.1440

There is a large farmer's market north of the city. This isn't surprising considering that many farms are in Laval just north of the city. Driving from Montreal, take highway 15 to the 440 exit (Laval Ouest). Stay on the service road and the market is on the right. It has 25 stands, with about half—depending upon whether it is the growing season or not—belonging to local farmers. There are also three butcher shops, a fishmonger, a bakery, and several stores selling cheese, fruit and vegetables, and gourmet foods.

Marché de l'Ouest
11600 De Salaberry
Dollard-des-Ormeaux (D.D.O.)
514.685.0119

A large unfocused market on the West Island. Not as busy as in previous years but there is a little bustle in the summer when farmers bring their trucks up to the doors. Stores range from good rug stores and jewelry stores to chains like Subway. Still, there are several excellent stores including the butcher store **La Préférence**, a branch of the Italian food and cheese chain **Cavallaro**, the wonderful **Maître Corbeau** for superb Quebec cheeses and unusual local food products, **Formosa** which has a wide range of Japanese and Chinese groceries and imported gifts (the Sekiryu sushi knives are bargains).

Ste-Anne's Saturday Market
In a parking lot on rue Ste-Anne in Ste-Anne-de-Bellevue at the corner of du Collège.

This small market is worthwhile stopping at when driving or biking through this lovely old community on the western tip of the island. The market is only open from about 10 a.m. to 2 p.m. on Saturdays. It is near the wonderful boardwalk that fronts the river in Ste-Anne. There are several stands of local foods, bread, crafts and Quebec wines from nearby vineyards. The Quinn Farm, just across the water on Île Perrot, regularly sells its produce here.

Guide to Shops and Restaurants

Absolut
5153 Décarie Blvd. (near Queen Mary)
Métro: Snowdon
514.486.4241
A small food store with an authentic Russian menu including dishes such as samsa, a large baked dumpling resembling an Indian samosa. Absolut also makes several kinds of pierogies, and large fritters called piroszki filled with cooked sauerkraut or potato. Eating on premises.

Adar
5458 Westminster (near Côte-St-Luc)
Métro: Villa Maria or bus 162
514.484.1189
Montreal's leading Sephardic bakery is in a strip mall off Côte-St-Luc Road and can be hard to see from the street. An excellent selection of baked goods and Jewish delicacies. Bourekas, challahs, strudel and coffee cakes, and sub sandwiches made with a variety of fillings including a peppery "spicy tuna."

Adonis
2001 Sauvé West (corner l'Acadie)
Métro : l'Acadie then bus 179
514.382.8606
705 Curé Labelle, Laval (corner Perron)
450.978.2333
4601 Sources, Dollard-des-Ormeaux
514.685.5050
Very large markets with a Middle Eastern focus. (The Sauvé branch is the largest.) Superb pastry sections, fresh produce, cheese sections with over a half dozen kinds of feta, large counters for nuts and imported spices, and butcher shops preparing kofta, sougouk and merguez sausages. Several easy-

to-prepare dishes to make at home including shwarma, taouk and shish-kebab are available. Friendly and knowledgeable service.

Afrodite
756 St-Roch St. (near l'Acadie)
Métro : Place des Arts or Parc then bus 80
514.274.5302
A long established Greek bakery in the heart of the old Greek community in Park Extension. Baklava, kourabiedes (sugar cookies), galaktaboureko (custard cakes), special cakes made to order.

Al-challal
475 Côte-Vertu, Ville St-Laurent
Métro : Côte-Vertu
514.747.4953
8500 Taschereau, Brossard (near Milton)
450.923.8568
An excellent large Middle Eastern supermarket: halal butchers, large pastry sections with baklava and kanafi, which are pre-pared daily. Good gourmet gift selection including imported sweets like Turkish Delight. Large deli counters with specialties like batsurma (Armenian sausage), pickled turnips, olives, several kinds of feta.

Aliments Exotiques
6695 Victoria (near Bouchard)
Métro: Plamondon
514.733.7577
Indian, Caribbean, and Sri Lankan imported products and fresh fruits and vegetables. Look for five-foot lengths of fresh sugar cane, yams, plantains, dried jack fruit, Trinidadian and Jamaican sweet potatoes (try each kind), coconut oil, spices, smoked herring, frozen kingfish and fresh goat meat. Heaps of chilis, ginger and garlic (also prepared ginger and garlic paste).

Ambrosia

4657 Samson, Chomedy Laval

450.686.2950

A beautiful pastry store with European and Greek delicacies. This is a great place if you are looking for a gift for a foodie with a sweet tooth. European favourites including eclairs, Black Forest and Opéra cakes are on display in glass cases on the left. Dozens of Greek pastries are on the right side of the store. Take a number when you go in because it may take a while to make a decision. Hand-made chocolate delicacies are brought out during holidays such as Christmas and Mother's Day. Imported comestibles from Greece include orino honey (from the mountains of Crete), loukoumia (similar to Turkish Delight) and spectacularly coloured glikot toy koualiou (pastry in a spoon) which are preserved fruits and nuts—watermelon, chestnut, almonds—in a honey syrup packaged in curvaceous glass jars and imported from Greece.

Amira

1445 Mazurette (near l'Acadie)

Metro: l'Acadie then bus 179

514.382.9823 / www.amira.ca

This is one of several great Middle Eastern markets tucked into a few small streets on the west side of l'Acadie. It's opposite the Marché Central, the huge wholesale market that has become the city's largest concentration of big box stores. Amira imports an extensive variety of products from the Middle East and has offices in Egypt. There is a large en vrac section with nuts, candies (the honey pecans are wonderful) olives, pickled vegetables, Durra jams from Syria, ghee, Turkish coffee pots, and a great spice section in the back. A small fresh produce section and Middle Eastern deli counter—try the spicy feta cheese and tomato dip.

Amore

6159 Sherbrooke West (near Grand)

Métro: Vendôme then bus 105

514.487.5104

Small Korean gift store with a few food products including teas, herbal products and beef jerky. The owner, Mme Chae Wha Lee, also runs a traditional Korean dance studio here.

Anatol Spice

6822 St-Laurent (near St-Zotique)
Métro: St-Laurent or de Castelnau then bus 55
514.276.0107

A compact, superbly-arranged bulk food and spice store. Almost every spice imaginable. Jimmy Hatzikakis specializes in serving grocers and restaurants but he is just as attentive to someone needing a small amount of mastica (for Greek holiday bread), freshly ground coffee, green peppercorns, Madagascar vanilla, large Israeli couscous or mini-pearls of tapioca.

Anjou-Québec

1025 Laurier West (corner Hutchison)
Métro: Place des Arts or Parc then bus 80
514.272.4065

Classic French-style butcher with a little extra: French-cut roasts and chops, a small selection of good cheese, fresh fish and shellfish. Charcuterie specialties include a super duck foie gras. Frozen sauces and complete dinners to go. Laurier is also a wonderful street for shopping and strolling.

Arawak Imports

5854 Sherbrooke West (corner Regent)
Métro: Vendôme then bus 105
514.488.6918

Salt cod, pig's foot, ackee, hot peppers, okra, squashes, plantains, shelves of hot sauces and sweet drinks imported from Jamaica, even Blue Mountain coffee. Get some tamarind balls (regular or spicy) for snacking as you leave the store. Plenty of cooking advice and everything you'll need to make an Island feast at home.

Asia Market
801 Somerset West
Ottawa
613.230.2329
Rice wine is easily and legally available in this well-stocked
Asian grocery in Ottawa.

Atelier de boulangerie de l'Est
There is no retail outlet, but bread is available in various stores.
514.488.3098
Bernard Bélanger makes small, delicious loaves: whole wheat,
multigrain, raisin, spelt, olive fougasses and other breads.
Look for them in selected cafés such as Café Esperanza at the
corner of St-Laurent Blvd. and St. Viateur, Café Rico (969
Rachel East) and Coop la Maison Verte at the corner of Sherbrooke West and Melrose. There is free home delivery for
orders of two loaves or more.

Atlantique
5060 Côte-des-Neiges (corner Queen Mary)
Métro : Guy-Concordia or Côte-des-Neiges then bus 165
514.731.4764
Delicatessen and pastry shop with a small café, good for
lunches. Butcher counter with homemade sausages: knockwurst, Vienna wurst, debrecziener, liverwurst. Smoked salmon
and fresh fish too. Lots of imported eastern European jams,
mustards, mini pumpernickel and rye loaves for canapes and
other delicacies.

B.J.'s Buttercrunch
514.484.7360, 514.481.4536
Bryna and Judy make only one thing—mouth-watering, nutty,
caramel buttercrunch. Eat this with caution. It is deliciously
addictive. Made-to-order gift packs range from $5 to $20.

Bassé Inc.
9360 Charles de Latour (near Chabannel)

Métro: l'Acadie then bus 179

514.387.8828

The slogan of the store is "we go nuts for you!" and the nuts are great, as is the selection of candy, spices, coffee, and imported delicacies like tamarind syrup and rose water. There are even unusual products like dried okra and eggplant. (Rehydrate these and use them for stews and rice dishes). What sets this store apart from others is that so many of the products are designed for gift giving. Drop by here for a food gift that is beautifully packaged or for something unique like a box of chewing gum from Jordan (with unusual flavours including licorice, cinnamon and coffee).

Batory Euro Deli

115 St-Viateur West (near St-Urbain)

Métro: St-Laurent or de Castelnau then bus 55

514.948.2161

This small deli (dwarfed by the massive St. Michael the Archangel church) has a friendly staff and home-style cooking. There is a wonderful variety of Polish specialties for take out or eating at the few tables in the store. Look for pierogies, ponchky (Polish donuts), sausages, soups, cabbage rolls, apple cake and poppy and cheese cakes. There is always a crowd on Sunday's after services. Closed Monday.

Bela Vista

68 des Pins East (corner Coloniale)

Métro: St-Laurent then bus 55

514.849.3609/ www.natas.ca

Portugese bakery noted for its pastéis de nata, made from a recipe used by the monks of Belém for centuries. A selection of cakes, pastries, sandwiches, café au lait and espresso, along with a few stools and outside tables make it worth the stop.

Betterbaking.com

www.betterbaking.com

This is a superb site for baking (bread, desserts, holiday

dishes). Visit regularly for discussions of ingredients, recipes and the ruminations of professional baker, full-time mother, and prolific cookbook writer Marcy Goldman.

Bilboquet
1311 Bernard West (near Outremont)
Métro: Place des Arts or Parc then bus 80
514.276.0414
For more than twenty years, this has been a local ice cream nirvana. More than three dozen kinds of home-made sorbets (they are dairy-free) and ice creams. Favourites include strawberry, vanilla, lychee, trichamp (a great combination of blueberry, raspberry and strawberry), praline, banana-cream and cacaphonie (chocolate, white chocolate and cashews). Small cones ($1.25) seem tiny, but the flavours are so intense that you may not want to eat too much, too quickly.

Binerie Mont-Royal, La
367 Mont-Royal East (near St-Denis)
Métro: Mont-Royal
514.285.9078
Traditional Quebec meals have been served here for half a century: oven-baked beans, gras de roti, tourtière, pudding chomeur. This is a small diner with room for barely more than a dozen. All dishes are available to go. The beans and tourtière can be kept in the freezer at home and reheat nicely.

Bonne Bouffe
5716 Sherbrooke West (near Wilson)
Métro: Vendôme then bus 105
514.488.3006
Platters filled with coco bread, patties, jerk chicken, goat and oxtail stews, and fried fish all pour out of the large kitchen and into this small store. Great in the summer when the sidewalk opens up with tables and everyone seems to eat outside.

Boucherie Capitol
Jean-Talon Market
Métro: Jean-Talon, or bus 55
514.276.1345
A must-stop selection of antipasti, breads, Italian pastas, reasonably-priced olive oils and vinegars and a great butcher shop with excellent veal and steaks, plus their own sausages, porchetta and slab pizza. Personal attention from the staff is excellent.

Boucherie du Marché Maisonneuve
4445 Ontario East (at Morgan)
Métro: Pie IX
514.256.6948
Sylvain Corbeil makes delicious tourtière, chicken and salmon pies, fresh sausage and steaks fresh-cut to order. The shop is small but has a large variety of products including foie de canard and maigret (breast). The staff readily offers cooking ideas and recipes.

Boucherie la Préférence
Marché de l'Ouest
11740 de Salaberry, Dollard-des-Ormeaux
514.683.5555
Les Halles d'Anjou
7500 Galleries d'Anjou Blvd.
514.355.5040
A full-service butcher with specialty items including freshly-made Italian sausage, rabbits, pork hocks, and meat aged several weeks before being cut to order.

Boucherie de Tours
Atwater Market
Métro: Lionel-Groulx
514.931.4406
A small, good French butcher shop that is attentive to individual requests. Large cooler for aging meat. Ribs and steaks

cut to order, fresh sausages, a tasty selection of patés, maigret de canard, dried sausages. Worth looking at specials and then wandering through the market to compare. Frankly, each butcher shop at the Atwater market has its favourite customers and all counters are worth stopping at.

Boucherie Westmount
5207 Sherbrooke West (corner Marlowe)
Métro: Vendôme then bus 105
514.481.1811
Small butcher shop offering organic beef, smoked turkey, aged steaks, free-range chicken and eggs, fresh sausages (try the chicken) made on the premises. Cooking advice freely offered. Chicken carcasses are sold separately and inexpensively for soups and stocks.

Boulangerie Arouche
917 Liege West (corner Stuart)
Métro: Place des Arts or Parc then bus 80
514.270.1092
One speciality here: lahmadjoun (Armenian pizza) made with lamb and served spicy or regular. Mostly to go but there is room to squeeze in and eat in the store.

Boulangerie Farhat Pita
7719 St-Laurent (near Villeray, across from Jarry Park)
Métro: St-Laurent or de Castelnau then bus 55
514.277.6268
A small Middle Eastern bakery with "Greek" pastries, lahmadjoun, spinach pies, kibbé, whole wheat and regular pitas, and ice cream— everything tastes wonderful. It is a great place to put together a picnic meal to carry across to the park or home.

Boulangerie Roma
6776 St-Laurent (near St-Zotique)
Métro: St-Laurent or Castelnau then bus 55
514.273.9357

The best ciabatta (sourdough) rolls in the city (they freeze well, too), slab pizza (try the eggplant and artichoke), sublime ricotta-filled cannoli and other Italian desserts made on the premises. Their pistachio, lemon, and vanilla gelati are particularly good. In the heart of Little Italy with great food and shopping all around.

Bucharest Delicatessen
4670 Decarie (corner Snowdon)
Métro: Snowdon
514. 481.4732
A large supermarket with a central and eastern European focus. Fresh and frozen pierogies, imported jams from Romania, Poland and Bulgaria, fruit syrups. A wide range of smoked hams, bacons, salamis and cold cuts; barrels of sauerkraut and pickles. Sandwiches are made to order at the deli counter.

Cacao Royal
5100 Sherbrooke West (corner Grey)
Métro: Vendôme or bus 24
514.488.2266
A young, trained chocolate-maker using imported Belgian Callebaut chocolate. Good truffles and other treats in the small store. Rich hot chocolate made to order. Unusual molds include illustrations from the Kama Sutra which make for inspiring Valentine's day gifts.

Café Ferreira Trattoria
1446 Peel (near de Maisonneuve)
Métro: Peel
514.848.0988/www.ferreiracafe.com
Carlos Ferreira's big bucks, great food, lavish service, over-the-top, high-modern-style restaurant featuring superb Portu-guese cooking and a wonderful selection of ports and wines by the glass. Excellent traditional dishes include an epicurean version of bacalhau (salt cod and potatoes).

Café Italia
6840 St-Laurent (near Dante)
Métro: St-Laurent or de Castelnau then bus 55
514.495.0059
One of the city's oldest Italian sports bars serving what many consider the best espresso in town. Freshly squeezed orange juice, grilled panetone, sandwiches made to order on Roma Bakery's ciabatta. A perfect spot during the European football season. Their coffee is also sold in bulk packages.

Cananut
1415 Mazurette (near l'Acadie)
Métro: l'Acadie then bus 179
514.388.8003
The aroma from freshly-roasted nuts and coffee wafts from the huge wholesale operation at the back of the building. The retail space is impressive with huge quantities of over a hundred varieties of dried fruits, nuts (including eight barrels of pistachios), lentils and spices. There are also olive oils, narghiles (water pipes), cooking supplies for couscous, and great advice from a very friendly staff.

Capital Q
707 H Street NW
Washington, DC 20001
202.347.8396
OK—this is not a Montreal restaurant. It's here because it worked itself into "Maple Smoke." More importantly, Capital Q shows that a great BBQ joint can thrive far from its roots. So why can't we have one here? Slow cooked pork ribs, fork-tender beef brisket, smoked turkey, and maybe side orders of collard greens and black-eyed peas (aka Texas caviar). Dubya would feel at home.

Caribbean Curry House
6892 Victoria (corner Mackenzie)
Métro: Plamondon then bus 124

514.733.0828

A Trinidadian restaurant with fabulous take-out. Come here for rotis, oxtail stew, curry goat, and especially the jerk chicken. Pleasant comfy dining room and a friendly staff will guide newcomers through the menu.

Cavallaro
4865 Sherbrooke West (near Victoria)
Métro: Vendôme or bus 24
514.484.0804

This is the Westmount franchise of the Cavallaro chain. An impressive array of vinegars (sherry, balsamic, white wine) and olive oils including a good house brand sold in bulk ("take me to your litre?"). And the breads: foccacia, baguettes, pizza, and challahs. Other stores are in Place Kirkland, Place Rose-mère, Pierrefonds, Galeries d'Anjou, and the Marché de l'Ouest. Each of the Cavallaro stores can stock different products but all have good deli and cheese counters. Imported specialty items such as Lavazza coffees, and a selection of custom-made frozen pastas are also available.

Charcuterie Hongroise
3843 St-Laurent (near Roy)
Métro: St-Laurent then bus 55
514. 844.6734

Long established on The Main. There are sausages, smoked brisket and ham, chicken and veal schnitzels steaming away and ready for sandwiches. Ask for a pickle too. Smoked bacon, sausages and Eastern European style cold cuts (which are dairy-free) are made in their own smokehouse. Also a good butcher shop for veal and pork specialties, sweet and spicy paprikas, imported jams and mustards.

Chez Benny
5071 Queen Mary (near Décarie)
Métro: Snowdon
514.735.1836

Strictly kosher. Kebabs, falafel, hamburgers, steaks and schnitzel. Great fries and a good crowd. Benny's has grown impressively over the years from a hole-in-the-wall Romanian snack bar to a large Middle Eastern cafeteria. Tasty and hearty food, well priced and a dynamite hot sauce.

Chez Clo
3199 Ontario East (corner Dézéry)
Métro: Préfontaine
514.522.5348
A wonderful Quebec-style diner that is a flashback to the 1950s with Saguenay-style tourtière, ragout de boulettes, salmon pie, pâté Chinois and pudding chômeur. It is not open in the evening.

Chez Louis in Jean-Talon Market
Métro: Jean-Talon or bus 55
514.277.4670
A top-flight greengrocer with the finest produce in the city. You will find fresh wild mushrooms, salicorne, varieties of potatoes, tomatoes and exotic fruits. Check out the names on the order books on the shelf. If it's good enough for the best chefs in town, it's good enough for my table.

Chilenita, La
152 Napoleon (corner de Bullion)
514.286.6075
4348 Clark (corner Marianne)
514.982.9212
For either location—Métro: St-Laurent or de Castelnau then bus 55
These small take-out bakeries and restaurants also call themselves "La Maison des Empanadas" and serve South American (mostly Chilean and Mexican) dishes and over a dozen kinds of empanadas: beef, chicken, several kinds of vegetarian (try the cheese and eggplant) and seafood. Plus

churrasco sandwiches, burritos, fajitas, and quesadillas. Open mostly during daytime hours—seldom in the evening.

Chopin
4200 Décarie (near Monkland)
Métro: Villa Maria
514.481.0302
A jewel of a small pastry shop and delicatessen with a European flavour. Homemade sausages, strudels, thick creamy Polish-style cheese cakes, imported soups and jams. Specialties include zurek (sour soup) and blueberry pierogies. Excellent sandwiches made to order. Great for lunch or tea. There are a few tables in the middle of the store and outside during warm weather.

Cinq-Saisons
Branches throughout Montreal
Upscale supermarkets featuring some of the best quality fruits and vegetables in the city. Look for fresh shiitake and oyster mushrooms, fresh herbs, and, in the winter, pricey but real tomatoes. Good cheese sections and butcher counters featuring Quebec lamb, locally-raised free-range chicken, and foie gras. Most stores have an extensive take-out salad bar.

Costco
Various locations including Marché Central and Bridge street in Pointe-St-Charles
All stores: 514.383.2626
A big-box retailer selling most things to many people. The food section carries brand-name items in extra-large economy-priced quantities. Costco also features local cooks and food suppliers for many of its fresh and packaged food products. Prices are generally lower than in regular stores, and the quality is uniformly high. There is an annual membership fee.

D.A.D.'s Bagels
5732 Sherbrooke West (corner Wilson)
Métro: Vendôme then bus 105
514.487.2454
Wood fired bagels 24/7, and fresh bread. Deli goodies include lox, cream cheese, karnatzle and other nosherei (snacks). Excellent Indian take-out (the owner is Sikh); vegetable and chicken curries, samosas, Tandoor chicken, Indian sweets. Eating on premises.

Deli Snowdon
5265 Decarie (corner Isabella)
Métro: Snowdon
514.488.9129 / www.Snowdondeli.ca
The Snowdon Deli has been serving great smoked meat sandwiches, matzoh ball soup, knishes, smoked turkey, sliced tongue, homemade apple strudel, bagels and lox, whitefish and carp platters, chopped liver, all-beef franks with a side of great fries and hot peppers and much more for over 50 years. Make sure you go through the correct door: eat on the right, take-out on the left. It gets crowded on Sunday morning.

Dima
Stores at the Jean-Talon and Maisonneuve markets and at 3623 Ontario East (corner Chambly)
Métros: Jean-Talon (for the Jean-Talon Market store), Pie IX (for the Maisonneuve Market), Joliette (for the Ontario East store)
514.274.3962
A nicely laid out "en vrac" store that sells well-known brands such as Costeña Latin American products and Valhorona chocolate at good prices. This is one-stop shopping for many kinds of legumes, pastas, lots of kinds of olives, oils and vinegars, coffee, teas, and spices. Call first if you are looking for something special.

Douceurs du Marché in Atwater Market
Métro: Lionel-Groulx
514.939.3902
A knockout of a food store. A special selection of olive oils, vinegars, spices, imported foods, Latin and Asian specialties, as well as Zyliss, Schlemmer Tops and other high quality cookware. Owners Glen Jones and René Lavallée take great delight in being the first to offer Montrealers unusual comestibles. They are knowledgeable and travel regularly to search out the best.

Dragon Beard Candy
85 de la Gauchetière West (near Clark)
Métro: Place d'Armes, or bus 55
Johnny Chin and his small staff make just one item, but they do it well and they make it fresh: Dragon Beard candy. This is a lovely dessert snack created from cornstarch, peanuts, and flavourings, pulled into wisps of endless thin threads and folded over until it's only a fluffy mouthful. A unique Chinatown treat and a must-stop after a full meal. The shop is really a tiny storefront that opens onto the street.

E.D. Foods Ltd.
6200 Trans-Canada
1.800.267.3333/www.ed-foods.com
E.D. Foods Ltd. is a soup, seasoning and food manufacturing company based in Pointe Claire. They make the house brand products for supermarkets and private labels. Their Montreal steak spice gets shipped around the world. This is not a retail store, so go on-line to shop. First-timers get free soup samples when they order.

Échoppe des Fromages, L'
12 Aberdeen, St-Lambert (near Victoria)
Métro: Longeuil and then bus 1, 15 or 16.
450.672.9701
Max Dubois is a second-generation cheese merchant and

affineur de fromage. Hundreds of cheeses, many made from raw milk and selected from small Quebec farms. During the winter, try the port-soaked Stilton. On the South Shore near the Victoria bridge. There is also a small luncheon menu with some well selected wines available by the glass.

Esprit de Carnival, L'
123 de la Commune West
Métro: Place d'Armes
514.875.1142
A large dairy bar with great fried dough. Surprisingly light and delicate. Try it simple, dusted with cinnamon and sugar—$2. For something more filling there is the Volcano—deep-fried honey balls with ice cream and a chocolate and/or caramel topping.

Euro-Plus
279 Lakeshore Drive (Bord-du-Lac), Pointe-Claire (near Cartier)
Bus: 211
514.694.4728.
A Dutch food specialty store with wonderful imported candies particularly chocolates and licorice; also smoked wursts, gouda cheeses, tubes of herring and smoked fish patés, and a good deli and pastry counter. There is a small café in the front with good luncheon specials and sandwiches. This is a great place to stop on weekends if you are bicycling along Lakeshore Drive.

Fairmont Bagel Bakery
74 Fairmount West (near St-Laurent)
Métro: St-Laurent or de Castelnau then bus 55
514.272.0667
Wood-fired bagels in almost any flavour imaginable: multigrain, garlic, onion, whole wheat, caraway, flax seed, even blueberry and cinnamon & raisin (oy!). Also basic poppy seed and sesame, of course. Open 24 hours.

Ferme Michaca
Jean-Talon Market
Métro: Jean-Talon or bus 55
(3026 Snaill, Athelston, QC, 450.264.4369)
Certified 100% organic vegetables, 90% of all other products also certified organic—grains, pulses, dried fruits, honey, maple syrup. Also sells flower and vegetable plants.

Fiesta-Pilipino
5980 Victoria (near de la Peltrie)
Métro: Plamondon then bus 124
514.341.7441
Small bakery with a variety of sweet breads and pastries including pandesal—a basic sweet bun, great with coffee—coconut buns, hopia (flaky pastry with a bean filling), also good cakes made to order.

Finesse
5945 Victoria (near Linton)
Métro: Plamondon then bus 124
514.735.1925
Strictly kosher quality chocolates made by Bryan and Tina Stutman. Truffles, holiday treats for Chanukah and Purim are a specialties. They even do chocolate-covered matzoh! A large variety of liquor-infused milk and dark chocolates. Parve chocolates are dairy-free. Specialty orders too.

Formosa
3343E Boulevard des Sources
(between Brunswick and de Salaberry)
514.683.5198
An all-purpose Asian grocery that is strong on Chinese and Japanese cooking utensils and supplies for meals. Hard to find items that are in stock here include dried galangal, roasted green peas (great for snacking), spring roll wrappers, banana leaves, and Serkiryu sushi knives. There are also cooking classes and great Asian gift items.

Foumagerie, La
4906 Sherbrooke West (corner Prince Albert)
Métro: Vendôme or bus 24
514.482.4100 / www.lafoumagerie.qc.ca
Excellent variety of cheeses. Raclette broilers and fondue sets rented out. Good charcuterie selection with locally made products such as tourtière, fresh baguettes and croissants, a small lunch counter with good coffee and freshly made sandwiches (anything with brie in it is delicious). There are a couple of tables with seating outside when it gets warm.

Foxy's
5987 Victoria (near Linton)
Métro: Plamondon then bus 124
514.739.8777
Popular neighbourhood café, particularly after shabbos (after sundown on Saturday night). Very good falafel, large portions (a half pita is quite filling, a full one is big enough to share). Strictly kosher.

Fromagerie du Deuxième in Atwater Market
Métro: Lionel Groulx
514.932.5532
Go upstairs at the market to see a wide selection of un-pasturized French and Quebec cheeses, plus lots of British cheddars and Stiltons. There is also a small charcuterie section with excellent duck foie patés as well as olive oils, vinegars and gourmet treats.

Fromagerie d'Exception
1218 Bernard West, Outremont (near Bloomfield)
Métro: Place des Arts or Parc then bus 80, or bus 160
514.279.9376
Until recently, this was the retail store for Montreal's best known affineur des fromages, Pierre-Yves Chaput. M. Chaput takes unpasteurized cheeses and ages them assiduously. Their flavours are strong, fresh tasting and quite remarkable com-

pared to what is available at most supermarket cheese counters. He now devotes his attention to "cheese finishing" and has ceased operating his own outlets. Many stores now carry Chaput cheeses. Exception has an excellent selection as well as other Quebec and French cheeses. Look for Tomme au Marc de raisin (covered with grape seeds) or wonderful Quebec varieties like Riopelle, a brie like triple-crême from Île-aux-grus and Valbert, a nutty cheese somewhat similar to a Swiss gruyére (and recently voted best cheese in Quebec) from the Lac St-Jean region. The store is spartan—wood and marble—with cheeses tucked into a wall fridge. The staff is helpful and willingly offers tasting samples and advice.

Fromagerie Hamel in Jean-Talon Market
Métro: Jean-Talon or bus 55
514.272.1161
Also at
2117 Mont-Royal East
Métro: Mont-Royal
514.521.3333
9196 Sherbrooke East
Métro: Honoré Beaugrand
514.355.6657
622 Notre-Dame, Repentigny
450.654.3578
There are several Hamel stores in the city but the Jean-Talon market branch is the oldest and largest. Many consider a trip to the market unfinished without a stop here to sample a few of their hundreds of cheeses. There is also a small eating area at the back of this store where you can take a break from shopping with a coffee and croissant, a plate of charcuterie and cheese, pasta or sandwiches. You can also rent a raclette grill—essential for an authentic Swiss dinner party.

Fromagerie du Marché Atwater in Atwater Market
Métro: Lionel-Groulx
514.932.4653

Large cheese store with a friendly staff. Try the tasting section in the back for an unusual Quebec goat cheese or raw milk import. Lagoyice knives and a few other unusual items. Also a good selection of antipasti, charcuterie, terrines, and local micro-brew beers. Owner Gilles Jordenais will organize wine-and-cheese tasting sessions upon request.

Fruiterie Milano
6862 St-Laurent (near Dante)
Métro: St-Laurent or de Castelnau then bus 55
514.273.8558
This is the small grocery store that took over the block. Everything is Italian, including staff and most of the customers. A wonderful selection of antipasti, cheeses, fruit and vegetables, pastas, imported and Canadian prosciutto, Italian mineral water, truffles, olives, every kind of panetone, pasta dishes and imported cooking giftware, a quality butcher shop, a vast selection of imported vinegars and olive oils. Also a choice of Italian pearly white arborio rice, the best for risotto.

Globe Restaurant
3455 St-Laurent (near Sherbrooke)
Métro: St-Laurent then bus 55, or bus 24
514.284.3823
Chef Fréderic Morin and his boss David Macmillan search the country for the best purveyors and freshest ingredients. The food is great, and Globe is always listed among the top restaurants in this town. But they also have a way with basics that makes the mouth water. Try the poutine. It's not listed on the menu and the waitress will probably laugh at you, but go ahead. If Morin is in the kitchen and he's not too busy, he'll make it—and like everything else here—you'll be amazed that something so simple can taste so good.

Gourmet Laurier
1042 Laurier West (near Hutchison)
Métro: Laurier then bus 51, or Place des Arts then bus 80

514.274.5601 / www.gourmetlaurier.com
Gerard Van Houtte's original coffee shop is now one-stop gourmet shopping for teas, baking chocolate, coffee, locally-made jams, kitchen tools, and giftware.

Haddad
12186 Laurentian (near de Salaberry), Ville St-Laurent
Métro: Côte Vertu then bus 151
514.745.5221
For 35 years this small Lebanese bakery has served up zatar pita, dolmas, tabboulé, knafé and a feast of appetizers and delicacies. There are even a few tables to sit at and munch on freshly-made lahmajoun—or enjoy a cup of coffee with a sweet swirl of M'chabak, a pastry flavoured with rose water.

Hoàng Oanh
1071 St-Laurent (corner René-Lévesque)
Métro: Place d'Armes
514.954.0053
7178 St-Denis (near Jean-Talon)
Métro: Jean-Talon
514.271.8668
Hoàng Oanh is a small chain of Vietnamese coffee shops specializing in bánh mì—Vietnamese sandwiches. They have one store in Toronto and two in Montreal. Ask for a frequent customer card. Eat ten bánh mì and the eleventh is free.

J&R Kosher Meat
Cavendish Mall, 5800 Cavendish
Métro: Plamondon then bus 161
514.369.2727
Aged steaks, great hot dogs, all beef salami, stuffed chicken, smoked meat, kanartzle dry sausage and all sorts of Jewish delicatessen goodies. Personal service. Strictly kosher.

Jardin du Cari
23 St-Viateur West (near St-Laurent)

Métro: St-Laurent or de Castelnau then bus 55

514.495.0565

Guyanese rotis are the pride of this small eat-in or take-out restaurant. The large flatbread rotis are stuffed with shrimp, goat, chicken, or chickpea and potato. The family recipe hot sauce is spectacular.

Jardin de Jade Poon Kai

67 de la Gauchetière West (near St-Laurent)

Métro: Place d'Armes, or bus 55

514.866.3127

This long-established Chinatown restaurant has a huge buffet and very large take-out section. Look for bao-ji (steamed buns), barbecued pork, and soups. Also lots of Chinese pastries to go. Jade is on a part of de la Gauchetière that is a pedestrian mall, but there is usually parking on side streets or on St-Laurent which is a block away.

Jerusalem Express

Cavendish Mall, 5800 Cavendish

Métro: Plamondon then bus 161

514.488.5382

Kosher Middle Eastern food stand in a food court—with plenty of seating nearby. Freshly-made salads, falafel, kebabs and shwarma. This is a great alternative to most of the mall fast food places.

Jos and Basile

152 Mozart East (corner Casgrain)

Métro: Jean-Talon, or bus 55

514.274.6358 / www.boucheriejosetbasile.com

A friendly family shop on the edge of Jean-Talon Market. Excellent butcher shop, good cheese selection, freshly-made calzone, homemade sausages, olive oil tastings and good prices on balsamic vinegars. There's a small hot-food counter and a few tables out front where you can have a coffee or bite to eat. Visit their web site to order on-line or see the weekly specials.

Kaizen Sushi Bar and KaizenTreehouse
4120 Ste-Catherine West (near Greene)
Métro: Atwater
514.932.5654 / www.kaizensushibar.com/Treehouse.html
In this restaurant complex, the sushi bar has spectacular 'traditional' California-Japanese sushi. The high-end Treehouse serves Japanese cuisine and fusion Asian.

Katsura Express
4822 Sherbrooke West
Métro: Vendôme then bus 105
514.487.1119
1104 de Maisonneuve West
Métro: Peel
514.842.4114
Spin-offs from Katsura, the long-established downtown Japanese restaurant, these are well-priced take-out sushi shops which also feature $8 bento boxes—small, meal-sized portions of Japanese dishes.

Kim Phat
3588 Goyer (corner Côte-des-Neiges)
Métro: Snowdon, then bus 165
514.737.2383
1875 Panama, Brossard (corner Taschereau)
450.923.9877
8080 Taschereau, Brossard
450.923.9973
3733 Jarry East (corner Pie IX)
Métro: Jarry, then bus 193
514.727.8919
The city's largest chain of Asian grocery stores has ingredients from across Southeast Asia and China. Impressive stores with fresh fish and meat counters (the chicken is often a bargain). Large sections for vegetables, spices and sauces, dried goods such as mushrooms and noodles. Vietnamese sandwiches sold during lunch hour.

Korean & Japanese Food

6151 Sherbrooke West (near Cavendish)
Métro: Vendôme then bus 105
514.487.1672

Korean and Japanese food items are primary in this expanding Korean grocery store. There is row upon row of sesame oils, soy and chili sauces, with kimchee made in the back, a large frozen meat selection which is precut for Korean barbecue, Mongolian hot pots, and other specific dishes. Look for the large selection of Japanese snacks near the door.

Kosher Quality Bakery

5855 Victoria (near Bourret)
Métro: Plamondon then bus 124
514.731.7883

Freshly-made breads, rolls, strudels and all sorts of great stuff for noshing. Challahs, poppyseed rolls, hamantaschen, prepared chickens, fish, and traditional Jewish delicacies ready for the table. It gets nuts here on Friday mornings as hordes of Montrealers come to get their weekend orders.

Kowloon Market

712 Somerest West, Ottawa
613.233.1108

Legal Chinese rice wine and all of the other Asian foodstuffs necessary for your kitchen.

Lahmadjoune Beyrouth-Yervan

420 Faillon East (near St-Denis)
Métro: Jean-Talon
514.270.1076

Falafal, spinach and cheese flatbreads, zatar pita, and crisp delicious lahmadjoune. Lots of other flatbread combinations too, all to go.

LaSalle Caribbean

408 Lafleur (near Clément)

Métro: Angrignon then bus 113
514.368.4808
Patties, jerk chicken, beans and rice, stews, rotis. Nice friendly place; many customers call here and order for take-out.

Maison du Bedouin

1616 Ste-Catherine West, Faubourg Ste-Catherine (at Guy)
Métro: Guy-Concordia
514.935.0236
Delicious North African food prepared with attention and skill. The daily specials with salad and rice might be succulent meatballs and gravy on couscous, or pastilla with almonds, chicken and rosewater. The not overly sweet doughnuts are served warm, with a drizzle of honey if requested—have one with a pot of real mint tea.

Maison Cakao

5090 Fabre (corner Laurier)
Métro: Laurier
514.598.2462
If you saw the film *Chocolate* you will feel at home here. Edith Gagnon runs a craft shop for chocolate lovers: chocolate encrusted with citrus or edged with bergamot (the flavour behind Earl Grey Tea) or sinful truffles, are only a few of the specialties here. And it is all beautifully wrapped. You can't leave here and not feel happy.

Maître Courbeau

11690 de Salaberry, Marché de l'Ouest, Dollard-des-Ormeaux (near Sources)
514.421.9944
1375 Laurier East
Métro: Laurier
514.528.3293
A gourmet store with a strong emphasis on Quebec products. The larger store, in the Marché de l'Ouest, has 250 cheeses, with a quarter of them from Quebec. Look for ten-year-old

port-infused Peron cheddar, dozens of local patés, Burnett maple syrup jelly from Sutton, Quebec, Haut-Panache low-fat gourmet sausages (pheasent, Thai-chili, etc.) and a large selection of Quebec wines.

Marché Akhavan
6170 Sherbrooke West (corner Grand)
Métro: Vendôme then bus 105
514.485.4887
An Iranian supermarket with a halal butcher (meat ground to order, lamb shanks, marinated kebabs ready-to-cook), a wide variety of feta cheeses, tsatsiki, and yogurt. Known for their choice of teas, imported juice concentrates (grape, pome-granate, sour cherry), nuts, spices, Iranian caviar, aged basmati rice. A large counter of Middle Eastern pastries and take out-dishes. Small selection of light meals can be eaten on the premises. Excellent service, and parking beside the store.

Marché Daou
4870 Sources, Dollard-des-Ormeaux (near Gouin)
514.685-8989
Full-service supermarket with a Lebanese tilt. Greek salads and combo platters ready-to-go near the cash, reasonably priced with half a dozen dishes including dolmas, hummus, tabouleh. Charcoal grill at the back turns out chickens on the spit, shwarma and kebabs ready for eating. There is a large vegetable section and pastry counter.

Marché des Saveurs du Québec in Jean-Talon Market
Métro: Jean-Talon or bus 55
514.271.3811
Run by the Drouin family, this is a great place for hard-to-find delicacies such as locally smoked ham, maple syrup, ice wine, cider and mead, mussels from les îles de la Madeleine, goat milk cheese and a full range of beers from local micro-breweries. Cheese and wine tastings are held regularly; call ahead to find out when.

Marché Farhat
5595 Côte-des-Neiges (near Côte-Ste-Catherine)
Métro: Guy-Concordia or Côte-des-Neiges then bus 165
514.738.4045

How much stuff can you fit into a small store? Start in the back with a Middle Eastern market crammed with olives and hard-to-find marinated lemons, sacks of semolina, fresh bread, labneh, Syrian cheese and much more. Then, as we move toward the street, there is a halal butcher counter, a grill for take-out dishes, and a couple of stools at the counter. The grill is a recent addition to this store—they use only charcoal. The aromas from the grilling chicken and marinated meats (available at the butcher counter) are fantastic. The mild but flavourful small Lebanese makanek sausages are a treat. Top off a plate with pickled vegetables and a pita, sit at the window counter and watch the world stroll by.

Marché Istanbul
8780 St-Laurent (near Cremazie)
Métro: Cremazie
514.276.7930

Turkish market with crafts, giftwares, a variety of excellent pastries and imported delicacies including a good selection of locum—Turkish Delight.

Marché Kim Hoa
4843 Sources, Pierrefonds
514.683.8878

Large all-purpose market geared toward Asian food. Perfect for fresh lemon grass, dried mushrooms, Thai basil, nuoc mam and other sauces essential for Thai and Vietnamese cooking. Copious vegetable and fruit sections and butcher and fish counters.

Marché Mit Thai Lao
942 Décarie, Ville St-Laurent
Métro: du College then bus 17; or Métro Côte-Vertu
514.748.9099

A superb Asian market with just about everything for Japanese, Thai, or South Asian cooking. Fresh lemon grass, galangal, durian ice cream, Thai mung bean candies, Vietnamese sandwiches, sticky rice, almost everything—except fish—for making sushi. Also udon noodles, won ton wrappers and homemade delicacies such as a fantastic Laotian hot sauce called chèo bung (look for it at the counter) and sompacka—tasty pickled cabbage somewhat like a mild version of Korean kimchee. The owners are friendly and willingly suggest cooking ideas. Few small Asian groceries have this variety.

Marché Norouz
5700 Sherbrooke West (corner Harvard)
Métro: Vendôme then bus 105
514.807.8747
A small Iranian store in N.D.G. Imported teas, nuts and dried fruits, homemade appetizers including meat and vegetable dolmas. The specialty here is Persian kebabs and grilled-to-order chicken and shish taouk. Eating on premises.

Marché Thai Hour
7130 St-Denis
Métro: Jean-Talon
514.271.4469
Busy supermarket with full service butcher and fish counter. Fresh fruits,vegetables, and all varieties of canned and frozen specialties to satisfy Thai, Vietnamese and West African tastes.

Marvellous Mustard Shop, The
109A Sparks Street, Ottawa
613.232.8777
Over 90 varieties of mustard, including a tasting bar, and a great little tea room too.

Ma's Place
5889 Sherbrooke West (near Clifton)
Métro: Vendôme then 105 bus

514.487.7488,
850 Decarie, Ville St-Laurent
Métro: Côte-Vertu
514.744.2011
Jerk chicken, ox-tail stew, goat roti, saltfish and ackee: all those authentic island foods are made in the small kitchen of this tiny restaurant. Lots of take-out and a few seats. Open 24-hours on the weekends at the Sherbrooke West location.

Mazurka
64 Prince Arthur East (near St-Laurent)
Métro: Sherbrooke or Métro St-Laurent then bus 55
514.844.3539
This is a great deal on Polish comfort food—pierogies, blintzes, potato pancakes. The daily special includes home-made soup and coffee at very reasonable prices. It's been around for decades, and with good reason.

Mr. Spicee
6889A Victoria (near Mackenzie)
Métro: Plamondon then bus 124
514.739.9714
Roti makers for many Caribbean restaurants in the city. Both the bread and the filling are called roti and Mr. Spicee fills theirs with curried goat, beef and chicken. Also delicious patties and sweet Caribbean drinks.

Miyamoto
382 Victoria (near Sherbrooke)
Métro: Vendôme
514.481.1952 / www.sushilinks.com
A well stocked Japanese food store with a wide selection of imported foods, Japanese snacking crackers (the ones with extra wasabi are a real hit), teapots and tools for making sushi. There is always a variety of sushi ready to go. The sushi is made on the premises and the staff can accommodate specific requests. Their web site with tips on sushi making is excellent.

Momesso
5562 Upper Lachine (corner Old Orchard)
Métro: Vendôme then bus 90
514.484.0005
There is only one thing you need to know; this snack bar serves the best sausage subs in the city. Also the same great seasoned meat on small hand-sized tomato-sauced pizzas. Get the hot sauce on the side if this is your first time. Maybe an espresso and sambucca after. A great sports bar with primo seating for World Cup football finals.

Momoi Bakery
6953 Victoria (near Mackenzie)
Métro: Plamondon
514.736.1925
A tiny Sri Lankan bakery hidden away, close to the underpass near Jean-Talon. Delicious and spicy cooking includes rotis, bread buns stuffed with fish, vegetable or chicken curry (warm them up and slice them before serving), chana dal, cookie-like appetizers, sweet banana balls, vegetable and meat rolls. There are also daily special take-outs such as rice and vegetable biryanyis selling for about $4.00. The owner, Nathan Path-manathan Sinnathan can also put together a Sri Lankan buffet selection for parties. Closed Mondays.

Montrealfood.com
Only available on the Internet at www.montrealfood.com. Eclectic food criticism by Nicholas Robinson, Barry Lazar, and others. The first venue for discussions about much of the material that appears in this book.

Montreal Pool Room
1200 St-Laurent (near Ste-Catherine)
Métro: St-Laurent or bus 55
"whydoyouwannaknowthephone?"
Montreal steamé (steamed hot dogs), great fries and, of course, poutine. Get the $5.16 trio and you may not eat anything else

all day. (Pool? Not for decades—for pool you must go to Metropool across the street.) Stools for a couple of dozen and 'authentic' atmosphere. A Montreal favorite since 1912.

Motta Bakery
315 Mozart East (near Henri-Julien)
Métro: Jean-Talon, or bus 55
514.270.5952
A neighbourhood institution, on the south-east corner of the Jean-Talon Market. Great for calzone, freshly baked goods, and a great variety of imported Italian treats. Motta has grown from being simply a bakery and features take-out and ready-to-heat Italian dishes. There are tables at the back and some outdoor tables for lunch and break-time munching.

Mourelatos
1621 St. Catherine West (near Guy)
Métro: Guy-Concordia
514.904.0300
1855 O'Brien, Ville St-Laurent (near Poirier)
Métro: Côte Vertu, bus 170
514.956.0100
4957 St-Jean, Pierrefonds
514.620.4200 / www.mourelatos.com
and other locations throughout Montreal
Family-run, high quality supermarkets with an emphasis on Mediterranean food. The web site includes recipes for many Greek dishes including souvlaki, fassolatha (bean stew) and spanakopita (spinach pie).

Mundial
7130 Casgrain (near Jean-Talon)
514.271.6171
Large Latino supermarket with a good butcher counter. Specialties include powdered horchata (rice) drinks, tamales, and cheeses. There's a small take-out section.

National Cheese
9001 Salley, LaSalle (near Dollard)
Métro: Angrignon then bus 113
514.364.5353 / www.nationalcheese.com
The wholesale outlet for Tre Stelle and other National Cheese products. Rich boconccini, good value for large blocks of Parmesan or Romano cheeses. Dozens of imported cheeses in stock, too. Also Italian olives, oils, vinegars, anchovies and pastas. Open to the public only on Saturdays, 8 a.m.- 4 p.m. Check out their web site for recipes, special promotions, with detailed information on dozens of cheeses.

National Food
4903 Sherbrooke West (near Prince Albert)
Métro: Vendome or bus 24
514.484.3541
Top-quality ingredients such as lemon grass, fresh herbs; fair-trade coffee and fresh produce and oriental foods sections. The homemade spring rolls go fast. Excellent take-out counter with freshly-made salads, curries and sushi rolls.

New Navarino
5563 Parc (near St-Viateur)
Métro: Place des Arts or Parc then bus 80
514.279.7725
This is a popular bakery and coffee shop for both the adjacent Mile End and Outremont crowd as well as for regulars from the burbs who can spend a quarter-hour looking for parking.The area has become increasingly trendy but New Navarino has kept high standards for more than 30 years. Spanakopita (spinach pie), thick crust Greek pizza, wonderful Greek pastries and cookies are always popular.

New Victoria Fish
6015 Victoria (near Van Horne)
Métro: Plamondon then bus 124
514.737.4873

A favourite fishmonger for people who used to live in the area and keep coming back. Not as large as some, but always high quality. Specialties include freshly ground gefilte fish to prepare at home. Maybe the best smoked salmon in the city (and always a slice to taste over the counter). The Greek restaurant next door, Yanni, is owned by the same family.

Olympico (aka Open da night)
124 St-Viateur West (corner Waverly)
Métro: Place des Arts then bus 80, or Métro St-Laurent then bus 55
514.495.0746
No menu. No liquor. Everyone comes here to shmooze and have great coffee.

Orange Julep
7700 Décarie (near Jean-Talon)
Métro : Namur
514.738.7486
Yes, the big orange ball you see driving up the Décarie expressway is a restaurant, not the sun setting in the north. Fries, hot dogs, hamburgers, and a thick, sweet orange drink—the julep—have made this old-fashioned drive-in famous for decades. Opening hours vary as the weather gets colder, but in the summer it is open 24/7—and on Wednesday and Thursday evenings the parking lot fills with classic cars. Worth a trip, even if it's out of the way.

Pacific Coast Wasabi
450-1050 Alberni Street
Vancouver, B.C., V6E 1A3 / www.wasabia.ca
The only grower of fresh wasabi (*wasabia japonica*)in Canada. As they say on their web site: "That lump of green paste sitting next to your sushi isn't wasabi!" $150 for 500 grams.

Paradis du fromage in Atwater Market
Métro: Lionel-Groulx
514.933.7422

A small cheese store with reasonable prices and a sampling stand outside on weekends. Middle Eastern pastries and other delicacies.

Pâtisserie de Gascogne
6095 Gouin West (near Laurentian)
514.331.0550
Colonnades Pointe-Claire, 940 St-Jean, Pointe-Claire
514.697.2626
4825 Sherbrooke West (near Grosvenor)
Métro: Vendôme or bus 24
514.932.3511
237 Laurier West (near Parc)
Métro: Place des Arts or Parc, then bus 80
514.490.0235
Several shops in the Montreal area. Fine chocolate, pastries cakes (a specialty), a small range of quality cheeses, baguettes and charcuterie. The massive chocolate Easter egg creations are always spectacular. Eating on premises at some locations.

Peregrina, La
4565 Belanger East (corner 30th)
Métro: St-Michel
514.721.0902
This Latino grocery store has a lunch counter wedged into the back and offers a variety of South American goodies every day. Papas rellenas is one of their best: cook a potato, mash it and then form it into a ball. Stuff this with hard-boiled egg and ground meat and then deep fry it. This is a common snack in Cuba or the Dominican Republic where it may be stuffed with cheese. Reheats well in the microwave or toaster oven.

Petit Alep, Le
191 Jean-Talon East (across from the Jean-Talon Market
Métro: Jean-Talon
514.270.6396
Le Petit Alep, and its older 'big brother' Alep, are at the centre of a thriving Middle Eastern community that includes spice

and grocery stores and several halal butchers. Sample an array of appetizers at Le Petit Alep such as muhammara (pomegranate and walnuts), tahini and tabouleh salads, sabenegh (spinach and onions) or homemade labneh (yoghurt) with honey.

Petit Milos, Le
5551 Parc (near St-Viateur)
Métro: Place des Arts or Parc then bus 80
514.274.9991
Imagine being in Greece with an array of appetizers before you; fresh fish and chicken coming off the grill, and shelves of beautifully presented imported foods. An off-shoot of the famed Milos restaurant, Le Petit Milos sells entrees, spices, Greek pasta and rice, Kythera honey and almonds, manouri cheese, and gift ideas. There are a few tables for eating.

Pho Rosemont
435 Rosemont (near St-Denis)
Métro: Rosemont
514.271.2696
A small restaurant with impeccable cuisine. Everything is made from scratch and it shows. Chicken brochettes, spring rolls, rice noodles. The soup (pho) is superb. (Ask for extra bo vien—small meatballs served in the soup).

Pizza Cachère Pita
6415 Décarie (between Van Horne and Plamondon)
Métro: Plamondon, bus 161
514.731.7482
Kosher pizza, falafel, Middle Eastern salads. The Tunisian tuna sandwich is spicy and delicious. This is a great place to grab a quick bite if you are browsing the incredible variety of small shops and ethnic groceries around Van Horne and Victoria. This is our city's immigrant heartland—what The Main (Boulevard St-Laurent) was to earlier generations.

Poissonnerie La Mer
1840 René-Lévesque East (corner Papineau)
Métro: Papineau
514.522.3003
Great fish, good prices, the first choice for many restaurants in the city. Look for wild salmon, oysters from France in season, sea urchins and other hard-to-find seafood as well as just about anything else you would expect to find in a fish market. Excellent service and good advice for aspiring chefs. Large fish restaurant next door.

Poisonnerie N.D.G. Fish Market
5611 Monkland
Métro: Villa-Maria then bus 103
514.481.3388
Sure there are lobsters and fresh fish, but it's the house-smoked salmon, fresh sushi with unusual toppings like Spanish caviar, and continual gastronomic experimentation by owner Cyrice Vigneau (smoked frog legs on one day) that make this shop different. Seasonal specialities include fresh lobster, B.C. wild salmon and products from the îles-de-la-Madeleine.

Poissonnerie René Marchand
1455 Victoria, St-Lambert (near Churchill)
Métro: Longueuil and then bus 1, 15 or 6
450.672.1231
A large variety of fresh and smoked fish, including several kinds of smoked salmon, mackerel, eel and whitefish. Store specialties include sushi and shrimp rillettes. Canned and prepared foods include concentrated lobster and fish chowders and fish stock (great for poaching salmon).

Poissonnerie Sherbrooke
5121 Sherbrooke (near Grey)
Métro: Vendôme then bus 105
514.486.5246
An impressive fish store (live lobsters and Malpeque and

Caraquet oysters in season, good smoked salmon, talapia, sword fish, snapper and usually at least a dozen other fresh varieties). Recently enlarged to include gourmet olive oils, vinegars and a decent-sized fresh vegetable section. There are also Greek specialties with excellent homemade koponistie (feta and sweet red pepper spread), taramosalata (fish roe, bread, lemon juice and olive oil spread) and tzatziki (yogurt, garlic and cucumber dip).

Première Moisson
1490 Sherbrooke West (near Mackay)
Métro: Guy-Concordia
514.931.6540
Over 12 branches in Montreal including the Atwater, Maisonneuve and Jean-Talon Markets, and Central Station. From basic baguettes to sourdough, croissants, nut breads, charcuterie and classic French pastries, plus famed fougasses (twisted olive or cheese loaves), over two dozen varieties all baked in wood-fired ovens. All of the stores have dining areas.

Pushap
5195 Paré (corner Mountain Sights)
Métro: Namur
514.737.4527
A Punjabi vegetarian restaurant and sweet shop. Samosas (with amazing tamarind sauce), pakoras and lots of other appetizers, sweets made on the premises such as jalebi (brilliant orange spirals), gulub jamun (dark pudding balls in a sugar syrup) and good carrot halva. Meals are filling and are usually presented on a thali—several items served on a segmented metal tray.

Quartier Perse
5899 Sherbrooke West
Métro: Vendôme, then bus 105
514.482.0009
4241 Décarie (original restaurant)

514.488.6367
Métro: Villa-Maria
A branch of the Quartier Perse on Décarie, this elegant small
storefront resto features dishes made to order and take-out.
A small selection of hot specials available daily. Room for a
dozen diners at the counter.

Quebec Smoked Meat Products (Nower Butchers)
1889 Centre (near Shearer)
Métro: Peel or Charlevoix then bus 107
514.935.5297
A delicatessen counter with smokers and racks of meat in
back. If you aren't eating at Schwartz's, chances are the
smoked meat is from here. Sensational sausages and unique
smoked meat hot dogs (you want these, you really do). Also
good bacon, smoked ham, pickles, sauerkraut, fresh rye bread
and lots of other deli products. Come after noon and ask to
buy the end cuts when pieces that are too small for the slicer
are often sold cheap.

Queues de Castor
127 de la Commune West
Métro : Place d'Armes
514.878.1222
Part of the beavertail chain of fast food, slightly leaden, foot-
long fried dough stands. There is another across the street
near the Imax theatre. Popular flavours include chocolate and
banana toppings at $4.50. Closed during the winter.

RamDas Food Ltd.
1503 Dollard, LaSalle (near Newman)
Métro: Angrignon then bus 113
514.364.3817
A large market with a great selection of Caribbean cooking
supplies: locally-produced Dolly & Mabel seasonings and
soups (jerk, ox tail, seafood), Busta Green Crush (and other
soft drinks from Trinidad), Aunt May's ginger beer syrup,

Matouk's hot sauce, dozens of varieties of dried lentils and rice, salt cod, and hot peppers.

Restaurant Émile Bertrand
1308 Notre-Dame West (near de la Montagne)
Métro: Guy then bus 57
514.935.0178
Hardly gourmet but this small snack bar gets special mention for its homemade spruce beer, the last of the artisanal root beer makers. While you're picking up a bottle, try their freshly-made hamburgers, all beef hot-dogs and above-average French fries.

Restaurant Shish Kebab
9394 l'Acadie (near Chabanel)
Métro: l'Acadie, then bus 179
514.858.6222
Wonderful Lebanese and Armenian kebabs (filet mignon, lamb, chicken), shish taouk, homemade sausages cooked in lemon, and the best baba ganouj.

Restaurant with No Name / Restaurant Sans Nom (Tortarella et Fils)
9700 St-Michel (near Sauvé)
Métro: Sauvé
514.389.6732
Luigi Tortarella and his father like to keep it simple. Delicious Italian food served in a small grocery store or in the grape vine-entwined terrace in the back. Imported specialties include porcini mushrooms, olive oil, marinated vegetables, pasta, aged balsamic vinegar. Make sure you try an espresso, among the best in the city. Open weekdays for lunch and Thursday to Saturday evenings for dinner (reservations essential). It's always a good idea to call ahead.

Roberto's
2221 Bélanger East (near de Lorimier)

Métro: Jean-Talon then bus 95

514.374.9844

Famous for homemade ice cream and gelati in an almost endless variety of flavours from coffee and nougat to melon and fresh fruit. There is also a full range of basic Italian dishes (pasta, veal, chicken, etc.) served after 5 p.m., but most people come here throughout the day for dessert. For an amazing treat ask for spaghetti-with-meatballs ice cream. The ice cream is forced through a ricer and and the cherries and sauce give it the meat sauce look.

Romados

115 Rachel East (corner de Bullion)

Métro: St-Laurent or de Castelnau then bus 55

514.849.1803

Portuguese bakery with good bread and rolls and a few desserts including creamy pastéis de nata. At the end of the store past the bread counter is a small kitchen serving great charcoal-grilled sausages, pork and chicken.

Rosie's Vermont Beef Jerky

231 St. Albans, Vermont

802.868.2877 / www.rosiesjerky.com

Maple-flavoured beef, teriyaki, sweet & spicy, Cajun—whatever flavour you like, Rosaire Laroche makes it. The family left Quebec generations ago and settled in Vermont. Rosie has been winning acclaim for his jerky made from beef strips, not processed meat. The taste is strong and meaty. The texture is chewy, a piece lasts a while. It doesn't dissolve into a mush like a lot of commercial jerky. Available in much of New England or, if you're driving through, in their smoke shops in Swanton and St. Alban's. However, it's best to call first.

Rotisserie Panama

789 Jean-Talon West (corner Outremont)

Métro: Parc or bus 92

514.276.5223

A restaurant that feels like the banquet scene from *My Big Fat Greek Wedding*. Lamb grilled on the spit on Friday and Saturday nights, fresh fish, chicken and unusual, but authentic dishes such as kokoretski (a traditional sausage made with organ meats) and bakaliaro tiganito (cod fritters). Reservations required on weekends.

Ruisseau, Le
12251 Laurentian (near Gouin)
Métro: Côte Vertu then bus 151
514.337.7066

An all-purpose Middle Eastern market with the bonus of a delightful, new Lebanese and Moroccan restaurant, with the same name, next door. In fact, you can be glancing at the marinated chicken and lamb at the butcher counter and unwittingly walk through a large archway and find that the same dish is being served a few steps away. Excellent variety of cheeses (labneh, feta, baldi), halal meats, nuts, spices, a good assortment of fruits and vegetables, imported cooking equipment, Turkish coffee makers, and water pipes.

St. Petersbourg Russian Delicatessen
5462 Sherbrooke West
Métro: Vendôme, then bus 105, 63, or 17
514.369.1377

A small store stuffed with goodies: Russian tea in elegant gift boxes, Polish blueberry juice, pickled mushrooms, baba with raisins, and chocolate-filled waffle cakes. The deli counters is replete with black bread, smoked chub, salted herring, salamis, cheeses, and, of course, caviar.

St-Viateur Bagel Shop
263 St-Viateur West (near Parc)
Métro: Place des Arts or Parc then bus 80
514.276.8044 / www. stviateurbagel.com

This is the place. For almost 50 years The Bagel Shop has baked the bagels that Montreal is known for. The lineup is a little daunting? Go to the wholesale bagel shop along the street at 158 St-Viateur West, or in Ville St-Laurent at 40 Marcel-Laurin. Same prices but seldom a lineup. There are also Bagel Shop cafés in the east and west ends of the city. But here is where it all started. Sesame and poppy seed bagels, matzoh boards; also lox, cream cheese, milk and eggs to go. Open 24/7.

Salerno
2411 Charland (corner St-Michel)
Métro: Sauvé then bus 121
514.384.9142
Salerno houses a large bakery and is open day and night, all the time. A wide selection of Italian products, freshly made desserts, a small deli section and great bakery products. Try the dessert calzone with a ricotta filling and a sugary crust. A few tables and chairs for an impromptu lunch or late-night snack.

Sami Fruits
232 Jean-Talon East in Jean-Talon Market
Métro : Jean-Talon or bus 55
514.278.5292
The fruit and vegetable emporium on the northern edge of the market sells more types of produce than seems possible. Good prices for fresh Moroccan mint and much else. Always crowded.

SAQ (Société des alcools du Québec)
Our government-run retail monopoly for wine and spirits, the Société des alcools du Québec (SAQ), offers us its products in various ways. Dépanneurs (corner stores) and supermarkets sell wine and beer but the wines are not vintage and are often imported in bulk by the SAQ and bottled here. SAQ retail outlets sell a wide variety of wines and spirits. The SAQ website (www.saq.com) features special promotions and indicates the availability of products at each store. There are several kinds of SAQ outlets, including standard retail stores,

express counters open late at night, and gourmet stores with unique products.

Here is a useful list of SAQ outlets:

SAQ Express stores stock 400 of the most popular products. Many of the white wines are already chilled—essential when you are on the way to a dinner party or BYOB restaurant. They are open every night until 10 p.m.

4128 St-Denis	514.845.5630
1034 Mont-Royal East	514.523.6117
6108 Sherbrooke West	514.489.6521
55 Mont-Royal West	514.843.7177
1108 Ste-Catherine West	514.861.7908
6394 Sherbrooke East	514.251.4711
10418 Lajeunesse	514.388-2726
2834 de Salaberry	514.336-7627
954 Décarie, Ville St-Laurent	514.747-2511
3699B St-Jean Boul., Dollard-des-Ormeaux	514.624.5384
6819 Newman Boul., Lasalle	514.595.0547

SAQ Signature is the deluxe wine and liquor outlet in Montreal. Unusual grappas, single malt Scotches, and some of the best wine in the city. Champagne by the magnum and larger bottles too. Montreal's Selection store downtown in Complexe Les Ailes de la Mode, 677 Ste-Catherine West, 514.282.9445 or (toll-free) 888.454.7007.

The *SAQ Depot* features bulk wines, gin, scotch, vodka and rum. You can bring your own wine bottles or buy them here too. Good value for unexceptional plonk, but vintage wines are also sold at discounts of up to 25%. Some excellent French and Italian wines at good prices. Worth the trip and plenty of parking space when you get there.
1001 Marché Central, 514.383.9954

The *SAQ outlets at the Jean Talon and Atwater Markets* have an excellent array of locally-produced products: wines from nearby vineyards, eau de vie from local orchards, ice ciders that are world class and hard to find elsewhere. The staff is keen and helpful. There are often tastings on weekend afternoons.

At the Jean Talon Market: 200 Jean-Talon East, 514.276.1512
At the Atwater Market:110 Atwater, 514.937.2068

Saum-Mom

1318 Mont-Royal East (near Chambord)
Métro: Mont-Royal then bus 97
514.526.1116

Saum-Mom (the name plays off the French words for salmon and summit) is a gourmet boutique that prepares salmon in dozens of ways—from their own salmon jerky and smoked salmon to patés and pies. The quality is high, even if the concept is unusual. Their gravlax is made with dill and sea salt only. Marinated for 24 hours, it has a clean, fresh taste. Many specialty stores also sell Saum-mom products.

Schwartz's Hebrew Delicatessen

3895 St-Laurent (near Duluth)
Métro: St-Laurent or de Castelnau then bus 55
514.842.4813

This is authentic Montreal—brined beef brisket, smoked, perfumed with peppers, steamed, cut by hand. Thickly stacked on rye bread. Order to go or eat here. Try the rib steak grilled over charcoal, served with liver, pickles and fries. The official soda is Cott's black cherry. No booze, no desserts, no loitering; and sometimes the line stretches around the block.

Serano

4136 du Souvenir, Chomedy Laval (near Labelle)
Métro: Henri-Bourassa then bus 40
450.681.7684

A large, well-established bakery catering to Montreal's growing Greek community (and Greek pastry lovers) in Laval since 1976. Look for sweet tzoureki bread (usually available at Easter, but made here year-round), bouyatsa custard-filled pastries, kourabiedes sugar coated cookies, freshly made cheese and spinach pies in warming ovens, thumb-sized mini-baklava (how mini can you eat?) and a chocolatier making superb bitter-sweet almond bark.

Slovenia Meat Poducts
6424 Clark (near Beaubien)
Métro: St-Laurent or de Castelnau then bus 55
514.279.8845
A combination butcher shop and delicatessen. Knockwursts and other sausages made here. Excellent smoked bacons, Eastern European jams, pickles. There are a few tables and a stand-up hot lunch counter at the side with an excellent selection of inexpensive dishes and hot meals such as goulash and several kinds of schnitzel to go.

Soto Express
510 McGill (near St-Jacques)
Métro: Square Victoria
514.866.8232 / www. soto.ca
Stores throughout Montreal.
Leading the way in store-front sushi operations, this is an off-shoot of the pricey Soto restaurant. Reasonably priced maki and sushi platters (about 20 pieces for two people). Also good miso soup and hot dishes such as grilled salmon served bento-style (in a container with rice and vegetables to go).

Stella Estrela
22 Duluth East (corner St-Dominique)
Métro: St-Laurent then bus 55
514.843.7012
Classic Portuguese bakery with a few tables to grab a coffee and something sweet: pastéis de nata, flan, arroz doce. Lots of good stuff. Opens early (usually 7 a.m.)

Sun Sing Lung
72A de la Gauchetière West (near St-Urbain)

Métro: Place d'Armes or bus 55

514.861.0815

Advice on Chinese cooking and a grocery store stocked with the basics. Superb barbecued pork, chicken and duck cooked in the back. Freshly made appetizers include egg rolls and steamed rice. Look in the freezer for dumplings, sausages and other dishes to take home.

Supermarché Andes

436 Bélanger East (near St-Denis)

Métro: Jean-Talon

514.277.4130

A butcher shop and grocery store with a wide selection of Latino products. The butcher shop has South American cuts of pork and beef, thin steaks, fresh chorizo sausages, stacks of tortillas, banana leaves, bottles of chipotle sauce, bags of masa and so much more— plus a cafeteria-style restaurant with a range of daily specials. Plantains, tamales, empanadas and other Latino goodies are available to go.

Sushi Shop

Throughout the city

www.sushishop.com

More a stand than a store, these small shops are popping up from Laval to Saint-Bruno. In Montreal they're in Holt Renfrew, the Atwater and Jean-Talon Markets, and on trendy streets including Monkland and Bernard. Freshly made takeout and quick service. Ready-to-go sushi packs are served from 11 to 2 p.m. and are good deals, starting at 11 pieces for $4.95. Eating on premises.

Tortillería Maya

5274 St-Laurent (near Fairmount)

Métro: St-Laurent or de Castelnau then bus 55

514.495.0606

Maya is a small, lively bakery pumping out fresh tortillas, tostadas and nachos every day. There is also a small lunch counter that serves a limited number of homemade Mexican takeout dishes.

Tranzo
6536 Somerled (near Cavendish)
Métro: Snowdon then bus 51
514.488.7907
Spit-roasted piglet is the specialty at this West-End butcher shop and gourmet food store. Also olive oils, imported pasta, Italian cheeses, antipasti to go.

Un, deux, trois chocolat
7010 Casgrain (across from Jean-Talon Market)
Métro: Jean-Talon or bus 55
514.803.3673
Owner Thierry Schickes is an artist working in chocolate. He makes only a few items: truffles, masks and edible but bizarre sculptures which he shows at his discretion. His work is whimsical and delicious.

Verger Pierre Gingras in Jean-Talon Market
(1132 Grande Caroline, Rougemont, QC   1.888.469.4954/ www.cidervinegar.com)
Métro : Jean-Talon or bus 55
Honey, beeswax, royal jelly; maple syrup and fudge and butter and jelly and suckers; apples and juice and syrup and muffins and butter, and pies and vinegar; and hand-made soap. Luscious.

Vieille Europe, La
3855 St-Laurent (near des Pins)
Métro: St-Laurent or de Castelnau then bus 55
514.842.5773
For New Yorkers reading this, think of Zabar's in Montreal. One-stop picnic shopping and gourmet feasting. Heady aromas as soon as you walk in, from wheels of cheese, racks of dry sausages and salamis, fresh peanut butter, dried fruits,

ground-to-order coffee roasted here (and many kinds of coffee makers), teas, herbs, spices, chocolate, and rows of imported jams and jellies.

Vinh Hing
939 Décarie, Ville St-Laurent (corner Côte Vertu)
Métro : Côte Vertu
514.748.7014
A tiny pastry store with good Vietnamese coffee, fresh bread and pastries, a limited menu featuring pho (soup).

Vrac du Marché in Atwater Market
Métro : Lionel Groulx
514.933.0202
This is a large self-serve store on the second floor of the market with a good variety of dried pastas, candies, flours, olive oils, and imported vinegars—and a fine spice and dried herb section. The staff is knowledgeable and helpful.

Vrai Délice
9897 St-Michel (near Sauvé)
Métro: Sauvé
514.955.9595
Bakery and pastry store tucked into a small mall in the north end of the city. Row upon row of freshly made baklava and petit-fours, palm-size vegetarian and meat pizzas (the chicken shwarma pizza is a fabulous appetizer) and a small take-out menu of specialties made fresh daily. A few chairs and tables are available for snacking.

William J. Walter Saucissier
Several locations including:
Les Halles d'Anjou, Galleries d'Anjou Shopping Centre
7500 des Galleries d'Anjou
514.351.6378
Atwater Market
Métro: Lionel-Groulx

514.933.4070
Jean-Talon Market
Métro: Jean-Talon or bus 55
514.279.0053

All are independent franchises drawing from a central kitchen that makes more than two dozen kinds of fresh sausages daily. Standards include knockwurst and wieners as well as spicy merguez and chorizo. Then there are unusual combinations like apple and bacon or broccoli and cheddar. At lunch time all the shops have several kinds piping hot, served with a choice of mustards and sauerkraut on a crusty roll.

Windmill Point Farm & Nursery
2103 Perrot, Ile Perrot
514.453-9757

The farm is open to the public during the summer and harvest season on Saturdays from 10 a.m. to 5 p.m. Ken Taylor has an organic experimental farm. Kiwis, Japanese pears, many kinds of squashes, apples, and other fruits and vegetables are grown here. Plants and root stock shipped throughout North America. The long-lost legendary Montreal Melon is being reintroduced at Windmill and seeds are sometimes available.

Shops & Restaurants Index

The Tastes of Montreal Index

Recipes Index

www.vehiculepress.com